Colloquy on Economic Man

Present at the colloquy (left to right): Adam Smith, Thomas Malthus, David Ricardo, Jeremy Bentham, John Stuart Mill, François Marie Charles Fourier, Claude Henri Saint-Simon, Auguste Comte, Karl Marx, and Pierre Joseph Proudhon.

Carrying on the Anatomical Studies

Left to right: Thorstein Veblen, Joseph Schumpeter, John Maynard Keynes, and Alfred Marshall.

The Making of Economic Society

fourth edition

Robert L. Heilbroner

Englewood Cliffs, New Jersey

The Making of Economic Society

fourth edition

PRENTICE-HALL, INC.

ACKNOWLEDGMENTS I am happy to acknowledge permission from the
New York Review of Books to use material on ecology,
the arms economy, and the multinational corporation. The
material first appeared (in somewhat different form) in its
pages. I should like to thank, as well, *Trans-action* for
permission to use material on social neglect in America,
published first in that journal and also to appear in a volume
of essays, *Is Law Dead?* to be published by the New York Bar
Association. Some of the material in this new edition
has also been published, in altered form, in my book
Between Capitalism and Socialism (Random House, Inc., 1970).

ISBN P 0-13-545756-4

C 0-13-545764-5

Library of Congress Catalog Card No.: 78-39216

10 9 8 7 6 5 4

LONDON PRENTICE-HALL INTERNATIONAL, INC.
SYDNEY PRENTICE-HALL OF AUSTRALIA, PTY. LTD.
TORONTO PRENTICE-HALL OF CANADA, LTD.
NEW DELHI PRENTICE-HALL OF INDIA PRIVATE LTD.
TOKYO PRENTICE-HALL OF JAPAN, INC.

CONTENTS

v

part THREE   The Challenge to the Market System

It is a little hard for us to imagine, but in the third decade of nineteenth century England, a knowledge of economics was part of a proper young lady's accomplishments. It was not a very profound knowledge (mainly it was gained from reading Miss Harriet Martineau's tracts), and it was not always very good economics—but that is not the point. In those days, economics was not only esteemed as important, but it was actually a *popular* study.

Today, alas, no such happy reputation precedes our subject. Not that the public estimation of economics has diminished; on the contrary, everyone admits that it was never more important, etc. But the very word has come to shed a pall. The student approaches his first economics course with apprehension; the layman is convinced that the whole thing is hopelessly beyond him.

In a way, both student and layman are quite right in thinking of economics as a difficult subject. When Auguste Comte classified the sciences of mankind in his general scheme of philosophy, he placed mathematics and the natural sciences at a lower stage of complexity than sociology or economics. This was not because Comte considered the logical structures of physics or chemistry to be simpler than those of the social sciences. It was because, despite their impressive architecture, these structures were founded on the solid ground of nature's dependable regularity and were thus blessedly free of human nature's undependable irregularity. Along the same line of reasoning, what made the social sciences appear so much more difficult to Comte was not their inner structure, their vocabulary, or their techniques. It was the fact that they had to form their intellectual architecture out of the stuff of human behavior itself.

Yet it is not this intrinsic and legitimate difficulty that frightens people away from economics. In fact, once its inner precincts have been invaded, these very difficulties—this challenging task of creating a "science" out of human behavior—lend fascination to the study. The problem, rather, is to crash the gates, to come to grips with this engrossing core of economics, in the first place. And here the trouble lies not within the discipline so much as in the routes by which it is usually approached.

One of the routes—that which the college student usually travels—is the road of economic theory. This is the traditional avenue into economics, but it is a very demanding and austere initiation. By dint of much hard work, the student learns about supply and demand and equilibrium and marginal cost curves; but when the textbook is closed and put away, somehow very little seems to stick. Despite the valiant efforts of his instructors, the formal apparatus of economics does not readily impart deep and unforgettable meanings to the average student, or root itself naturally into the "real world." The regrettable result is that the facts and formulae soon fade, leaving only a memory of economics as a very hard course.

But the other route to economics is equally unsatisfactory. This is the route of general events, past or present. Here is where the ordinary person comes into contact with economic matters, whether in newspaper headlines or as part of the background to a biography or a book on general history. And here the difficulty is the obverse of the first. To come into touch with economics as an immediate issue of past or present is to see it only as a series of isolated problems and, more bewildering yet, to face those problems without the larger framework of knowledge needed to understand what they are all about.

If this diagnosis is correct, the remedy suggests itself. The isolated problems of economics must first be joined into a connected flow, which is to say, they must be viewed in the light of *history*. But that is not enough. In turn, the movement of history must be further lit by the generalizing insights of economic *theory*. In other words, economics should be approached from a point of view in which theory explains and enlightens the facts of history and in which history illustrates and substantiates the abstractions of theory.

This little book is an attempt to present some of the basic content of economics in this mingled light of theory and history. Thus it begins with an effort to bring history home by a broadside exposure to some of the more sobering and disturbing aspects of history's cutting edge—the present. In our first chapter, "America Today," the relevant issues of our time are laid out for unsparing examination. Here is poverty, the military economy, pollution, racism, and other unpleasant realities of American life, presented not as a rounded picture of our life today, but as a direct confrontation with the facts to which economics must address itself.

What does economics have to say about these problems? In part the answer lies in an understanding of technical economic theory, of which we can give only a few hints in these pages. *But more important than the technical apparatus, which the aspiring economist will soon master, is an understanding of the historic process that has produced these facts.* It is to this central problem that our subsequent chapters address themselves. By the time we have finished Chapter 4 we will not be in a position to "explain" all the problems of America Today, but we will be in a position to view these problems from a perspective of social change that should make us *ready* to learn about them as professional economists.

I should like to add a word to my professional readers. With but minor emendations, this text comprises the first and last parts of *The Economic Problem*—a full-scale text in which this account of economic history serves as the setting for teaching basic macro and micro economics. That text was, however, a good many years in the writing, and when the first portion of it was completed, it was published as a book in itself—in fact, as this very book. Subsequently the macro and micro portions of the text also found separate publication, and only later were the three books (and a good deal of other material) welded together in their originally conceived form.

To my great pleasure, *The Making of Economic Society* had a happy reception upon its appearance, encouraging enough to make me believe that it should be continued as a separate book. Although summaries and questions appended to each chapter make the book a little "like a textbook," I hope that this psychological obstacle will be outweighed by the advantages, both for student and teacher, in dealing with and weighing the subject matter. Finally, as before, I hope that my readers will not hesitate to write to me when they discover me in error or in what they consider to be mistaken emphases. The best way a teacher learns, I have discovered, is through his students, and I am eager to continue my education at your hands.

ROBERT L. HEILBRONER

Prologue

We Americans tend to think of ourselves as members of the richest society on earth. And so we are, for by the measure usually employed to count riches—gross national product—the American economy is beyond doubt the wealthiest in the world. In the winter of 1970, gross national product (GNP) crossed the trillion dollar mark for the first time in our history. Per capita, that amounted to approximately $5,000 for every man, woman, and child in the land. This is one third higher than the next richest country, Sweden; 40 percent higher than the next after Sweden: Canada; more than double that of West Germany; almost four times that of the Netherlands; and incomparably greater than the per capita GNP of India, which amounts to the equivalent of one week's American income per Indian—per year.[1]

Yet, these gargantuan figures mask a seamy side of American life. The wealth is there—but so is an extraordinary carelessness in its use; so that far from enjoying the highest standard of general well-being of any nation on earth, we find that our overall riches coexist with a degree of social neglect comparable to that of some of the poorest nations on earth.[2]

Take, for example, what is probably the most meaningful indicator of social welfare—the sheer statistical chances of remaining alive in a given society. Since the United States spends a higher proportion of its GNP on health services than any other nation, we might suppose that life expectancy in this country would be the highest in the world. It is not. In 1965 the United States ranked 22nd in male life expectancy and 10th in female life expectancy. Perhaps even more shocking, it ranked 24th in infant survival, putting it roughly at the level of Hong Kong.[3]

Or take the quality, rather than the "quantity," of life as an indicator of relative well-being. There exists no official index of the extent of slums or

[1] *Statistical Abstract of the United States* (Washington, D.C.: U.S. Bureau of the Census, 1970), p. 810. Let the reader be warned that intercountry comparisons of GNP are very shaky for various technical reasons. Nevertheless, GNP is the most commonly used measure of comparative international well-being.

[2] See R. Heilbroner, "The Roots of Social Neglect in the United States" in *Is Law Dead?* ed. Eugene Rostow (New York: Simon & Schuster, 1971).

[3] *Toward a Social Report* (Washington, D.C.: Department of Health, Education and Welfare, 1969), pp. 1-13; also N. Glazer "Paradoxes of Health Care," *The Public Interest,* No. 22 (Winter 1971), 72.

urban decay here or in other nations, but anyone who has traveled abroad knows that to match the lower depths of the New York, Detroit, Chicago, or any large American city one must visit not Europe but the underdeveloped world. To put it the other way around, any traveler knows that the general cleanliness and decency to be found in virtually *all* Scandanavian, West German, Swiss, or Dutch cities is simply not to be found in *any* large United States city at all.

Nor is it merely a matter of urban blight. The rural slums in America also vie with those of the underdeveloped world in sheer misery and neglect. Nearly a quarter of the (white) population of eastern Kentucky, for example, cannot read or write;[4] and malnutrition to the point of actual starvation has been discovered in some sections of the South and Southwest (including the presence of kwashiorkor, an illness formerly associated only with areas of extreme privation such as Central Africa).

Thus, if we are the richest nation in the world, we are also one of the more socially neglectful—ignorant of, or acquiescent in, conditions that other, less wealthy nations no longer tolerate.

POVERTY

This brings us to the broad problem of poverty in America. Poverty is, of course, a relative concept. A Calcutta family of street-dwellers would consider itself unimaginably well-off if it were given rupees equal to welfare payments made to a family in Mississippi (1969: $47 per month). A Mississippi family on welfare, transported to New York (average welfare per month $248) might also feel prosperous (a situation that helps explain the influx of rural poor to the big cities). So, too, some Americans who are officially "poor" may have incomes higher than those of some Norwegians who think of themselves as comfortable—perhaps because no Norwegian suffers the ill effects of slum conditions so common in America.

Yet, with all the problems of defining poverty, few would call the present U.S. definition extravagant. The U.S. Department of Labor establishes a poverty threshold that ranges from an income of $1,748 for a single

[4] Paul Good, *The American Serfs* (New York: Putnam, 1968), p. 166.

person living in a metropolitan area to $5,789 for a city-dwelling family of seven ($2.27 per person per day). By this definition, about 10 percent of urban Americans in 1968 were poor. The poverty threshold is appreciably lower for rural areas ($1,487 for a single person; $4,916 for a seven-member family), where 23 percent of all families fall below the threshold. For the nation as a whole, roughly one family in seven is officially considered "poor," and perhaps double that number "near-poor."[5]

But these overall figures dilute what poverty means to those who suffer from it, for the incidence of poverty is not random. It affects some groups much more severely than others. In 1968, for example, among families headed by a person 65 or older, 31 percent were poor. Among Negro families, 33 percent were poor; and among families (black or white) in which no adult male breadwinner was present, almost 39 percent were poor. For large groups of Americans, in other words—the aged, the blacks, the broken families—poverty is more likely to be a near-normal state of affairs than an unhappy accident. Put differently, whereas 41 percent of all white American families enjoy incomes of more than $10,000 a year, only 19 percent of Negro families have reached this degree of modest affluence; and whereas only 9 percent of white families fall below $3,000 a year, 24 percent of Negro families are clustered in this lowest range.[6]

Because of this clustering we cannot regard poverty with complacency, secure in the knowledge that the problem will gradually disappear. Although poverty has been slowly shrinking within American society as a whole, it rose 5 percent from 1969 to 1970, reversing a 10-year trend. Furthermore, poverty is not shrinking in certain critical areas. As the racial composition of the cities changes, for example, the concentration of poverty becomes worse, not better. It is estimated that we can expect an *additional* 1.4 million nonwhite poor children in our central cities by 1985.[7] What effect that will have on the crime rate, the drug problem, and the general civility of those cities can be imagined.

Poverty must be considered an aspect of social neglect by any nation affluent enough to eliminate it. And for Americans, this is perhaps the most disturbing aspect of all, for the elimination of poverty in America would not be a difficult task. To transfer enough money to bring all officially "poor" families up to the poverty threshold level would require approximately $10 to $15 billions per annum—between 1 and 1.5 percent of our GNP. Alternatively, if the 85 percent of households who are not poor would acquiesce in having the *growth* in their annual incomes reduced from an average of about 3 percent a year to about 2.5 percent, allowing the difference to be trans-

[5] *Statistical Abstract of the United States,* (1970), p. 327. See also *Economic Report of the President* 1969 (Washington, D.C.), p. 151*f*; and Anthony Downs, *Who Are the Urban Poor?* (Washington, D.C.: Committee for Economic Development, 1970), *passim.*

[6] *Statistical Abstract,* 1970, p. 328.

[7] Downs, *Who Are the Urban Poor?* p. 55.

ferred to the poor, within less than five years all families below the poverty line would have been brought up to levels of minimum decency.[8]

But so far no such willingness has been visible, either within Congress or in any "grass roots" movement. As one observer has bitterly commented: "The middle class knows that the economists are right when they say that poverty could be eliminated if only we will it; they simply do not will it."[9]

Now let us turn to another aspect of our economic troubles. It is that perhaps 8 to 9 percent of the trillion dollars of total output of the American economy consists of military goods and services—missiles, bombs, planes, tanks, payrolls of the armed forces, military subsidies to foreign nations, and the like. The "perhaps" refers to the fact that we cannot give a very precise estimate of total military spending, because its full extent is only now being revealed. Recently, for example, the Senate Foreign Relations Committee discovered that direct and indirect military assistance to foreign nations for 1971 totalled $6.9 billion, whereas the item for Military Assistance in the President's Budget Message to Congress listed it at only $625 million. It was discovered as well that under the Food for Peace Program, $691 million had been transferred to foreign nations *for the purchase of arms;* that the United States had spent $1.5 billion in supporting South Vietnamese currency, of which $680 million was lost because of an overvaluation of that currency; and that the Pentagon had a surplus weapons stock worth $17 billion.[10]

After listening to three days of testimony with regard to the hitherto undisclosed flow of military assistance abroad, a senator said: "Most of us in Washington have seen a lot of mismanagement in government programs. But military assistance is the first program I have come across that appears to be characterized by unmanagement.... In some respects, the United States has been transformed from an 'arsenal of democracy' to a gigantic discount supermarket with no check-out counters, no store managers—only clerks who blithely deliver to foreign governments of practically any political persuasion whatever they happen to see and like."

If there is much that we do not yet know about the extent of our military economy, what we do know is sobering enough. The Department of Defense (DOD) is the largest planned economy outside the Soviet Union. Its property—plant and equipment, land, inventories of war and other commodities—amounts to some $202 billion, equal to about 8 percent of the assets of the entire American economy. It owns 39 million acres of land, roughly an area the size of Hawaii. It rules over a population of 4 million—direct employees or soldiers—and spends an "official" budget of over $75 billion, a

THE MILITARY ECONOMY

[8] *Economic Report of the President,* 1969, p. 160.

[9] Adam Walinsky in *The New Republic,* July 4, 1964, p. 15.

[10] Reported in *Sane World* (February 1971); figures from hearings before the Joint Subcommittee on Economy in Government (January 1971).

budget three-quarters as large as the entire gross national product of Great Britain.[11]

This makes the DOD richer than any small nation in the world and, of course, incomparably more powerful. That part of its assets represented by nuclear explosives alone gives it the equivalent of six tons of TNT for every living inhabitant of the globe, to which must be added the awesome military power of its "conventional" weapons. The conventional explosives dropped in Indochina *before* the extension of the war to Laos amounted to well over 3 million tons, or 50 percent *more* than the total bomb tonnage dropped on all nations in both European and Pacific theaters during World War II.

The DOD system embraces both men and industry. In 1969 the men (and women) included, first, some 3 million soldiers deployed in 2,257 bases or locations abroad and at home, plus another one million civilians located within the United States and abroad. No less important are at least 2.3 million civilian workers who are directly employed on war production, in addition to a much larger number employed in the secondary echelon of defense-related output. This does not include still further millions who owe their livelihood to the civilian services they render to the military. Symptomatic of the pervasive influence of military spending is the rise in unemployment in Connecticut to 8.1 percent of the labor force when a first small effort was made in 1971 to cut back on military output. What would be the effect of a major contraction in defense spending is a problem we will have to defer for later consideration, but no one denies that such a major contraction—*unless counteracted by vigorous expansion of peacetime spending*—could plunge this country into a severe depression.

The web of DOD expenditures extends to more areas of the economy than one might think. One expects Lockheed Aircraft, with 88 percent of its sales to the government, to be a ward of the DOD, which explains why the government agreed to rescue the company from bankruptcy in 1971 with an enormous advance of funds. One does not expect the DOD to show up as the source of some 44 percent of the revenues of Pan Am or to be, through its Post Exchange (PX) system the third largest marketing chain in the country, just after Sears Roebuck and the A&P; or to be a major factor in the construction business, spending more for military housing facilities between 1956 and 1967 than the total spent by federal government on all other public housing.[12]

All in all, some 22,000 firms are prime contractors with the DOD, although the widespread practice of subcontracting means that a much

[11] Adam Yarmolinsky, *The Military Establishment* (New York: Harper, 1971), p. 10. Note that this *excludes* the military component in our AID program, any military portion of NASA, and all CIA expenses. For further data on DOD employment and on the extent and distribution of military expenditure, see *Economic Report of the President,* 1971, pp. 42–49, and Seymour Melman, *Pentagon Capitalism* (New York: McGraw-Hill, 1970), pp. 72–73, 79.

[12] Melman, *Pentagon Capitalism,* pp. 72–73, 79.

larger number of enterprises—perhaps 100,000 in all—look to defense spending for a portion of their income. Within the main constituency, however, a very few firms are the bastion of the DOD economy. The hundred largest defense contractors supply about two-thirds of the $40-odd billion of manufactured deliveries; and within this group, an inner group of ten firms by themselves accounted for 30 percent of the total. Incidentally, many of these largest contractors owe not only their sales to the military economy, but a considerable portion of their capital as well. As of 1967, defense contractors used $2 billion worth of government-owned furniture and office machines, $4.7 billion worth of government-owned materials, and over $5 billion worth of government plant and equipment, on all of which they were allowed to make profits just as if they were using their own property.[13]

The military establishment, as the largest single customer in the economy, not only supports a central core of industry but also penetrates that core with 2,072 retired military officers who were employed in 1969 by the 95 biggest contractors (the 10 largest firms averaging 106 officers each). Meanwhile, the establishment has a powerful political arm as well. The DOD employs some 339 lobbyists on Capitol Hill and (a conservative estimate) some 2,700 public relations men in the U.S. and abroad. This close political relationship undoubtedly has some bearing on the Pentagon's requests for funds being given, until recently, only the most cursory congressional inspection, leading among other things to cost "overruns" of $24 billion on 38 weapons systems.

This is not to say, of course, that the United States does not need a strong defense capability today. But at what point does a "defense" capability become an instrument for aggressive use in its own right? To what extent has the sheer weight of military power been the cause of the *fifty* acts of military intervention officially listed since the end of World War II?[14]

To these questions we will return in Chapter 14, for it is clear that our military-industrial subeconomy poses a tremendous problem for (perhaps *of*) American capitalism. Meanwhile, it is worth pondering the words of Professor Seymour Melman, a well-known expert on military economics:

Rarely does a single social force have a controlling influence in changing, swiftly, the character of life in a large and complex society. The expansion of the Pentagon and its state-management is such a force. Failing decisive action to reverse the economic and other growth of these institutions, then the parent state, if it is saved from nuclear war, will surely become the guardian of a garrison-like society dominated by the Pentagon and its state-management."[15]

[13] Melman, *Pentagon Capitalism*, p. 80.
[14] Yarmolinsky, *The Military Establishment*, Chaps. 13, 14; also *The Pentagon Watchers*, Leonard Rodberg and Derek Sherer, eds. (Garden City, N.Y.: Doubleday, 1970), pp. 99-140, 143.
[15] Melman, *Pentagon Capitalism*, p. 227.

Neglect, poverty, militarism are aspects of American society to which critics have been sensitive for some time. But with startling swiftness, a new, almost wholly overlooked problem has come to the fore. This is the problem of pollution, the frightening rate at which we are narrowing the margin of safety in the air we breathe, the water we drink, the wastes we discharge into the environment.

ITEM: *Annual throwaway list:*

214 million tons of carbon monoxide, sulfur oxides, hydrocarbons, particulates, and nitrous oxides (over a ton per American)

55 billion tin cans (275 for each of us)

20 billion bottles (100 apiece)

65 billion metal and plastic bottle caps (325 each)

7 million cars (our annual output has to go *somewhere* after 100,000 miles or so)

10 million tons of steel and iron scrap (an average of 1,000 pounds each)

150 million tons of garbage and trash (4.1 pounds per person daily)

3 billion tons of tailings, mine debris, and waste (4 tons for each of us each day)

ITEM: In August, 1969, inhabitants of Los Angeles and St. Louis were warned against indulging in any kind of exercise, including jogging, golf, etc., because deep breathing was dangerous.

ITEM: Nitrates and phosphates in fertilizers and detergents cause water pollution problems that are beyond the control of present technology. The use of these chemicals is estimated to increase by tenfold before the year 2000. Professor Barry Commoner, ecologist, predicts a major agricultural crisis in the United States from this source alone within 50 years.

ITEM: It is estimated that by the year 2000, there will be, at any time, some 3,000 six ton trucks in transit carrying dangerous radioactive wastes to burial sites.

ITEM: With 6 percent of the world's population, the United States annually consumes about 40 percent of the world's output of raw materials and discharges into the environment about the same percentage of the world's waste products. Thus each American is roughly the equivalent of seven Asians or Africans or South Americans in his ecological disturbance. There are, in round numbers, some 2.2 billion inhabitants of Asia, Africa, and South America. What does this imply for the long-run chances of economic development in those areas? What does it imply about the long-run acceptable levels of economic "development" in the United States?[16] Clearly, here is a situation in which something must "give." Will it be the chance for economic development for the world's peoples, or will it be our profligate use of resources?

[16] See Paul and Anne Ehrlich, *Population, Resources, Environment* (San Francisco: Freeman, 1970), *passim.*

The troubles of the United States, it must be clear, are closely intertwined. This is why it is difficult to deal with them individually. Social neglect is closely associated with poverty; and the failure to cope with social neglect and poverty are both connected with the vast military claim on our output; and all these in turn aggravate, and are aggravated by, the increasing pollution of the environment. Hence it is perhaps redundant to single out the special miseries of the ghetto as something apart from the issues we have already considered. Yet ghetto life, with its violence, its crime, its concentrated squalor, takes us more closely than any issue we have previously considered into what is surely one of the most troublesome problems that America faces today—racial discrimination. Let us therefore take a moment to sketch out its dimensions and peculiar difficulties.

How many people live in the black ghettos? No one is exactly sure. We have discovered that the census counts may be off by at least 10 percent in neighborhoods where addresses are often impermanent and where citizens avoid interviews by census takers, fearing them to be investigators from the welfare department, bill collectors, or process servers. But a reasonably reliable estimate puts the number of ghetto citizens at about 14 million, as of 1970. More important, because there continues to be an in-migration of blacks from the depressed rural South, we can expect the number to grow rapidly during the next decade. By 1985, the ghetto population is likely to have risen to over 20 million (and because of the high birthrate, will reach 17 million, even if in-migration comes to a halt).[17]

Life in the ghetto is mean, hard, and poor. Crime rates are higher than elsewhere in the country. Housing is scarcer and more expensive. Living is not cheap but expensive: a Federal Trade Commission study has revealed that prices in Washington, D.C., ghetto stores averaged $255 for each $100 of wholesale cost, compared with $159 for stores in nonghetto areas of the city.[18]

Typically, unemployment is rife in the ghetto. In 1970, the unemployment rate in poor urban neighborhoods was 60 percent higher than in the country at large. Among black teenagers, it reached a catastrophic level of 42 percent.[19] And even this may be an understatement of the problem, for a study of the slum labor market in New York City in 1966 revealed a "subemployment" rate that was three times higher than the official "unemployment" figure.[20] (This is a rate that takes into consideration the special problems of very low-wage employment and of the failure of official statistics to report on those who were so discouraged that they were no longer even looking for work.)

[17] W.K. Tabb, *The Political Economy of the Ghetto* (New York: Norton, 1970), p. 8: Carolyn Shaw Bell, *The Economics of the Ghetto* (New York: Pegasus, 1970), *passim.*

[18] *Tabb, ibid.,* pp. 38–40; Bell, *ibid.,* pp. 142–43.

[19] *The New York Times,* Jan. 25, 1971, p. 1.

[20] *Poverty and Economic Development in New York City,* First National City Bank (December 1968), p. 25.

Perhaps worst of all is the outlook for those who grow up in the ghetto and want to escape. The same New York City study revealed how tragically mismatched were the skills (or lack of skills) offered by the ghetto resident and those wanted by the outside world.

TABLE 1 • 1

THE SKILLS
GAP

	Occupational distribution of ghetto unemployed, 1966	Estimated job openings, 1965–1975
White collar	13.6%	65.7%
Craftsmen	2.8	7.4
Operatives	14.7	7.7
Service	16.6	18.6
Laborers and others	52.3	0.6

Source: First National City Bank, op cit., p. 12.

As the table shows, in only one category—service—was the prospective demand for labor roughly in line with the skills that were available. This meant a reasonable employment prospect for maids, restaurant workers, bellhops, and the like—among the lowest-paid occupations in the nation. As for the common laborer, who comprised over half the "skill pool" of the New York ghetto, the outlook for his services was bleak indeed—less than 1 percent of the estimated new jobs would fall in that category. Conversely, for the widest job market in the outside world, the white-collar trades that will offer over two-thirds of the new jobs over the decade ahead—the ghetto was able to offer only one-seventh of its residents as adequately trained. If these figures have any meaning at all, it is that ghetto poverty is here to stay, short of a herculean effort to retrain the trapped ghetto resident.

PROBLEMS VS.
SOLUTIONS

This is not a balanced view of America, and it is not meant to be. On the one hand it omits everything that is reassuring or healthy on our economic scene; but it also omits areas in which economic problems remain to be explored. Unemployment *outside* the ghetto; the seemingly intractable problem of inflation; the power of giant corporations and strategically located labor unions; the relationship of rich America to the economies of the underdeveloped world—all these and still other problems remain for examination.

Hence what we have covered is no more than a partial inventory of America's debits and none of its credits. More important, we have only described in a journalistic way the things that are troubling America's conscience and we have as yet made no effort to probe into their origins or to assess their consequences. In short, we have done little more than make explicit some of the questions that we have in mind when we ask "Is economics relevant?" and some of the problems to which a textbook on economics should address itself.

Now it is time to conclude this initial plunge into some of the realities of the American scene, and to prepare ourselves for the lengthy and careful analysis that is to follow. That analysis will take us with disconcerting suddenness from the concerns of today to those of the ancient—and yet, as we will see, not entirely "remote"—past. We are going to take a detour through history before we come out again upon the present, to look around with new perspectives on today's problems. Throughout this journey through economic history we shall be dealing with problems in some ways different from those we have raised in this first documentary view of America. Yet, by the time we have completed our historical and analytical tour, I hope that America's problems will be understandable in ways that they were not before we started.

There remains only one question before we embark on our historical search. It is the question of what is the root cause of the panorama of problems we have encountered in America Today. All through the 1960s we tended to think of these problems as faults and flaws within an essentially sound economic system, for which specific remedies could be found. But in the 1970s a more disturbing question is in the air. It asks: are the problems the consequence of the system itself? Can our kind of economic society produce a decent, peaceful, compassionate way of life? *Or can the troubles of our time be corrected only drastically, by dismantling American capitalism and creating a new economic system?*

That is the fundamental question to which this entire book is ultimately directed. But it is not a question to be taken on at once. To cope with it, we will need to draw on a considerable understanding of economic history. Hence, only when we have gained some perspective on capitalism will we attempt to risk an answer to a question so profound and momentous as whether American capitalism is salvageable, despite its problems.

So we shall have to complete a course of study before the final answer. But meanwhile, I trust that one thing has become indisputably clear: that economics is concerned with dramatic and decisive issues that are likely to affect you for the rest of your life. Many years ago, when I wrote *The Worldly Philosophers,** I said:

A man who thinks that economics is only a matter for professors forgets that this is the science that has sent men to the barricades. A man who has looked into an economics textbook and concluded that economics is boring is like a man who has read a primer on logistics and decided that the study of warfare must be dull.

I hope that this book will not be boring and that those who read it will not conclude that economics had best be left to the professordom, because the problems of America Tomorrow will depend to no small degree on the economic understanding of those who are studying America Today.

CONCEPTS, WORDS, AND QUESTIONS

All the following chapters end with summaries of key concepts—to help you focus on the important propositions in that chapter—key words to add to your vocabulary, and questions to make you think out for yourself the main points at issue. But in this first chapter, I think a summary is out of place, and questions are premature. This is not a chapter to be "studied," but one to be thought about. If it has made you angry or troubled, it has served its purpose. Now you are in the right mood to begin to study modern economics itself.

* At the front of the book, the reader will find a gallery of those sometimes very worldly and sometimes out-of-this worldly characters drawn by Bernarda Bryson. I am grateful to the *Scientific American* for permission to use one of Miss Bryson's drawings.

The emergence

of modern

economic

society

Having decided on our course of exploration, it would be convenient if we could immediately begin to examine our economic past. But not quite yet. Before we can retrace economic history, we need to know what economic history *is*. And that, in turn, requires us to take a moment to clarify what we mean by economics and by the economic problem itself.

The answer is not a complicated one. Economics is essentially the study of a process we find in all human societies—"the" economic problem is simply *the process of providing for the material well-being of society.* In its simplest terms, economics is the study of how man earns his daily bread.

This hardly seems like a particularly exciting subject for historical scrutiny. Indeed, when we look back over the pageant of what is usually called "history," the humble matter of bread hardly strikes the eye at all. Power and glory, faith and fanaticism, ideas and ideologies are the aspects of the human chronicle that crowd the pages of history books. If the simple quest for bread is a moving force in human destiny, it is well concealed behind what one philosopher historian has called "that history of international crime and mass murder which has been advertised as the history of mankind."[1]

Yet, if man does not live by bread alone, it is obvious that he cannot live without bread. Like every other living thing, the human being must eat—the imperious first rule of continued existence. And this first prerequisite is less to be taken for granted than at first appears, for the human organism is not, in itself, a highly efficient mechanism for survival. From each hundred calories of food it consumes, it can deliver only about twenty calories of mechanical energy. On a decent diet, man can produce just about one horsepower-hour of work daily, and with that he must replenish his exhausted body. With what is left over, he is free to build a civilization.

As a result, in many countries, the sheer continuity of human existence is far from assured. In the vast continents of Asia and Africa, in the Near

---

[1] Karl Popper, *The Open Society and Its Enemies,* 3rd ed. (London: Routledge, 1957), II, 270.

East, even in some countries of South America, brute survival is the problem that stares humanity in the face. Millions of human beings have died of starvation or malnutrition in our present era, as countless hundreds of millions have died over the long past. Whole nations are acutely aware of what it means to face hunger as a condition of ordinary life; it has been said, for example, that the Egyptian fellah, from the day he is born to the day he dies, never knows what it is to have a full stomach. In many of the so-called underdeveloped nations, the life span of the average person is less than half of ours. Not many years ago, an Indian demographer made the chilling calculation that of one hundred Asian and one hundred American infants, more Americans would be alive at age sixty-five than Indians at age *five!* The statistics, not of life but of premature death throughout most of the world, are overwhelming and crushing.

Thus we can see that economic history must focus on the central problem of survival and on how man has solved that problem. For most Americans, this may make economics seem very remote. Few of us are conscious of anything resembling a life-or-death struggle for existence. That it might be possible for us to experience severe want, that we might ever know in our own bodies the pangs of hunger experienced by an Indian villager or a Bolivian peon is a thought nearly impossible for most of us to entertain seriously.

Short of a catastrophic war, it is highly unlikely that many of us ever will know the full meaning of the struggle for existence. Nonetheless, even in our prosperous and secure society, there remains, however unnoticed, an aspect of life's precariousness, a reminder of the underlying problem of survival. *This is our helplessness as economic individuals.*

For it is a curious fact that as we leave the most impoverished peoples of the world, where the human being with his too few calories scratches out for himself a bare subsistence, we find the economic insecurity of the individual many times multiplied. The solitary Eskimo, Bushman, Indonesian, Nigerian, left to his own devices, will survive a considerable time. Living close to the soil or to his animal prey, such an individual can sustain his own life, at least for a while, singlehanded. With a community numbering only a few hundred, he can live indefinitely. Indeed, a very large percentage of the human race today lives in precisely such fashion—in small, virtually self-contained peasant communities that provide for their own survival with a minimum of contact with the outside world. This large portion of mankind suffers great poverty, but it also knows a certain economic independence. If it did not, it would have been wiped out centuries ago.

When we turn to the New Yorker or the Chicagoan, on the other hand, we are struck by exactly the opposite condition, by a prevailing ease of material life coupled with an extreme *dependence* on others. We can no longer envisage the solitary individual or the small community surviving unaided in the great metropolitan areas where most Americans live, unless they loot warehouses or stores for food and necessities. The overwhelming majority of Americans have never grown food, caught game, raised meat, ground grain into flour, or even fashioned flour into bread. Faced with the challenge of clothing themselves or building their own homes, they would be hopelessly untrained and unprepared. Even to make minor repairs in the machines which surround them, they must call on other members of the community whose business it is to fix cars or repair plumbing or whatever. Paradoxically, perhaps, the richer the nation, the more apparent is this inability of its average inhabitant to survive unaided and alone.

DIVISION OF LABOR

There is, of course, an answer to the paradox. We survive in rich nations because the tasks we cannot do ourselves are done for us by an army of others on whom we can call for help. If we cannot grow food, we can buy it; if we cannot provide for our needs ourselves, we can hire the services of someone who can. This enormous *division of labor* enhances our capacity a thousandfold, for it enables us to benefit from other men's skills as well as our own.

Along with this invaluable gain, however, comes a certain risk. It is a sobering thought, for example, that we depend on the services of less than 150,000 men—only one out of every five hundred people working in the nation—to provide us with that basic commodity, coal. An even smaller number of workers—only one third as many—are responsible for running the locomotives that haul all the nation's rail freight and passenger service. A still smaller number—roughly 20,000—comprises our total commercial aircraft pilot crew. A failure of any one of these very small groups to perform its functions would cripple us: in the case of airplane pilots, slightly; in the case of locomotive engineers, badly; in the case of coal miners, perhaps disastrously. As we know, when from time to time we face a bad strike, our entire economic machine may falter because a strategic group ceases to perform its accustomed tasks.

Thus along with the abundance of material existence as we know it goes a hidden vulnerability: our abundance is assured only insofar as the organized cooperation of huge armies of people is to be counted upon. Indeed, our continuing existence as a rich nation hinges on the tacit precondition that the mechanism of social organization will continue to function effectively. *We are rich, not as individuals, but as members of a rich society, and our easy assumption of material sufficiency is actually only as reliable as the bonds that forge us into a social whole.*

Strangely enough, then, we find that man, not nature, is the source of most of our economic problems, at least above the level of subsistence. To be sure, the economic problem itself—that is, the need to struggle for existence—derives ultimately from the *scarcity* of nature. If there were no scarcity, goods would be as free as air, and economics—at least in one sense of the word—would cease to exist as a social preoccupation.

And yet if the scarcity of nature sets the stage for the economic problem, it does not impose the only strictures against which men must struggle. For scarcity, as a felt condition, is not solely the fault of nature. If Americans today, for instance, were content to live at the level of Mexican peasants, all our material wants could be fully satisfied with but an hour or two of daily labor. We would experience little or no scarcity, and our economic problems would virtually disappear. Instead, we find in America—and indeed in all industrial societies—that as the ability to increase nature's yield has risen, so has the reach of human wants. In fact, in societies such as ours, where relative social status is importantly connected with the possession of material goods, we often find that "scarcity" as a psychological experience and goad becomes more pronounced as we grow wealthier: our desires to possess the fruits of nature race out ahead of our mounting ability to produce goods.

Thus the "wants" that nature must satisfy are by no means fixed. But, for that matter, nature's yield itself is not a constant. It varies over a wide range, depending on the social application of human energy and skill. Scarcity is therefore not attributable to nature alone but to "human nature" as well; and economics is ultimately concerned not merely with the stinginess of the physical environment, but equally with the appetite of the human being and the productive capability of the community.

Hence we must begin a systematic analysis of economics by singling out the functions that social organization must perform to bring human nature into social harness. And when we turn our attention to this fundamental problem, we can quickly see that it involves the solution of two related and yet separate elemental tasks:

1. *A society must organize a system to assure the production of enough goods and services for its own survival.*
2. *Society must also arrange the distribution of the fruits of its production so that more production can take place.*

These two tasks of economic continuity are, at first look, very simple.* But it is a deceptive simplicity. Much of economic history, as we shall see, is concerned with the manner in which various societies have sought to cope with these elementary problems; and what strikes us in surveying their attempts is that most of them were partial failures. (They could not have been total failures, or society would not have survived.) Hence it behooves us to look more carefully into the two main economic tasks, to see what hidden difficulties they may conceal.

Production and Distribution Problems

MOBILIZING
EFFORT

What are the obstacles that a society encounters in organizing a system to produce the goods and services it needs?

Since nature is usually stingy, it seems that the production problem must be essentially one of applying engineering or technical skills to the resources at hand, of avoiding waste and utilizing social effort as efficaciously as possible.

This is indeed an important task for any society, and a great deal of formal economic thought, as the word itself suggests, is devoted to economizing. Yet this is not the core of the production problem. Long before a society can even concern itself about using its energies "economically," it must first marshal the energies to carry out the productive process itself. That is, *the basic problem of production is to devise social institutions that will mobilize human energy for productive purposes.*

This basic requirement is not always so easily accomplished. For example, in the United States in 1933, the energies of nearly thirteen million people—one-quarter of our work force—were not directed into the produc-

---

* In a more technical treatment of the Economic Problem, it is customary to note that the production problem is itself a twofold task, involving both a choice of different *ends* to which effort may be put and also of different *methods* by which those ends may be sought. Here, where the challenge of social organization is emphasized, we combine these two tasks into a single overarching concern.

tion process at all. Although these unemployed men and women were eager to work, although empty factories were available for them to work in, despite the existence of pressing wants, somehow a terrible and mystifying breakdown short-circuited the production process, with the result that an entire third of our previous annual output of goods and services simply disappeared.

We are by no means the only nation that has, on occasion, failed to find work for willing workers. In the very poorest nations, where production is most desperately needed, we frequently find that unemployment is a chronic condition. The streets of the Asian cities are thronged with people who cannot find work. But this, too, is not a condition imposed by the scarcity of nature. There is, after all, an endless amount of work to be done, if only in cleaning the filthy streets or patching up the homes of the poor, building roads, or digging ditches. Yet, what seems to be lacking is a social mechanism to put the unemployed to work.

Both these examples point out to us that the production problem is not solely a physical and technical struggle with nature. On these "scarcity" aspects of the problem will depend the speed with which a nation may forge ahead and the level of well-being it can reach with a given effort. But the original mobilization of productive effort itself is a challenge to its *social organization*, and on the success or failure of that social organization will depend the volume of the human effort that can be directed to nature.

But putting men to work is only the first step in the solution of the production problem. Men must not only be put to work; they must be put to work *in the right places*. They must produce the goods and services that society needs. Thus, *in addition to assuring a large enough quantity of social effort, the economic institutions of society must also assure a viable allocation of that social effort.*

In a nation such as India or Bolivia, where the great majority of the population is born in peasant villages and grows up to be peasant cultivators, the solution to this problem offers little to vex our understanding. The basic demands of society—food and fiber—are precisely the goods that its peasant population "naturally" produces. But in an industrial society, the proper allocation of effort becomes an enormously complicated task. People in the United States demand much more than bread and cotton. They need, for instance, such things as automobiles. Yet no one "naturally" produces an automobile. On the contrary, in order to produce one, an extraordinary spectrum of special tasks must be performed. Some people must make steel; others must make rubber. Still others must coordinate the assembly process itself. And this is but a tiny sampling of the far from "natural" tasks that must be performed if an automobile is to be produced.

As with the mobilization of its total production effort, society does not always succeed in the proper allocation of its effort. It may, for instance, turn out too many cars or too few. Of greater importance, it may devote its energies to the production of luxuries while large numbers of its people are starving. Or it may even court disaster by an inability to channel its productive effort into areas of critical importance. In the early 1950s, for instance, the British suffered a near economic collapse because they were unable to get enough of their workers to mine coal.

Such allocative failures may affect the production problem quite as seriously as a failure to mobilize an adequate quantity of effort, for a viable society must produce not only goods, but the right goods. And the allocative question alerts us to a still broader conclusion. It shows us that the act of production, in and of itself, does not fully answer the requirements for survival. Having produced enough of the *right* goods, society must now *distribute* those goods so that the production process can go on.

DISTRIBUTING
OUTPUT

Once again, in the case of the peasant who feeds himself and his family from his own crop, this requirement of adequate distribution may seem simple enough. But when we go beyond the most primitive society, the problem is not always so readily solved. In many of the poorest nations of the East and South, urban workers have often been unable to deliver their daily horsepower-hour of work because they have not been given enough of society's output to run their human engines to capacity. Worse yet, they have often languished on the job while granaries bulged with grain and the well-to-do complained of the ineradicable laziness of the masses. At the other side of the picture, the distribution mechanism may fail because the rewards it hands out do not succeed in persuading people to perform their necessary tasks. Shortly after the Russian Revolution, some factories were organized into communes in which managers and janitors pooled their pay, and from which all drew equal allotments. The result was a rash of absenteeism on the part of the previously better-paid workers and a threatened breakdown in industrial production. Not until the old unequal wage payments were reinstituted did production resume its former course.

As was the case with failures in the production process, distributive failures need not entail a total economic collapse. Societies can exist—and indeed, in the majority of cases, do exist—with badly distorted productive and distributive efforts. It is only rarely, as in the instances above, that maldistribution actively interferes with the actual ability of a society to staff its production posts. More frequently, an inadequate solution to the distribution problem reveals itself in social and political unrest or even in revolution.

Yet this, too, is an aspect of the total economic problem. For if society is to insure its steady material replenishment, it must parcel out its production in a fashion that will maintain not only the capacity but the willingness to go on working. And thus again we find the focus of economic inquiry directed to the study of human institutions. For a viable economic society, we can now see, is not only one which can overcome the stringencies of nature, but one which can contain and control the intransigence of human nature.

The Three Solutions to the Economic Problem

Thus to the economist, society presents itself in what is to us an unaccustomed aspect. Underneath the problems of poverty or pollution or the arms economy, he sees a process at work that he must understand before he can turn his attention to the issues of the day, no matter how pressing. That process is society's basic *mechanism for survival*, a mechanism for accomplishing the complicated tasks of its production and distribution necessary for its own continuity.

But the economist sees something else as well, something that at first seems quite astonishing. Looking not only over the diversity of contemporary societies, but back over the sweep of all history, he sees that man has succeeded in solving the production and distribution problems in but three ways. That is, within the enormous diversity of the actual social institutions that guide and shape the economic process, the economist divines but three overarching *types* of systems which separately or in combination enable humankind to solve its economic challenge. These great systemic types can be called economies run by *Tradition*, economies run by *Command*, and economies run by the *Market*. Let us briefly see what is characteristic of each.

TRADITION

Perhaps the oldest and, until a very few years ago, by far the most generally prevalent way of solving the economic challenge has been that of tradition. It has been a mode of social organization in which both production and distribution were based on procedures devised in the distant past, rigidified by a long process of historic trial and error, and maintained by heavy sanctions of law, custom, and belief.

Societies based on tradition solve the economic problems very manageably. First, they deal with the production problem—the problem of assuring that the needful tasks will be done—by assigning the jobs of fathers to their sons. Thus a hereditary chain assures that skills will be passed along and jobs will be staffed from generation to generation. In ancient Egypt, wrote Adam Smith, the first great economist, "every man was bound by a principle of religion to follow the occupation of his father and was supposed to commit the most horrible sacrilege if he changed it for another."[2] And it was not merely in antiquity that tradition preserved a productive orderliness within society. In our own Western culture, until the fifteenth or sixteenth centuries, the hereditary allocation of tasks was also the main stabilizing force within society. Although there was some movement from country to town and from occupation to occupation, birth usually determined one's role in life. One was born to the soil or to a trade; and on the soil or within the trade, one followed in the footsteps of one's forebears.

Thus tradition has been the stabilizing and impelling force behind a great repetitive cycle of society, assuring that society's work would be done each day very much as it had been done in the past. Even today, among the less industrialized nations of the world, tradition continues to play this immense organizing role. In India, for example, until very recently, one was born to a caste which had its own occupation. "Better thine own work is, though done with fault," preached the Bhagavad-Gita, the great philosophic moral poem of India, "than doing other's work, even excellently."

Tradition not only provides a solution to the production problem of society, but it also regulates the distribution problem. Take, for example, the Bushmen of the Kalahari Desert in South Africa who depend for their livelihood on their hunting prowess. Elizabeth Marshall Thomas, a sensitive observer of these peoples, reports on the manner in which tradition solves the problem of distributing their kill.

The gemsbok has vanished ... Gai owned two hind legs and a front leg, Tsetchwe had meat from the back, Ukwane had the other front leg, his wife had one of the feet and the stomach, the young boys had lengths of intestine. Twikwe had received the head and Dasina the udder.

It seems very unequal when you watch Bushmen divide the kill, yet it is their system, and in the end no person eats more than any other. That day Ukwane gave Gai still another piece because Gai was his relation, Gai gave meat to Dasina because she was his wife's mother ... No one, of course, contested Gai's large share, because he had been the hunter and by their law that much belonged to him. No one doubted that he would share his large amount with others, and they were not wrong, of course; he did.[3]

The manner in which tradition can divide a social product may be, as the illustration shows, very subtle and ingenious. It may also be very crude and, by our standards, harsh. Tradition has often allocated to women, in nonindustrial societies, the most meager portion of the social product. But

---

[2] *The Wealth of Nations* (New York: Modern Library, 1937), p. 62.
[3] *The Harmless People* (New York: Knopf, 1959), pp. 49-50.

however much the end-product of tradition may accord with, or depart from, our accustomed moral views, we must see that it is a workable *method of dividing society's production.*

Traditional solutions to the economic problems of production and distribution are most commonly encountered in primitive agrarian or nonindustrial societies where, in addition to serving an economic function, the unquestioning acceptance of the past provides the necessary perseverance and endurance to confront harsh destinies. Yet even in our own society, tradition continues to play a part in solving the economic problem. It plays its smallest role in determining the distribution of our own social output, although the persistence of such traditional payments as tips to waiters, allowances to minors, or bonuses based on length of service are all vestiges of old traditional ways of distributing goods, as is the differential between men's and women's pay for equal work.

More important is the continued reliance on tradition, even in America, as a means of solving the production problem—that is, in allocating the performance of tasks. Much of the actual process of selecting an employment in our society is heavily influenced by tradition. We are all familiar with families in which sons follow their fathers into a profession or a business. On a somewhat broader scale, tradition also dissuades us from certain employments. Sons of American middle-class families, for example, do not usually seek factory work, even though factory jobs may pay better than office jobs, because blue-collar employment is not in the middle-class tradition.

Thus, even in our society—clearly not a "traditional" one—custom provides an important mechanism for solving the economic problem. But now we must note one very important consequence of the mechanism of tradition. *Its solution to the problems of production and distribution is a static one.* A society that follows the path of tradition in its regulation of economic affairs does so at the expense of large-scale rapid social and economic change.

Thus the economy of a Bedouin tribe or a Burmese village is in few essential respects changed today from what it was a hundred or even a thousand years ago. The bulk of the peoples living in tradition-bound societies repeat, in the daily patterns of their economic life, much of the routine that characterized them in the distant past. Such societies may rise and fall, wax and wane, but external events—war, climate, political adventures and misadventures—are mainly responsible for their changing fortunes. Internal, self-generated economic change is but a small factor in the history of most tradition-bound states. *Tradition solves the economic problem, but it does so at the cost of economic progress.*

A second manner of solving the problem of economic continuity also displays an ancient lineage. This is the method of imposed authority, of

COMMAND

economic command. It is a solution based not so much on the perpetuation of a viable system by the changeless reproduction of its ways, as on the organization of a system according to the orders of an economic commander-in-chief.

Not infrequently we find this authoritarian method of economic control superimposed upon a traditional social base. Thus the Pharaohs of Egypt exerted their economic dictates above the timeless cycle of traditional agricultural practice on which the Egyptian economy was based. By their orders, the supreme rulers of Egypt brought into being the enormous economic effort that built the pyramids, the temples, the roads. Herodotus, the Greek historian, tells us how the Pharaoh Cheops organized the task.

[He] ordered all Egyptians to work for himself. Some, accordingly, were appointed to draw stones from the quarries in the Arabian mountains down to the Nile, others he ordered to receive the stones when transported in vessels across the river. . . . And they worked to the number of a hundred thousand men at a time, each party during three months. The time during which the people were thus harassed by toil lasted ten years on the road which they constructed, and along which they drew the stones; a work, in my opinion, not much less than the Pyramid.[4]

The mode of authoritarian economic organization was by no means confined to ancient Egypt. We encounter it in the despotisms of medieval and classical China which produced, among other things, the colossal Great Wall, or in the slave labor by which many of the great public works of ancient Rome were built. Of course, we find it today in the dictates of the communist economic authorities. In less drastic form we find it also in our own society; for example, in the form of taxes—that is, in the preemption of part of our income by the public authorities for public purposes.

Economic command, like tradition, offers solutions to the twin problems of production and distribution. In times of crises, such as war or famine, it may be the only way in which a society can organize its manpower or distribute its goods effectively. Even in America, we commonly declare martial law when an area has been devastated by a great natural disaster. On such occasions we may press people into service, requisition homes, impose curbs on the use of private property such as cars, or even limit the amount of goods a family may consume.

Quite aside from its obvious utility in meeting emergencies, command has a further usefulness in solving the economic problem. Unlike tradition, the exercise of command has no inherent effect of slowing down economic change. Indeed, the exercise of authority is the most powerful instrument society has for *enforcing economic change.* Authority in modern China or Russia, for example, has effected radical alterations in the systems of pro-

[4] *Histories*, trans. Cary (London: 1901), Book II, p. 124.

duction and distribution. But again, even in our own society, it is sometimes necessary for economic authority to intervene into the normal flow of economic life, to speed up or bring about change. The government may, for instance, utilize its tax receipts to lay down a network of roads that will bring a backwater community into the flux of active economic life. It may undertake an irrigation system that will dramatically change the economic life of a vast region. It may deliberately alter the distribution of income among social classes.

To be sure, economic command which is exercised within the framework of a democratic political process is very different from that which is exercised by a dictatorship: there is an immense social distance between a tax system controlled by Congress and outright expropriation or labor impressment by a supreme and unchallengeable ruler. Yet whilst the means may be much milder, the *mechanism* is the same. In both cases, command diverts economic effort toward goals chosen by a higher authority. In both cases it interferes with the existing order of production and distribution, to create a new order ordained from "above."

This does not in itself serve to commend or condemn the exercise of command. The new order imposed by the authorities may offend or please our sense of social justice, just as it may improve or lessen the economic efficiency of society. Clearly, command can be an instrument of a democratic as well as of a totalitarian will. There is no implicit moral judgment to be passed on this second of the great mechanisms of economic control. Rather, it is important to note that no society—certainly no modern society—is without its elements of command, just as none is devoid of the influence of tradition. *If tradition is the great brake on social and economic change, so economic command can be the great spur to change.* As mechanisms for assuring the successful solution to the economic problem, both serve their purposes, both have their uses and their drawbacks. Between them, tradition and command have accounted for most of the long history of man's economic efforts to cope with his environment and with himself. The fact that human society has survived is testimony to their effectiveness.

THE MARKET

But there is also a third solution to the economic problem, a third way of maintaining socially viable patterns of production and distribution. This is the *market organization of society*—an organization that, in truly remarkable fashion, allows society to insure its own provisioning with a minimum of recourse either to tradition or command.

Because we live in a market-run society, we are apt to take for granted the puzzling—indeed, almost paradoxical—nature of the market solution to the economic problem. But assume for a moment that we could act as economic advisers to a society that had not yet decided on its mode of economic organization. Suppose, for instance, that we were called on to act as consultants to one of the new nations emerging on the continent of Africa.

We could imagine the leaders of such a nation saying, "We have always experienced a highly tradition-bound way of life. Our men hunt and cultivate the fields and perform their tasks as they are brought up to do by the force of example and the instruction of their elders. We know, too, something of what can be done by economic command. We are prepared, if necessary, to sign an edict making it compulsory for many of our men to work on community projects for our national development. Tell us, is there any other way we can organize our society so that it will function successfully—or better yet, more successfully?"

Suppose we answered, "Yes, there is another way. Organize your society along the lines of a market economy."

"Very well," say the leaders. "What do we then tell people to do? How do we assign them to their various tasks?"

"That's the very point," we would answer. "In a market economy, no one is assigned to any task. In fact, the main idea of a market society is that each person is allowed to decide for himself what to do."

There is consternation among the leaders. "You mean there is no assignment of some men to mining and others to cattle raising? No manner of designating some for transportation and others for weaving? You leave this to people to decide for themselves? But what happens if they do not decide correctly? What happens if no one volunteers to go into the mines, or if no one offers himself as a railway engineer?"

"You may rest assured," we tell the leaders, "none of that will happen. In a market society, all the jobs will be filled because it will be to people's advantage to fill them."

Our respondents accept this with uncertain expressions. "Now look," one of them finally says, "let us suppose that we take your advice and allow our people to do as they please. Let's talk about something specific, like cloth production. Just how do we fix the right level of cloth output in this 'market society' of yours?"

"But you don't," we reply.

"We don't! Then how do we know there will be enough cloth produced?"

"There will be," we tell him. "The market will see to that."

"Then how do we know there won't be *too much* cloth produced?" he asks triumphantly.

"Ah, but the market will see to that too!"

"But what is this market that will do these wonderful things? Who runs it?"

"Oh, nobody runs the market," we answer. "It runs itself. In fact there really isn't any such *thing* as 'the market.' It's just a word we use to describe the way people behave."

"But I thought people behaved the way they wanted to!"

"And so they do," we say. "But never fear. They will want to behave the way you want them to behave."

"I am afraid," says the chief of the delegation, "that we are wasting our time. We thought you had in mind a serious proposal. What you suggest is inconceivable. Good day, sir."

Could we seriously suggest to such an emergent nation that it entrust itself to a market solution of the economic problem? That will be a problem to which we shall return at the very end of our book. But the perplexity which the market idea would rouse in the mind of someone unacquainted with it may serve to increase our own wonderment at this most sophisticated and interesting of all economic mechanisms. How does the market system assure us that our mines will find miners, our factories workers? How does it take care of cloth production? How does it happen that in a market-run nation each person can indeed do as he wishes and, withal, fulfill needs that society as a whole presents?

Economics, as we commonly conceive it and as we shall study it in much of this book, is primarily concerned with these very problems. Societies that rely primarily on tradition to solve their economic problems are of less interest to the professional economist than to the cultural anthropologist or the sociologist. Societies that solve their economic problems primarily by the exercise of command present interesting economic questions, but here the study of economics is necessarily subservient to the study of politics and the exercise of power.

It is a society that solves its economic problems by the market process that presents an aspect especially interesting to the economist. Clearly, many (although not all) of the problems we encounter in America today have to do with the workings or misworkings of the market system. And precisely *because* our contemporary problems often arise from the operations of the market, we study economics itself. Unlike the case with tradition and command, where we quickly grasp the nature of the economic mechanism of society, when we turn to a market society we are lost without a knowledge of economics. For in a market society it is not at all clear that even the simplest problems of production and distribution will be solved by the free interplay of individuals without guidance from tradition or command; nor is it clear how and to what extent the market mechanism is to be blamed for society's ills—after all, we can find poverty and neglect and pollution and armaments in nonmarket economies too!

In subsequent parts of this book we shall analyze these puzzling questions in more detail. But the task of our initial exploration must now be clear. As our imaginary interview with the leaders of an emergent nation has suggested, the market solution appears very strange to someone brought up in the ways of tradition or command. Hence the question arises: how did the market solution itself come into being? Was it imposed, full-blown, on our society at some earlier date? Or did it arise spontaneously and without forethought? This is the focusing question of economic history to which we now turn, as we retrace the evolution of our own market system out of the tradition and authority dominated societies of the past.

KEY CONCEPTS AND KEY WORDS

Provisioning wants

1. Economics is the study of how man assures his material sufficiency, of how societies arrange for their *material provisioning.*

Scarcity

2. Economic problems arise because the wants of most societies exceed the gifts of nature, giving rise to the general condition of *scarcity.*

3. Scarcity, in turn (whether it arises from nature's stinginess or man's appetites) imposes two severe tasks on society:

Production

a) It must mobilize its energies for *production*—producing not only enough goods, but the right goods, and

Distribution

b) It must resolve the problem of *distribution,* arranging a satisfactory solution to the problem of Who Gets What?

Division of labor

4. These problems exist in all societies, but they are especially difficult to solve in advanced societies in which there exists a far-reaching *division of labor.* Men in wealthy societies are far more socially interdependent than men in simple societies.

5. Over the course of history, there have evolved three types of solutions to the two great economic problems. These are *Tradition, Command,* and the *Market System.*

Tradition

6. Tradition solves the problems of production and distribution by enforcing a continuity of tasks and rewards through social institutions such as the caste system. *Typically, the economic solution imposed by Tradition is a static one,* in which little change occurs over long periods of time.

Command

7. Command solves the economic problem by imposing allocations of effort or reward by *governing authority.* Command can be a means for achieving rapid and far-reaching economic *change.* It can take extreme totalitarian or mild democratic forms.

Market

8. The market system is a complex mode of organizing society in which order and efficiency emerge "spontaneously" from a seemingly uncontrolled society. We shall investigate the market system in great detail in the chapters to come.

QUESTIONS

1. If everyone could produce all the food he needed in his own backyard, and if technology were so advanced that we could all make anything we wanted in our basements, would an "economic problem" exist?

2. Suppose that everyone were completely versatile—able to do everyone else's work just as well as his own. Would a division of labor still be useful in society? Why?

3. Modern economic society is sometimes described as depending on "organization men" who allow their lives to be directed by the large corporations for which they work. Assuming that this description has some glimmer of truth, would you think that modern society should be described as one of Tradition, Command, or the Market?

4. In what way do your own plans for the future coincide with or depart from the occupations of your parents? Do you think that the so-called generational split is observable in all modern societies?

5. Economics is often called the science of scarcity. How can this label be applied to a society of considerable affluence such as our own?

6. What elements of Tradition and Command do you think are indispensable in a modern industrial society? Do you think that modern society could exist without any dependence on Tradition or without any exercise of Command?

7. Much of production and distribution involves the creation or the handling of *things.* Why are production and distribution *social* problems rather than engineering or physical problems?

8. Do you consider man's wants to be insatiable? Does this imply that scarcity must always exist?

9. Take the main problems that disturbed us in "America Today": neglect, poverty, armaments, pollution, racial discrimination. To what extent do you find such problems in societies run by Tradition? By Command? What is your feeling about the responsibility the market system bears for these problems in America?

"Nobody ever saw a dog make a fair and deliberate exchange of one bone for another with another dog," wrote Adam Smith in *The Wealth of Nations*. "Nobody ever saw one animal by its gestures and natural cries signify to another, this is mine, that yours; I am willing to give this for that."[1]

Smith was writing about "a certain propensity in human nature . . . ; the propensity to truck, barter, and exchange one thing for another." That such a propensity exists as a universal characteristic of humankind is perhaps less likely than Smith believed, but he was certainly not mistaken in putting the act of exchange at the very center of his scheme of economic life. For there can be no doubt that exchange, buying and selling, lies at the very heart of a market society such as he was describing. And so, as we now begin to study the rise of the market society, what could be more natural than to commence by tracing the pedigree of markets themselves?

It comes as something of a surprise, perhaps, to discover how very ancient is that pedigree. Men have traded with one another at least as far back as the last Ice Age. We have evidence that the mammoth-hunters of the Russian steppes obtained Mediterranean shells in trade, as did also the Cro-Magnon hunters of the central valleys of France. In fact, on the moors of Pomerania in northeastern Germany, archeologists have come across an oaken box, replete with the remains of its original leather shoulder strap, in which were a dagger, a sickle head, and a needle—all of Bronze Age manufacture. According to the conjectures of experts, this was very likely the sample kit of a prototype of the traveling salesman, an itinerant representative who collected orders for the specialized production of his community.[2]

And as we proceed from the dawn of civilization to its first organized societies, the evidences of trade and of markets increase rapidly. As Miriam Beard has written:

Millennia before Homer sang, or the wolf suckled Romulus and Remus, the bustling damkars (traders) of Uruk and Nippur . . . were buckling down to business. Atidum the merchant, in need of enlarged office facilities, was agreeing to rent a suitable

---

[1] Smith, *The Wealth of Nations*, p. 13.
[2] *Cambridge Economic History of Europe* (Cambridge: Cambridge University Press, 1952), II, 4.

location from Ribatum, Priestess of Shamash, for one and one-sixth shekels of silver per year—so much down and the rest in easy installments. Abu-wakar, the rich shipper, was delighted that his daughter had become Priestess of Shamash and could open a real estate office near the temple. Ilabras was writing to Ibi: "May Shamash and Marduk keep thee! As thou knowest, I had issued a note for a female slave. Now the time to pay is come."[3]

Thus at first glance it seems as if we can discover evidences of a market society deep in the past. But these disconcerting notes of modernity must be interpreted with caution. If markets, buying and selling, even highly organized trading bodies were well-nigh ubiquitous features of ancient society, they must not be confused with the equally ubiquitous presence of a *market society.* Trade existed as an important adjunct to society from earliest times, but the fundamental impetus to production, or the basic allocation of resources among different uses, or the distribution of goods among social classes was largely divorced from the marketing process. That is, *the markets of antiquity were not the means by which those societies solved their basic economic problems.* They were subsidiary to the great processes of production and distribution rather than integral to them; they were "above" the critical economic machinery rather than within it. As we shall see, between the deceptively contemporary air of many markets of the distant past and the reality of our contemporary market economy lies an immense distance over which society would take centuries to travel.

The Economic Organization of Antiquity

We must ourselves traverse that distance if we are to understand how contemporary market society came into being and, indeed, if we are to understand what it is. For only by immersing ourselves in the societies of the past, only by seeing how they did, in fact, solve their economic prob-

---

[3] *A History of the Business Man* (New York: Macmillan, 1938), p. 12.

lems, can we begin to understand clearly what is involved in the evolution of the market society which is our own environment.

Needless to say, it would make an enormous difference which of the many pre-market societies of the past we visited as general observers. To trace economic history from the monolithic temple-states of Sumer and Akkad to the "modernity" of classical Greece or Rome is to undertake a cultural journey of fantastic distance. Yet, traveling only as economic historians, we will find that it makes much less difference in which of the societies of antiquity we light. For as we examine these societies, we can see that underlying their profound dissimilarities of art or political rule or religious belief, there are equally profound similarities of economic structure, similarities we call to mind less frequently because they are in the "background" of history and rarely adorn its more exciting pages. But these identifying characteristics of economic organization are the ones that now interest us as we turn our gaze to the past. What is it that we see?

AGRICULTURAL
FOUNDATION
OF ANCIENT
SOCIETIES

The first and perhaps the most striking impression is the overwhelmingly agricultural aspect of all these economies.

In a sense, of course, all human communities, no matter how industrialized, live off the soil: all that differentiates the "agricultural" society from the "industrial" is the number of the nonagricultural population that its food growers can support. Thus an American farmer, working a large acreage with abundant equipment, maintains more than thirty nonfarmers; while an Asian peasant, tilling his tiny plot with little more than a stick-plow, is often hard pressed to sustain his own family.

Over all of antiquity the capacity of the agricultural population to sustain a nonfarming population was very limited. Exact statistics are unavailable, but we can project backwards to the situation that prevailed in all these ancient nations by looking at the underdeveloped regions of the world today where the levels of technique and the productivity of agriculture bear a close—too close—resemblance to antiquity. Thus in India, in Egypt, in the Philippines, Indonesia, Brazil, Colombia, Mexico, we find that it takes two farm families to support one nonfarm family; while in tropical Africa, a survey tells us: "the productivity of African agriculture is still so low that it takes anywhere from two to ten people—men, women, and children—to raise enough food to supply their own needs and those of *one* additional—non-food-growing—adult."[4]

Antiquity was not *that* badly off; indeed at times it produced impressive agricultural outputs. But neither was it remotely comparable to American farm productivity with its enormous capacity to support a nonagricultural population. All ancient economic societies were basically rural econo-

[4] George H. T. Kimble, *Tropical Africa* (New York: Twentieth Century Fund, 1960), I, 572. (Italics added.)

mies. This did not preclude, as we shall see, a very brilliant and wealthy urban society nor a far-flung network of international trade. Yet the typical economic personage of antiquity was neither trader nor urban dweller. He was a tiller of the soil, and it was in his rural communities that the economies of antiquity were ultimately anchored.

But this must not lead us to assume that economic life was therefore comparable to that of a modern agricultural community like Denmark or New Zealand. Contemporary farmers, like businessmen, are very much bound up in the web of transactions characteristic of a market society. They sell their output on one market; they buy their supplies on another. The accumulation of money, and not of wheat or corn, is the object of their efforts. Books of profit and loss regularly tell them if they are doing well or not. The latest news of agricultural technology is studied and put into effect if it is profitable.

None of this properly describes the "farmer" of ancient Egypt, of antique Greece or Rome, or of the great Eastern civilizations. With few exceptions, the tiller of the soil was a peasant, and a peasant is a social creature very different from a farmer. He is not technologically alert but, on the contrary, clings with stubborn persistence—and often with great skill—to his well-known ways. He must, since a small error might mean starvation. He does not buy the majority of his supplies but, to a large extent, fashions them himself; similarly, he does not produce for a "market," but principally for himself. Finally, he is often not even free to consume his own crop, but typically must hand over a portion—a tenth, a third, half, or even more—to the owner of his land.

For in the general case, the peasant of antiquity did not own his land. We hear of the independent citizen—farmers of classical Greece and republican Rome, but these were exceptions to the general rule in which peasants were but tenants of a great lord. And even in Greece and Rome, the independent peasantry tended to become swallowed up as the tenantry of huge commercial estates. Pliny mentions one such enormous estate or latifundium (literally: broad farm) with a quarter of a million livestock and a population of 4,117 slaves.

Hence the peasant, who was the bone and muscle of the economies of antiquity, was in himself a prime example of the nonmarket aspect of these economies. Although some cultivators freely sold a portion of their own crop in the city marketplaces, the great majority of agricultural producers scarcely entered the market at all. For many of these producers—especially when they were slaves—this was, accordingly, an almost cashless world, where a few coppers a year, carefully hoarded and spent only for emergencies, constituted the only link with a world of market transactions.*

* This is not, let us note, only an ancient condition. Traveling in Morocco, John Gunther reported of the local peasant-serfs: "formerly they got no wages—what would they need money for—but this is changing now." *Changing now—in 1953! (Inside Africa.* New York: Harper, 1955, p. 104.)

Thus, whereas the peasant's legal and social status varied widely in different areas and eras of antiquity, in a broad view the tenor of his economic life was singularly constant. Of the web of transactions, the drive for profits of the modern farmer, he knew little or nothing. Generally poor, tax-ridden and oppressed, prey to nature's caprices and to the exploitation of war and peace, bound to the soil by law and custom, the peasant of antiquity—as the peasant today who continues to provide the agricultural underpinnings to the civilizations of the East and South—was dominated by the economic rule of tradition. His main stimulus for change was command—or, rather, obedience. Labor, patience, and the incredible endurance of the human being were his contributions to civilization.

ECONOMIC LIFE OF THE CITIES

The basic agricultural cast of ancient society and its typical exclusion of the peasant-cultivator from an active market existence makes all the more striking another common aspect of economic organization in antiquity. This is the diversity, vitality, and ebullience of the economic life of the cities.

Whether we turn to ancient Egypt, classical Greece, or Rome, we cannot help but be struck by this contrast between the relatively static countryside and the active city. In Greece, for example, a whole panoply of goods passed across the docks of the Piraeus: grain from Italy, metal from Crete and even Britain, books from Egypt, perfume from still more distant origins. Isocrates, in the *Panegyricus,* boasts: "The articles which it is difficult to get, one here, one there, from the rest of the world; all these it is easy to buy in Athens." So, too, Rome developed a thriving foreign and domestic commerce. By the time of Augustus, 6,000 loads of ox-towed barges were required to feed the city annually,[5] while in the city forum a crowd of speculators converged as on "an immense stock exchange."[6]

Thus something which at least superficially approximated our own society was visible in many of the larger urban centers of antiquity. And yet we must not be beguiled into the conclusion that this was a market society similar to our own. In at least two respects the differences were profound.

The first of these was the essentially restricted character and scope of the market function of the city. Unlike the modern city, which is not only a receiver of goods shipped in from the hinterlands but also an important exporter of goods and services back to the countryside, the cities of antiquity tended to assume an economically parasitic role vis-à-vis the rest of the economy. Much of the trade that entered the great urban centers of Egypt, Greece, and Rome (over and above the necessary provisioning of the city masses) was in the nature of luxury goods for its upper classes, rather than raw materials to be worked and then sent out to a goods-consuming

[5] *Cambridge Economic History of Europe,* II, 47.
[6] W. C. Cunningham, *An Essay on Western Civilization* (New York: 1913), p. 164.

economy. The cities were the vessels of civilization; but as centers of economic activity, a wide gulf separated them from the country, making the cities enclaves of economic life rather than nourishing components of integrated rural-urban economies.

Even more important was a second difference between the ancient city economies and a contemporary market society. This was their reliance on *slave labor*.

For slavery on a massive scale was a fundamental pillar of nearly every ancient economic society. In Greece, for instance, the deceptively modern air of the Piraeus masks the fact that much of the purchasing power of the Greek merchant was provided by the labor of 20,000 slaves who labored under sickening conditions in the silver mines of Laurentium. At the height of "democratic" Athens, it is estimated that at least one-third of its population were slaves. In Italy of 30 B.C., some 1,500,000 slaves—on the latifundia, in the galleys, the mines, the "factories," the shops—provided a major impetus in keeping the economic machinery in motion.[7] Seneca even tells us that a proposal that they wear special dress was voted down lest recognizing their own number, they might know their strength.

Slaves were not, of course, the only source of labor. Groups of free artisans and workmen, often banded together in *collegia* or fraternal bodies, also serviced the Roman city, as did similar free workmen in Greece and elsewhere. In many cities, especially latter-day Rome, a mass of unemployed (but not enslaved) laborers provided a source of casual work. Yet, without the motive power of the slave, it is doubtful if the brilliant city economies of the past could have been sustained. And this brings us to the central point. It is that the flourishing market economy of the city rested atop an economic structure run by tradition and command. Nothing like the free exercise and interplay of self-interest guided the basic economic effort of antiquity. If an astonishingly modern urban market structure greets our eye, we must not forget that its merchants are standing on the shoulders of innumerable peasants and slaves.

The presence of great agglomerations of urban wealth amid a far poorer rural setting alerts us to another characteristic of ancient economic society. This is the special relationship between its wealth and its underlying economic organization.

In any society, wealth implies that a *surplus* has been wrung from nature, that a social organization has not alone solved its economic produc-

---

[7] K. J. Beloch, *Die Bevölkerung der Griechisch-Römischen Welt* (Leipzig: 1886), p. 478.

tion problem but has achieved a margin of effort above that required for its own existence. Perhaps what first astonishes us when we regard the civilizations of the ancient world is the size of surplus which could be got from a basically poor peasant population. The temples of the ancient Assyrian kings, the extraordinary treasures of the Aztecs, the pyramids and pleasure craft of the Pharaohs of Egypt, the Acropolis of Athens, and the magnificent roads and architecture of Rome all testify to the ability of an essentially agricultural civilization to achieve a massive surplus, to pry considerable amounts of labor loose from the land, support it at whatever low level, and put it to work building for posterity.

But the stupendous achievements of the past testify as well to something else. The surplus productive potential that society manages to achieve (whether by technology or by adroit social organization) can be applied in many directions. It can be directed to agricultural improvements, such as irrigation ditches or dams, where it is apt to increase the bounty of the harvest still further. It can be applied to the tools and equipment of the city workman, where it is apt to raise his ability to produce. Or the surplus may be used to support a nonworking religious order or a class of courtiers and idle nobility. If it were not for its amazing capacity to produce a surplus, the United States could never support its armed forces—anymore than the U.S.S.R. could, if *its* economy did not also give rise to more output than it required for sheer self-perpetuation.

Thus the social form taken by the accumulation of wealth reveals a great deal about any society. "To whom does the surplus accrue?" is a question which invariably sheds important light on the structure of power within that society.

To whom did the wealth of antiquity accrue? At first glimpse it seems impossible to answer in a phrase. Emperors, nobles, religious orders, merchant traders—all enjoyed the wealth of antiquity at one time or another. But at second look, an interesting and significant generalization becomes possible: most wealth did not go to those who played a strictly *economic* role. Although there are records of clever slaves in Egypt and Rome who became wealthy, and although rich merchants and bankers are visible throughout the annals of antiquity, theirs was not the primary route to wealth. Rather, *in ancient civilization wealth was generally the reward for political, military, or religious power or status, and not for economic activity.*

There was a reason for this. Societies tend to reward most highly the activities they value most highly; and in the long and turbulent centuries of antiquity, political leadership, religious tutelage, and military prowess were unquestionably more necessary for social survival than trading *expertise*. In fact, in many of these societies, economic activity itself was disdained as essentially ignoble. As Aristotle wrote in his *Politics*, "in the best-governed polis . . . the citizens may not lead either the life of craftsmen or of traders, for such a life is devoid of nobility and hostile to perfection of character." It was a theme on which Cicero would later expand in his essay *De Officiis* (Book I).

The toil of a hired worker, who is paid only for his toil and not for artistic skill, is unworthy of a free man and is sordid in character. For in his case, money is the price of slavery. Sordid too is the calling of those who buy wholesale in order to sell retail, since they would gain no profits without a great deal of lying.... Trade on a small retail scale is sordid, but if it is on a large wholesale scale including the import of many wares from everywhere and their distribution to many people without any misrepresentation, it is not to be too greatly censured....

Especially, added the great lawyer, "if those who carry on such trade finally retire to country estates, after being surfeited or at least satisfied with their gains."

Over and above the lesser social function of the merchant compared with the general, the consul, or the priest, this disdain of wealth obtained from "ignoble" economic activity reflected an economic fact of great importance: society had not yet integrated the production of wealth with the production of goods. Wealth was still a surplus to be seized by conquest or squeezed from the underlying agricultural population; it was not yet a natural adjunct of a system of continuously increasing production in which some part of an expanding total social output might accrue to many classes of society.

And so it would be for many centuries. Until the smallest as well as the largest activities of society would receive their price tag, until purchases and sales, bids and offers would penetrate down to the lowest orders of society, the accumulation of wealth would always remain more a matter of political, military, or religious power than of economics. To sum it up: *in premarket societies, wealth tended to follow power; not until the market society would power tend to follow wealth.*

Before we move on to view the economic system of antiquity in transition and evolution, we must ask one more question. What did contemporary economists think of it?

The answer we find is an interesting one: there were no contemporary "economists." Historians, philosophers, political theorists, writers on manners and morals abounded during the long span of history we here call "antiquity," but economists, as such, did not exist. The reason is not far to seek. The economics of society—that is, the mode by which society organized itself to meet the basic tasks of economic survival—were hardly such as to provoke the curiosity of a thoughtful man. There was little or no "veil" of money to pierce, little or no complexity of contractual relationship in the marketplace to unravel, little or no economic rhythm of society to interpret. As the harvest flourished, as the justice or injustice of the tax

"ECONOMICS"
AND SOCIAL
JUSTICE IN
ANTIQUITY

gathering system varied, as the fortunes of war and politics changed, so went the lot of the peasant proprietor, the slave, the petty craftsman, and trader. As relative military strength rose or fell, as individual merchants fared luckily or otherwise, as the arts prospered or declined, so went the pulse of trade. As his prowess in war or politics permitted, as his chance at ransoms, local monopolies, or marriage dictated, so fared the individual acquisitor of wealth. In all of this there was little to tax the analytic powers of social observers.

If there was a problem of economics—aside from the eternal problems of poor harvests, fortunes of war, etc.—it was inextricably mingled with the problem of social justice. As far back as the early Assyrian tablets, we have records of reformers who sought to alleviate taxes on the peasantry, and throughout the Bible—indeed, down through the Middle Ages—a strain of primitive communism, of egalitarian sharing, runs through the background of religious thought. In the Book of Leviticus, for example, there is mentioned the interesting custom of the *jubilee* year, one year in each fifty, in which the Israelites were to "return to each man unto his possession."* But despite the fact that religion was concerned with riches and poverty, and thus with the distributive problem of economics, the span of antiquity saw little or no systematic inquiry into the *social system* which produced riches or poverty. If riches were an affront, this was due to the personal failings of greedy men; and if social justice were to be obtained, it must be achieved by personal redistribution, by alms and charity. The idea of an "economic" study of society, as contrasted with a political or moral one, was conspicuous largely by its absence.

There was, however, one exception which we should note. Aristotle, the great pupil of Plato, turned his powerful scrutiny to economic affairs, and with him the systematic study of economics, as such, truly begins. Not that Aristotle, any more than the majority of the Church fathers, was a radical social reformer. Much is summed up in his famous sentence: "From the hour of their birth, some are marked out for subjection, others for rule."[8] But the student of the history of economic thought turns first to Aristotle for questions whose treatment he can subsequently trace down through the present time: questions such as "What is value?" "What is the basis of exchange?" "What is interest?"

We will not linger here over Aristotle's formulations of these ideas. But one point we might note, for it accords with what we have already seen of the attitude of antiquity to economic activity itself. When Aristotle examined the economic process, he differentiated it into two branches—not

---

* That is, lands which had been forfeited in debt, etc., were to be restored to their original owners. The wrath of the later prophets such as Amos indicates that the injunction must have been observed largely in the breach.

[8] *Politics*, Book I.

production and distribution, as we have done, but *use* and *gain*. More specifically, he differentiated between *oeconomia*—whence "economics," and *chrematistike*, from which we have no precise derivative term. By *oeconomia* the Greek philosopher meant the art of household management, the administration of one's patrimony, the careful husbanding of resources. *Chrematistike*, on the other hand, implied the use of nature's resources or of human skill for acquisitive purposes: *chrematistike* was trade for trade's sake, economic activity that had as its motive and end not use, but profit. Aristotle approved of *oeconomia* but not of *chrematistike*, and within the scope of the essentially limited market structure of antiquity, where the city trader all too frequently exploited the country peasant, it is not hard to see why. The much more difficult problem of whether a market society, in which *everyone* strives for gain, might warrant approval or disapproval never appears in Aristotle's writings, as it never appeared in ancient history. The market society with its genuinely perplexing questions of economic order and economic morality had yet to come into being. Until it did, the philosophy needed to rationalize that order was understandably lacking.

Economic Society in the Middle Ages

Our conspectus of economic organization has thus far scanned only the great civilizations of antiquity. Now we must turn in somewhat closer focus to a society far nearer in time and, what is more important, immediately precedent to ours in terms of social evolution. This is the vast expanse of history we call the Middle Ages, an expanse which stretches over and describes the Western world, from Sweden to the Mediterranean, "beginning" with the fall of Rome and "ending" with the Renaissance.

Modern scholarship emphasizes more and more the diversity which characterizes that enormous span of time and space, a diversity not alone of social appearance from century to century but of contrast from locality to locality within any given period. It is one thing to speak of "life" in the Middle Ages if one has in mind a tenth century peasant community in Normandy where, it is estimated, the average inhabitant probably never saw more than two hundred or three hundred persons in his lifetime or commanded a vocabulary of more than six hundred words,[9] and another if we mean the worldly city of Florence about which Boccaccio wrote so engagingly.

Even more relevant for our purposes is the need to think of the Middle Ages in terms of economic variety and change. The early years of feudal

[9] George G. Coulton. *Medieval Village, Manor and Monastery* (New York: Harper, Torchbooks, 1960), p. 15.

economic life are very different from the middle or later years, particularly insofar as general well-being is concerned. The commencement of feudalism coincided with a period of terrible retrenchment, deprivation, depopulation. During the fifth century the population of Rome actually fell from 1,500,000 to 300,000. But by the twelfth century, towns had again expanded (after 600 years!) to the limits of their old Roman walls and even spilled out beyond; and by the beginning of the fourteenth century, a very considerable prosperity reigned in many parts of Europe.* Then came a series of catastrophes: a ghastly two-year famine in 1315; thereafter, in 1348, the Black Death, which carried off between one-third and two-thirds of the urban population; a century-long devastating struggle between England and France and among the petty principalities of Germany and Italy. All of these misfortunes pulled down the level of economic existence to dreadful depths. Neither stasis nor smooth linear progress, but enormous and irregular secular tides mark the long history of feudalism, and they caution us against a simplistic conception of its development.

Our purpose, however, is not to trace these tides, but rather to form a generalized picture of the *economic structure* which, beneath the swings of fortune, marks the feudal era as a unique way-station of Western economic history. And here we can begin by noting the all-important development which underlay the genesis of that economic structure. *This was the breakdown of large-scale political organization.*

For as Rome "fell" and as successive raids and invasions from north, east, and south tore apart the European countryside, the great administrative framework of law and order was replaced by a patchwork quilt of small-scale political entities. Even in the ninth century, when Charlemagne's Holy Roman Empire assumed such impressive dimensions on the map, beneath the veneer of a unified "state" there was, in fact, political chaos: neither a single language nor a coordinated central government nor a unified system of law, coinage, or currency nor, most important, any consciousness of "national" allegiance bound the statelets of Charlemagne's day into more than temporary cohesion.

We note this striking difference between antiquity and the Middle Ages to stress the tremendous economic consequences that came with political dissolution. As safety and security gave way to local autarky and anarchy, long voyages of commodities became extremely hazardous, and the once vigorous life of the great cities impossible. As a common coin and a common law disappeared, merchants in Gaul could no longer do business with merchants in Italy, and the accustomed network of economic connec-

* There is some evidence that in England around the year 1500, real wages for common laborers achieved a level that they would not again surpass for at least three centuries. (*Economica*, November 1956, pp. 296–314.)

tions was severed or fell into disuse. As disease and invasion depopulated the countryside, men turned of necessity to the most defensive forms of economic organization, to forms aimed at sheer survival through self-sufficiency. A new need arose, a need to compress the viable organization of society into the smallest possible compass. For centuries this insularity of economic life, this extreme self-reliance would be the economic hallmark of the Middle Ages.

The need for self-sufficiency brought with it a new basic unit of economic organization: the *manorial estate.*

What was such an estate like? Typically, it was a large tract of land, often including many thousands of acres, which was "owned" by a feudal lord, spiritual or temporal.* The word "owned" is properly in quotation marks, for the manor was not first and foremost a piece of economic property as such. Rather, it was a social and political entity in which the lord of the manor was not only landlord, but protector, judge, police chief, administrator. Although himself bound into a great hierarchy in which each lord was some other lord's servant (and even the pope was *servus servorum Dei)*, the feudal noble was, within the confines of his own manor, quite literally "lord of the land." He was also undisputed owner and master of many of the people who lived on the land, for the serfs (or villeins) of a manor, although not slaves, were in many respects as much the property of the lord as were his (or their) houses, flocks, or crops.

At the focal point of the estate was the lord's homestead, a great manor house, usually armed against attack from marauders, walled off from the surrounding countryside, and sometimes attaining the stature of a genuine castle. In the enclosed courtyard of the manor were workshops in which cloth might be spun or woven, grapes pressed, food stored, simple ironwork or blacksmithing work performed, coarse grain ground. Extending out around the manor was a patchwork of fields, typically subdivided into acre or half-acre "strips," each with its own cycle of crops and rest. Half or more of all of these belonged directly to the lord; the remainder "belonged," in various senses of that legal term, to the hierarchy of free, half-free, and unfree families who made up an estate.

The exact meaning of the word "belonged" hinged on the obligations and rights accruing to a serf, a freeman, or whatever other category one might be born into. Note however that even a freeman who "owned" his land could not sell it to another feudal lord. At best, his ownership meant

* That is, the lord might be the abbot or the bishop of the locality, or he might be a secular personage, a baron who came into his possessions by inheritance or by being made a knight and given lands for exceptional service in battle or for other reasons.

that he could not himself be displaced from his land short of extraordinary circumstances. A lesser personage than a freeman did not even have this security. A typical serf was literally tied to "his" plot of land. He could not, without specific permission and, usually, without specific payment, leave his homestead for another, either within the domain of the manor or within that of another. With his status came, as well, a series of obligations which lay at the very core of the manorial economic organization. These consisted of the necessity to perform labor for the lord—to till his fields, to work in his shops, to provide him with a portion of one's own crop. From manor to manor, and from age to age, the labor-dues varied: in some localities they amounted to as much as four or even five days of labor a week, which meant that only by the labor of a serf's wife or children could his own fields be maintained. And finally, the serfs owed small money-payments: head taxes, like the *chevage;* death-duties, like the *heriot;* or *merchet,* a marriage fee, or dues to use the lord's mill or his ovens.

There was, however, an extremely important *quid pro quo* for all of this. If the serf gave the lord his labor and much of the fruits of his toil, in exchange the lord provided some things which the serf alone could not have obtained.

The most important of these was a degree of physical security. It is difficult for us to reconstruct the violent tenor of much of feudal life, but one investigator has provided a statistic which may serve to make the point. Among the sons of English dukes, 46 percent of those born between 1330 and 1479 died violent deaths. Their life expectancy when violent death was excluded was 31 years; when violent death was included, it was but 24 years.[10] The peasant, although not a warrior and therefore not occupationally exposed to the dangers of continual combat, assassination, etc., was pre-eminently fair prey for the marauding lord, defenseless against capture, unable to protect his poor possessions against destruction. Hence we can begin to understand why even free men became serfs by "commending" themselves to a lord who, in exchange for their economic, social, and political subservience, offered them in return the invaluable cloak of his military protection.

In addition, the lord offered a certain element of *economic* security. In times of famine, it was the lord who fed his serfs from the reserves in his own manorial storehouses. And, although he had to pay for it, the serf was *entitled* to use the lord's own beasts and equipment in cultivating his own strips as well as those of the lord himself. In an age when the average serf possessed almost no tools himself, this was an essential boon.[11]

[10] T. H. Hollingsworth, "A Demographic Study of the British Ducal Families," *Population Studies,* XI (1957–58). I am indebted to Dr. Goran Ohlin for this reference.

[11] For a picture of life among the various classes in medieval Europe, one might turn to Eileen Power's *Medieval People* (Garden City, N.Y.: Doubleday, Anchor Books, 1954), a scholarly but

These facts should not incline us to an idyllic picture of feudal life. The relation between lord and serf was often and even usually exploitative in the extreme. Yet we must see that it was also mutually supportive. Each provided for the other services essential for existence in a world where over-all political organization and stability had virtually disappeared.

Despite the extreme self-sufficiency of manorial life, there is much here that resembles the economic organization of antiquity.

To begin with, like those earlier societies, this was clearly a form of economic society organized by tradition. Indeed, the hand of custom—the famous "ancient customs" of the medieval manor court which served frequently as the counsel for the otherwise undefended serf— was never stronger. Lacking strong unified central government, even the exercise of command was relatively weak. As a result, the pace of economic change, of economic development, although by no means lacking, was extremely slow during the early years of the medieval period.

Second, even more than with antiquity, this was a form of society which was characterized by a striking absence of money transactions. Unlike the latifundium of Rome, which sold its output to the city, the manor supplied only itself, and perhaps a local town. No manorial estate was ever quite so self-sufficient that it could dispense with monetary links with the outside world; even serfs bought a few commodities and sold a few eggs; and the lord, on occasion, had to buy considerable supplies which he could not produce for himself. But on the whole, very little money changed hands. As Henri Pirenne, an authority on medieval economic history, has put it:

. . . the tenants paid their obligations to their lord in kind. Every serf . . . owed a fixed number of days of labour and a fixed quantity of natural products or of goods manufactured by himself, corn, eggs, geese, chickens, lambs, pigs, and hempen, linen or woollen cloth. It is true that a few pence had also to be paid, but they formed such a small proportion of the whole that they cannot prevent the conclusion that the economy of the domain was a natural economy . . . since it did not engage in commerce it had no need to make use of money. . . .[12]

charming account of the reality of human existence which lies behind history. For a sense of the violent tenor of the times, see J. Huizinga, *The Waning of the Middle Ages* (Garden City, N.Y.: Doubleday, Anchor Books, 1954), Chap. I. Let me call attention also to two other books that convey a vivid sense of feudal economic life. One is by H. S. Bennett, *Life on the English Manor* (Cambridge: Cambridge University Press, 1965); the other, by Marc Bloch, *French Rural History* (Berkeley: University of California Press, 1966). *French Rural History,* especially, is one of the real masterworks of economic history.

[12] *Economic and Social History of Medieval Europe* (New York: Harcourt, Harvest Books, 1956), p. 105.

It would, however, be a misrepresentation of medieval life to conclude that cash and cash transactions and the bargaining of a market society were wholly foreign to it. Rather, as was the case with antiquity, we must think of medieval economic society as consisting of a huge, static, virtually moneyless foundation of agricultural production atop which flourished a considerable variety of more dynamic activities.

For one thing, in addition to manors, there also existed the shrunken descendants of Roman towns (and as we shall later see, the nuclei of new towns) and these small cities obviously required a network of markets to serve them. Every town had its stalls to which peasants brought some portion of their crop for sale. More important, towns were clearly a different social unit from manors, and the laws and customs of the manors did not apply to their problems. Even when towns fell under manorial protection, townspeople little by little won for themselves freedom from feudal obligations of labor and, more important, from feudal obligations of law.* In contrast to the "ancient customs" of the manor, a new, evolving "law of merchants" regulated much of the commercial activity within the town walls.

Another locus of active economic life was the fair. The fair was a kind of traveling market, established in fixed localities for fixed dates, in which merchants from all over Europe conducted a genuine international exchange. Held usually but once a year, the great fairs were tremendous occasions, a mixture of social holiday, religious festival, and a time of intense economic activity. At some fairs, like those at Champagne in France or Stourbridge in England, a wide variety of merchandise was brought for sale: silks from the Levant, books and parchments, horses, drugs, spices. Anyone who has ever been to the Flea Market, the famous open-air bazaar outside Paris, or to a country fair in New England or the Middle West has savored something of the atmosphere of such a market. One can imagine the excitement which fairs must have engendered in the still air of medieval life.

And finally, within the towns themselves, we find the tiny but highly important centers of medieval "industrial" production. For even at its grandest, the manor could not support every craft needed for its maintenance, much less its extension. The services or products of glaziers and masons, expert armorers and metalworkers, fine weavers and dyers had to be bought

---

* Hence the saying "City air makes men free"; for the serf who escaped to a city and remained there a year and a day was usually considered to have passed from the jurisdiction of his lord to that of the city burghers.

when they were needed, and typically they were to be found in the medieval institutions as characteristic of town life as the manors themselves were of life in the country.

These institutions were the *guilds*—trade, professional, and craft organizations of Roman origins. Such organizations were the "business units" of the Middle Ages; in fact, one could not usually set oneself up in "business" unless one belonged to a guild. Thus the guilds were a kind of exclusive union, but not a union of workers so much as of managers. The dominant figures in the guild were the guildmasters—independent manufacturers, working in their own houses and banding together to elect their own guild government which then laid down the rules concerning the internal conduct of affairs. Under the master guildsmen were their few journeymen (from the French *journée* or day), who were paid by the day, and their half-dozen or so apprentices, ten to twelve years old, who were bound to them for periods of three to twelve years as their legal wards. In time, an apprentice could become a journeyman and then, at least in medieval romance, graduate to the status of a full-fledged guildmaster on completion of his "masterpiece."

Any survey of medieval town life delights in the color of guild organization: the broiders and glovers, the hatters and scriveners, the shipwrights and upholsterers, each with its guild hall, its distinctive livery, and its elaborate set of rules. But if life in the guilds and at the fairs provides a sharp contrast with the stodgy life on the manor, we must not be misled by surface resemblances into thinking that it represented a foretaste of modern life in medieval dress. It is a long distance from the guild to the modern business firm, and it is well to fix in mind some of the differences.

In the first place, the guild was much more than just an institution for organizing production. While most of its regulations concerned wages and conditions of work and specifications of output, they also dwelt at length on "noneconomic" matters: on the charitable contributions expected from each member, on his civic role, on his appropriate dress, and even on his daily deportment. Guilds were the regulators not only of production but of social conduct: when one member of the mercer's guild in London "broke the hed" of another in an argument over some merchandise, both were fined £10 and bonded for £200 not to repeat the disgrace. In another guild, members who engaged in a brawl were fined a barrel of beer, to be drunk by the rest of the guild.

But between guild and modern business firm there is a much more profound gulf than this pervasive paternalism. *Unlike a modern firm, the purpose of a guild was not first and foremost to make money.* Rather, it was to preserve a certain orderly way of life—a way which envisaged a decent income for its master craftsmen but which was certainly not intended to allow any of them to become a "big" businessman or a monopolist. On the contrary, guilds were specifically designed to ward off any such outcome of an uninhibited struggle among their members. The terms of service, the wages, the route of advancement of apprentices and journeymen were all fixed by custom. So, too, were the terms of sale: a guild member who cornered the supply of an item was guilty of *forestalling,* for which rigorous penalties were invoked, and one who bought wholesale to sell at retail was similarly punished for the faults of *engrossing* or *regrating.* Thus competition was strictly limited and profits were held to prescribed levels. Advertising was forbidden, and even technical progress in advance of one's fellow guildmen was considered disloyal.

In the great cloth guilds of Florence in the fourteenth century, for instance, no merchant was permitted to tempt a buyer into his shop or to call out to a customer standing in another's doorway, nor even to process his cloth in a manner different from that of his brethren. Standards of cloth production and processing were subject to the minutest scrutiny. If a scarlet dye, for instance, were found to be adulterated, the perpetrator was condemned to a crushing fine and, failing payment, to loss of his right hand.[13]

Surely the guilds represent a more "modern" aspect of feudal life than the manor, but the whole temper of guild life was still far removed from the goals and ideals of modern business enterprise. There was no free play of price, no free competition, no restless probing for advantage. Existing on the margin of a relatively moneyless society, the guilds perforce sought to take the risks out of their slender enterprises. Their aim was not increase, but preservation, stability, orderliness. As such, they were as drenched in the medieval atmosphere as the manors.

MEDIEVAL ECONOMICS

Beyond even these differences, we must note a still deeper chasm between medieval economic society and that of a market economy. This is the gulf between a society in which economic activity is still inextricably mixed with social and religious activity, and one in which economic life has, so to speak, emerged into a special category of its own. In our next chapter we shall be talking about the ways in which a market society creates a special sphere of economic existence. But as we complete our introduction to medieval economic society, the main point to which we should pay heed is that no such special sphere then existed. *In medieval society, economics was a subordinate and not a dominant aspect of life.*

And what was dominant? The answer is, of course, that in economic matters as in so many other facets of medieval life, the guiding ideal was religious. It was the Church, the great pillar of stability in an age of disorder, that constituted the ultimate authority on economics, as on most other matters.

But the economics of medieval Catholicism was concerned not with the credits and debits of successful business operation so much as with the

[13] G. Renard, *Histoire du Travail à Florence* (Paris: 1913), pp. 190 ff.

credits and debits of the souls of business operators. As R. H. Tawney, one of the great students of the problem, has written:

. . . the specific contributions of medieval writers to the technique of economic theory were less significant than their premises. Their fundamental assumptions, both of which were to leave a deep imprint on social thought of the sixteenth and seventeenth centuries, were two: that economic interests are subordinate to the real business of life, which is salvation; and that economic conduct is one aspect of personal conduct, upon which, as on other parts of it, the rules of morality are binding. Material riches are necessary . . . since without them men cannot support themselves and help one another . . . But economic motives are suspect. Because they are powerful appetites men fear them, but they are not mean enough to applaud them. Like other strong passions, what they need, it is thought, is not a clear field, but repression. . . .[14]

Thus what we find throughout medieval religious thought is a pervasive uneasiness with the practices of economic society. Essentially, the Church's attitude toward trade was wary and nicely summed up in the saying: "Homo mercator vix aut numquam Deo placere potest"—the merchant can scarcely or never be pleasing to God.

We find such a suspicion of business motives in the Church's concern with the idea of a "just price." What was a just price? It was selling a thing for what it was worth, and no more. "It is wholly sinful," wrote Thomas Aquinas, "to practise fraud for the express purpose of selling a thing for more than its just price, inasmuch as a man deceives his neighbor to his loss."[15]

But what *was* a thing "worth"? Presumably, what it cost to acquire it or make it. Suppose, however, that a seller had himself paid too much for an article—then what was a "just price" at which he might resell it? Or suppose a man paid too little—was he then in danger of spiritual loss, offsetting his material gain?

These were the questions over which the medieval "economist-theologians" mulled, and they testify to the mixture of economics and ethics, characteristic of the age. But they were not merely theoretical questions. We have records of the dismay that economic theology brought to actual participants in the economic process. One St. Gerald of Aurillac in the tenth century, having bought an ecclesiastical garment in Rome for an unusually low price, learned from some itinerant merchants that he had picked up a "bargain"; instead of rejoicing, he hastened to send to the seller an additional sum, lest he fall into the sin of avarice.[16]

[14] *Religion and the Rise of Capitalism* (New York: Harcourt, 1947), p. 31.

[15] A. E. Monroe, ed., "Summa Theologica," in *Early Economic Thought* (Cambridge, Mass.: Harvard University Press, 1924), p. 54.

[16] Henri Pirenne, *Economic and Social History of Medieval Europe* (New York: Harcourt, Harvest Books, 1956), p. 27.

St. Gerald's attitude was no doubt exceptional. Yet if the injunction to charge fair prices did not succeed in staying men's appetites for gain, it did stay their unbridled enthusiasm. Men in ordinary business frequently stopped to assess the condition of their moral balance sheets. Whole towns would, on occasion, repent of usury and pay a heavy amend, or merchants like Gandoufle le Grand would, on their deathbeds, order restitution made to those from whom interest had been extracted. Men of affairs in the twelfth and thirteenth centuries occasionally inserted codicils in their wills urging their sons not to follow their footsteps into the snares of trade, or they would seek to make restitution for their commercial sins by charitable contributions. One medieval merchant of London founded a divinity scholarship with £14 "forasmoche as I fynde myn conscience aggrugged that I have deceived in this life divers persons to that amount."[17]

Thus the theological cast of suspicion injected a wholly new note into the moneymaking process. For the first time it associated the making of money with *guilt*. Unlike the acquisitor of antiquity who unashamedly reveled in his treasures, the medieval profiteer counted his gains in the knowledge that he might be imperiling his soul.

Nowhere was this disapproval of moneymaking more evident than in the Church's horror of usury—lending money at interest. Moneylending had, since Aristotle's day, been regarded as an essentially parasitic activity, an attempt to make a "barren" commodity, money, yield a return. But what had always been a vaguely disreputable and unpopular activity became, under Church scrutiny, a deeply evil one. Usury was decreed to be a *mortal* sin. At the Councils of Lyons and Vienne in the thirteenth and fourteenth centuries, the usurer was declared a pariah of society, to whom no one, under pain of excommunication, might rent a house, whose confession might not be heard, whose body might not have Christian burial, whose very will was invalid. Anyone even defending usury was to be suspected of heresy.

These powerful churchly sentiments were not produced merely by theological scruples. On the contrary, many of the Church's injunctions against both usury and profiteering arose from the most secular of realities. Famine, the endemic scourge of the Middle Ages, brought with it the most heartless economic gouging; loans commanded 40 and 60 percent—for bread. Much of the dislike of profit seeking and interest taking rose from its identification with just such ruthless practices, with which medieval times abounded.

Finally, another, perhaps even more fundamental, reason underlay the disrepute of gain and profit. This was the essentially static organization of economic life itself. Let us not forget that that life was basically agricultural

---

[17] S. L. Thrupp, *The Merchant Class in Medieval London* (Chicago: University of Chicago Press, 1948), p. 177. Also Renard, *Histoire du Travail à Florence*, pp. 220 ff.

and that agriculture, with its infinite complexity of peasant strips, was far from efficient. To quote once more from Henri Pirenne:

. . . the whole idea of profit, and indeed the possibility of profit, was incompatible with the position occupied by the great medieval landowner. Unable to produce for sale owing to the want of a market, he had no need to tax his ingenuity in order to wring from his men and his land a surplus which would merely be an encumbrance, and as he was forced to consume his own produce, he was content to limit it to his needs. His means of existence was assured by the traditional functioning of an organization which he did not try to improve.[18]

What was true of the country was also true of the city. The idea of an *expanding* economy, a *growing* scale of production, an *increasing* productivity was as foreign to the guildmaster or fair-merchant as to the serf and lord. Medieval economic organization was conceived as a means of reproducing, but not enhancing, the material well-being of the past. Its motto was perpetuation, not progress. There is little wonder that in such a static organization, profits and profitseeking were viewed as essentially disturbing rather than welcome economic phenomena.

Prerequisites of Change

We have traced the broad outlines of the economic organization of the West roughly up to the tenth or twelfth century. Once again it is wise to emphasize the diversity of currents concealed within a landscape we have too often been forced to treat as undifferentiated. At best, our journey into antiquity and the Middle Ages can give us a few glimpses of the prevailing flavor of the times, a sense of the ruling economic climate, of the main institutions and ideas by which men organized their economic efforts.

But one thing is certain. We are very far from the temper and tempo of modern economic life. The few stirrings we have witnessed in the slow world of the manor and the town are but the harbingers of a tremendous change which, over the course of the next centuries, would dramatically alter the basic form of economic organization itself, replacing the old ties of tradition and command with new ties of market transactions.

We shall have to wait until our next chapter to witness the actual process of change itself. But perhaps it will help us put into focus both what we have already seen and what we are about to witness if we anticipate our line of advance. We now have an idea of a pre-market society, a society in

[18] *Economic and Social History of Medieval Europe*, p. 63.

which markets exist but which does not yet depend on a market mechanism to solve the economic problem. What changes will be required to transform such a society into a true market economy?

1. *A new attitude toward economic activity will be needed.*

For such a society to function, men must be free to seek gain. The suspiciousness and unease which surrounded the ideas of profit, of change, of social mobility must give way to new ideas which would encourage those very attitudes and activities. In turn this meant, in the famous words of Sir Henry Maine, that the *society of status* must give way to the *society of contract*, that the society in which men were born to their stations in life must give way to a society in which they were free to define those stations for themselves.

Such an idea would have seemed to the medieval mind without any possible rationale. The idea that a general free-for-all should determine men's compensations, with neither a floor to prevent them from being ground down nor a ceiling to prevent them from rising beyond all reason, would have appeared senseless—even blasphemous. If we may listen again to R. H. Tawney:

To found a science of society upon the assumption that the appetite for economic gain is ... to be accepted, like other natural forces ... would have appeared to the medieval thinker as hardly less irrational or less immoral than to make the premise of social philosophy the unrestrained operation of such necessary human attributes as pugnacity or the sexual instinct.[19]

Yet some such freeing of the quest for economic gain, some such aggressive competition in the new contractual relationship of man to man would be essential for the birth of a market society.

2. *The monetization of economic life will have to proceed to its ultimate conclusion.*

One prerequisite of a market economy should by now be clear: such an economy must involve the process of exchange, of buying and selling, at every level of society. But for this to take place men must have the wherewithal to enter a market; that is, they must have cash. And, in turn, if society is to be permeated with cash, men must earn money for their labors. In other words, *for a market society to exist, nearly every task must have a monetary reward.*

Even in our highly monetized society we do not pay for every service: most conspicuously not for the housekeeping services of a wife. But all through the pre-market era, the number of unpaid services—the amount of

[19] *Religion and the Rise of Capitalism*, pp. 31-32.

work performed by law without monetary compensation—was vastly larger than in our society. Slave labor was, of course, unpaid. So was most serf labor. Even the labor of apprentices was remunerated more in kind, in food and lodging, than in cash. Thus probably 70 to 80 percent of the actual working population of an ancient or medieval economy labored without anything resembling full payment in money.

Clearly, in such a society the possibilities for a highly involved exchange economy were limited. But a still more important consequence must be noted. The absence of a widespread monetization of tasks meant the absence of a widespread *market for producers*. Nothing like the flow of "purchasing power" which dominates and directs our own productive efforts could be forthcoming in a society in which money incomes were the exception rather than the rule.

3. *The pressures of a free play of market "demand" will have to take over the regulation of the economic tasks of society.*

All through antiquity and the Middle Ages, as we have seen, tradition or command solved the economic problem. These were the forces that regulated the distribution of social rewards. But in a market society, another means of control must rise to take their place. *An all-encompassing flow of money demand, itself stemming from the total monetization of all economic tasks, must become the great propulsive mechanism of society.* Men must go to their tasks not because they are ordered there, but because they will make money there; and producers must decide on the volume and the variety of their output not because the rules of the manor or the guild so determine, but because there is a market demand for particular things. From the top to the bottom of society, in other words, a new marketing orientation must take over the production and distribution tasks. The whole replenishment, the steady provisioning, the very progress of society must now be subject to the guiding hand of a universal demand for labor and goods.

What forces would ultimately drive the world of medieval economic organization into a world of money, of universal markets, of profit-seeking? The stage is now set for us to attempt to answer this profoundly important and difficult question. Let us turn to a consideration of the causes capable of effecting so vast a change.

KEY CONCEPTS AND KEY WORDS

1. **We must differentiate between markets, which have a very ancient pedigree, and market societies, which do not.** *In a market society, the economic problem itself*—both production and distribution—*is solved by means of a vast exchange between buyers and sellers.* **Many ancient societies had markets, but these markets did not organize the fundamental activities of these societies.**

Markets

2. The economic societies of antiquity had several features in common, which contrast sharply with those of modern market economies:
   • They rested on an agricultural base of *peasant farming.*

   • Their cities were—from an economic point of view—parasitic *centers of consumption, not active centers of production.*
   • *Slavery* was a common and very important form of labor.

   • They produced very considerable *surplusses.*

3. As a result, in the economic societies of antiquity we find the economic side of life subservient to the political side. Priest, warrior, and statesman were superior to merchant or trader; *wealth followed power,* not—as in market societies to come—the other way around.

4. Medieval economic life emerged from the catastrophic disorganization that followed the decline of Roman law and order. It was characterized by a unique form of organization called the *manorial* system in which:
   • *Local lords were the centers of political, military, economic, and social power.*
   • *Most peasants were bound as serfs* to a particular lord, for whom they were required to work and to whom they owed both labor and taxes or dues.
   • *Physical security* against brigands or other lords was provided by the lord, as well as some economic security in times of distress.

5. *The manorial system,* particularly in its earlier days (sixth to tenth centuries), *was a static economic system,* in which monetary payments played only a minor role. Self-sufficiency was the main purpose and the most outstanding characteristic of the manor.

6. Side by side with the manor existed the economic life of the *towns.* Here monetary exchange always played a more important role, as did the organization of a more active economic life in the institution of *fairs.*

7. The *guild* was the main form of organizing production in the towns and cities. *Guilds were very different from modern-day businesses,* insofar as they discouraged competition or profit seeking and sought to impose general rules on the methods of production, rates of pay, practices of marketing, and so on.

8. All through medieval times the church—the main social organization of the age—was suspicious of buying and selling activity. In part this reflected a dislike of the exploitative practices of the times, in part it was a consequence of an ancient contempt for moneymaking (remember Aristotle's dislike of *chrematistike*) and especially for money-lending (usury). The religious leaders of the day worried about "just" prices, and did not admit that unregulated buying and selling gave rise to just prices.

9. Three profound and pervasive changes would be needed to convert medieval society into a market society:
   • *A new attitude toward moneymaking* as a legitimate activity would have to replace the medieval suspicion of profit seeking.

   • *The web of monetization would have to expand* beyond its narrow confines—that is, buying and selling would have to control the output of all products and the performance of nearly all tasks.
   • The flux of *"demand" and "supply" would have to be allowed to take over the direction of economic activity* from the dictates of lords and the usages of custom.

1. What differences, if any, characterize the economic attitudes and behavior of the American farmer and the American businessman? Can this comparison also describe the behavior and attitude of the Egyptian peasant and the Egyptian merchant? What accounts for the difference between the two societies?

2. Julius Caesar and J. P. Morgan were both wealthy and powerful men. What is the difference in the origins of their wealth and their power? Does power still follow wealth in modern economic societies? Does wealth still follow power in nonmarket societies? If not, why not?

3. To what uses was the surplus of society put in ancient Rome? In feudal society? In modern America? In the U.S.S.R.? What significance attaches to these different uses? What do they tell us about the structure of these societies?

4. What do you think of the validity of Aristotle's distinction between economic activity for *use* and *gain*?

5. In what ways is a serf a different *economic* creature from a modern farm worker? How is a slave different from an industrial worker?

6. What changes would have to take place within a guild before it resembled a modern business?

7. The Bible has numerous hostile references to moneymaking—"It is easier for a camel to go through the eye of a needle than for a rich man to enter into the kingdom of God." How do you account for this ancient churchly antipathy toward wealth? Is religion today still suspicious of moneymaking? Why?

8. Is the idea of a "just" price (or a "just" wage) still encountered in our own society? What is usually meant by these terms? Do you think these ideas are compatible with a market system?

9. The manorial system persisted for nearly 1,000 years. Why do you think change was so slow in coming?

10. Ancient Greece and Rome are a great deal more "modern" in their temper than feudal Europe. Yet neither was remotely a modern economic system. Why not?

Tradition, changelessness, order—these were the key concepts of economic society in the Middle Ages, and our preceding chapter introduced us to this unfamiliar and static way of economic life. But our purpose in this chapter is different. It is no longer to describe those factors which preserved the economic stability of medieval society, but to identify those forces which eventually burst it asunder.

Once again we need to begin with a word of caution. Our chapter spans an immense variety of historical experience. We must beware of thinking that the forces of change which dominate this chapter were identical from region to region or from century to century, or that the transition which they effected was uniform throughout the broad expanse of Europe. On the contrary, the great evolution which we will witness in these pages was not sharp and clear, but muddy and irregular. At the same time that the first evidences of a truly modern market society were beginning to manifest themselves in the medieval cities of Italy or Holland, the most archaic forms of feudal relationship still persisted in the agricultural sectors of these nations, and indeed in the city life of other nations. We must bear in mind that the historic processes of this chapter extended from the tenth to the seventeenth (and even eighteenth and nineteenth) centuries and manifested themselves in no two countries in precisely the same way.

With these cautions in mind, now let us turn to the great evolution itself. What agents were powerful enough to effect the major historic changes needed to bring about a market society?

THE ITINERANT MERCHANT

We meet the first of these forces of change in an unexpected guise. It is a small irregular procession of armed men, jogging along one of the rudimentary roads of medieval Europe: standard-bearer with colors in the lead, then a military chief, then a group of riders carrying bows and swords, and finally a caravan of horses and mules laden with casks and bales, bags and packs.

CHAPTER

Someone unacquainted with medieval life might easily take such a troop for part of the baggage train of a small army. But he would be mistaken. These were not soldiers but merchants, the traveling merchants whom the English of the twelfth century called "pie-powers," from *pieds poudreux,* dusty feet. No wonder they were dusty; many of them came immense distances along routes so bad that we know of one instance where only the intervention of a local ecclesiastical lord prevented the "road" from being plowed up as arable land. In their bags and packs were goods which had somehow made a perilous journey across Europe, or even all the way from Arabia or India, to be sold from town to town, or from halt to halt, as these merchant adventurers wound their way across the medieval countryside.

And adventurers they were indeed. For in the fixed hierarchies of the great manorial estates of Europe there was no natural place for these unlanded peddlers of goods, with their unfeudal attributes of calculation and (often very crude) bookkeeping and their natural insistence on trade in money. The traveling merchants ranked very low in society. Some of them, without doubt, were the sons of serfs, or even runaway serfs themselves. Yet since no one could prove their bondage, they had, if only by default, the gift of "freedom." It is no wonder that in the eyes of the nobility, the merchants were upstarts and a disturbing element in the normal pattern of things.

Yet no one would have dispensed with their services. To their brightly canopied stalls at the fairs flocked the lords and ladies of the manors as well as the Bodos and Ermentrudes of the fields. After all, where else could one buy pepper, or purple dye, or acquire a guaranteed splinter from the Cross? Where else could one buy the marvelous cloths woven in Tuscany or learn such esoteric words, derived from the Arabic, as "jar" or "syrup"? If the merchant was a disturbing leaven in the mix of medieval life, he was also the pinch of active ingredient without which the mixture would have been very dull indeed.

We first note the traveling merchant in Europe in the eighth and ninth century, and we can follow his progress until the fourteenth and fifteenth century. By this time, largely through the merchants' own efforts, commerce was sufficiently organized so that it no longer required these itinerant journeyers.* For what these travelers brought, together with their wares, was the first breath of commerce and commercial intercourse to a Europe which had sunk to an almost tradeless and self-sufficient manorial stagnation. Even to towns as minuscule and isolated as Forcalquier in France—a dot on the map without so much as a road to connect its few hundred souls to the outer world—these hardy traders beat their path: we know from a primitive book of accounts that in May, 1331, thirty-six itinerant merchants visited Forcalquier to transact business at the home and "shop" of one Ugo Teralh, a notary.[1] And so, in a thousand isolated communities, did they slowly weave a web of economic interdependence.

URBANIZATION

An important by-product of the rise of the itinerant merchant was the slow urbanization of medieval life, the creation of new towns and villages. When the traveling merchants stopped, they naturally chose the protected site of a local castle or burg, or of a church. And so we find growing up around the walls of advantageously situated castles—in the *foris burgis,* whence *faubourg,* the French word for "suburb"—more or less permanent trading places, which in turn became the inner core of small towns. Nestled close to the castle or cathedral wall for protection, the new burgs were still not "of" the manor. The inhabitants of the burg—the burgesses, burghers, bourgeois—had at best an anomalous and insecure relation to the manorial world within. As we have seen, there was no way of applying the time-hallowed rule of "ancient customs" in adjudicating their disputes, since there *were* no ancient customs in the commercial quarters. Neither were there clear-cut rules for their taxation or for the particular degrees of fealty they owned their local masters. Worse yet, some of the growing towns began to surround themselves with walls. By the twelfth century, the commercial burg of Bruges, for example, had already swallowed up the old fortress like a pearl around a grain of sand.

Curiously, it was this very struggle for existence in the interstices of feudal society which provided much of the impetus for the development of a new social and economic order within the city. In all previous civilizations, cities had been the outposts of central government. Now, for the first time,

---

* Records of an order for goods placed on the occasion of a funeral of a Swedish nobleman in 1328 include saffron from Spain or Italy, caraway seed from the Mediterranean, ginger from India, cinnamon from Ceylon, pepper from Malabar, anise from southern Europe, and Rhine and Bordeaux wines. The order was placed for immediate delivery from one local merchant, despite the fact that Sweden was then a laggard and even primitive land. Cf. Fritz Rorig, *Mittelalterliche Weltwirtschaft* (Jena: 1933), p. 17. (I am again indebted to Dr. Goran Ohlin for this reference.)

[1] *Cambridge Economic History of Europe,* II, 325-26.

they existed as independent entities outside the main framework of social power. As a result, they were able to define for themselves—as they *had* to define for themselves—a code of law and social behavior and a set of governing institutions which were eventually to displace those of the feudal countryside.

The process was long drawn out, for the rate of growth of towns was often very slow. In the nearly two centuries between 1086 and 1279, for example, the town of Cambridge, England, added an average of but one house *per year*.[2] One important reason for this almost imperceptible rate of expansion was the difficulty of moving men or materials over the terrible roads. Not the least consequence of the decline of Roman power had been the decay of its once magnificent system of highways, the very stones of which were pilfered for building materials during the years of worst social disorganization. Until the roads recovered, economic movement was perforce limited and limping. And it is worth remarking that in many parts of Europe, a system of transportation as efficient as that of ancient Rome was not enjoyed until the eighteenth or even nineteenth centuries.

Yet if growth was slow, it was steady; and in some locales it was much faster than in Cambridge. During the 1,000 years of the Middle Ages nearly 1,000 towns were fathered in Europe, a tremendous stimulus to the commercialization and monetization of life, for each town had its local marts, its local toll gates, often its local mint; its granaries and shops, its drinking places and inns, its air of "city life" which contrasted so sharply with that of the country. The slow, spontaneous growth of urban ways was a major factor in introducing a marketing flavor to European economic life.

The rise of the itinerant merchant and the town were two great factors in the slow evolution of a market society out of medieval economic life; a third factor was the Crusades.

THE CRUSADES

It is an ironic turn to history that the Crusades, the supreme religious adventure of the Middle Ages, should have contributed so much toward the establishment of a society to which the Church was so vigorously opposed. If we consider the Crusades, however, not from the point of view of their religious impulse, but simply as great expeditions of exploration and colonization, their economic impact becomes much more understandable.*

The Crusades served to bring into sudden and startling contact two very different worlds. One was the still slumbering society of European

---

[2] George Gordon Coulton, *Medieval Panorama* (New York: World Publishing, Meridian Books, 1955), p. 285.

* We might note here some of the complex interaction of the process we are watching. For the Crusades were not only a cause of European economic development, but also a *symptom* of the development which had previously taken place.

feudalism with all its rural inertia, its aversion to trade, and its naïve conceptions of business; the other was the brilliant society of Byzantium and Venice, with its urban vitality, its unabashed enjoyment of money-making, and its sophisticated business ways. The Crusaders, coming from their draughty castles and boring manorial routines, thought they would find in the East only untutored heathen savages. They were astonished to be met by a people far more civilized, infinitely more luxurious, and much more money-oriented than they.

One result was that the simple-minded Crusaders found themselves the pawns of commercial interests which they little understood. During the first three Crusades, the Venetians, who provided ships, gulled them as shamelessly as country bumpkins at a fair. The fact that they were fleeced, however, did not prevent the Crusaders from reaching the Holy Land, albeit with inconclusive results. But in the notorious Fourth Crusade (1202–1204) Dandolo, the wily 94-year-old Doge of Venice, managed to subvert the entire religious expedition into a gigantic plundering operation for Venetian profit.

First Dandolo held up the voyagers for an initial transportation price of 85,000 silver marks, an enormous sum for the unmoneyed nobility to scrape up. Then, when the funds had been found, he refused to carry out his bargain until the Crusaders agreed first to attack the town of Zara, a rich commercial rival of Venice. Since Zara was a *Christian*, not an "infidel" community, Pope Innocent III was horrified and suggested that the attack be directed instead against heathen Egypt. But Egypt was one of Venice's best customers, and this horrified Dandolo even more. The Crusaders, stranded and strapped, had no choice: Zara soon fell—after which, at Dandolo's urging, Christian Constantinople was also sacked. The "heathen" Orient was never reached at all, but Venice profited marvelously.

It was not only Venice which gained, however. The economic impact on the Crusaders themselves was much more formidable than the religious. On many this impact was disastrous, as knights who had melted down their silver plate to join the Crusades came back penniless to their ruined manor houses. To others, however, the Crusades brought a new economic impetus. When in 1101, for example, the Genoese raided Caesarea, a Palestinian seaport, 8,000 soldiers and sailors reaped a reward of some forty-eight *solidi* each, plus two pounds of pepper—and thus were 8,000 petty capitalists born.[3] And in 1204 when Constantinople fell, not only did each knight receive twenty marks in silver as his share of the booty, but even the squires and archers were rewarded with a few marks each.

Thus the Crusades provided an immense fertilizing experience for Europe. The old, landed basis of wealth came into contact with a new moneyed basis which proved much more powerful. Indeed, the old conception of life itself was forcibly revised before a glimpse of an existence not

[3] *Cambridge Economic History of Europe,* II, 306.

only wealthier, but gayer and more vital. As a means of shaking a sluggish society out of its rut, the Crusades played an immense role in speeding along the economic transformation of Europe.

Yet another factor in the slow commercialization of economic life was the gradual amalgamation of Europe's fragmented economic and political entities into larger wholes. As the disintegration of economic life following the break-up of the old Roman Empire had shown, a strong economic society requires a strong and broad political base. Hence as political Europe began its slow process of reknitting, once again its economic tempo began to rise.

One of the most striking characteristics of the Middle Ages, and one of its most crippling obstacles to economic development, was the medieval crazy quilt of compartmented, isolated areas of government. Over a journey of a hundred miles, a traveling merchant might fall under a dozen different sovereignties, each with different rules, regulations, laws, weights, measures, money. Worse yet, at each border there was apt to be a toll station. At the turn of the thirteenth and fourteenth centuries there were said to be more than thirty toll stations along the Weser River and at least thirty-five along the Elbe; along the Rhine, a century later, there were more than sixty such toll stations, mostly belonging to local ecclesiastical princes: Thomas Wykes, an English chronicler, described the system as "the raving madness of the Teutons." But it was not only a German disease. There were so many toll stations along the Seine in France in the late fifteenth century that it cost half its final selling price to ship grain 200 miles down the river.[4] Indeed, among the European nations, England alone enjoyed an internally unified market during the middle and late Middle Ages. This was one powerful contributory factor to England's emergence as the first great European economic power.

The amalgamation of Europe's fragmented markets was essentially a political as well as an economic process; it followed the gradual centralization of power which changed the map of Europe from the infinite complexity of the tenth century to the more or less "modern" map of the sixteenth. Here, once again, the burgeoning towns played a central and crucial role. It was the city burghers who became the allies of the nascent monarchies, thereby disassociating themselves still further from their local feudal lords while, in turn, supplying the shaky monarchs with an absolutely essential prerequisite for kingship: cash.

Thus monarch and bourgeois combined to bring about the slow growth of centralized governments, and from centralized government, in turn, came not alone a unification of law and money but a direct stimulus to the

[4] *Ibid,* pp. 134-35.

development of commerce and industry as well. In France, for example, manufacturing was promoted by royal patronage of the famous Gobelin tapestry and Sevres porcelain works, and business was created for innumerable craftsmen and artisans by the demands of the royal palaces and banquet halls. In other fields, growing national power also imparted a new encouragement: navies had to be built, armies had to be equipped, and these new "national" armed forces, many of whom were mercenaries, had to be paid. All this set into faster motion the pumps of monetary circulation.

Another economic impetus given by the gradual consolidation of political power was the official encouragement of exploration. All through the long years of the Middle Ages a few intrepid adventurers, like Marco Polo, had beat their way to remote regions in search of a short route to the fabled riches of India; and as a matter of fact, by the early fourteenth century the route to the Far East was well enough known so that silk from China cost but half the price of that from the Caspian area, only half the distance away.

Yet the network of all these hazardous and brave penetrations beyond Europe formed only the thinnest of spider webs. There still remained the systematic exploration of the unknown, and this awaited the kingly support of state adventurers. Columbus and Vasco da Gama, Cabral and Magellan did not venture on their epoch-making journeys as individual merchants (although they all hoped to make their fortunes thereby) but as adventurers in fleets bought with, and equipped by, royal money, bearing the royal mark of approval, and sent forth in hope of additions to the royal till.

The economic consequences of those amazing adventures were incalculably great. For one thing, they opened up an invigorating flow of precious metals into Europe. Gold and silver, coming from the great Spanish mines in Mexico and Peru, were slowly redistributed to other nations as Spain paid in gold specie for goods it bought abroad. As a result, prices rose throughout Europe—between 1520 and 1650 alone, it is estimated that they increased 200 to 400 percent, bringing about both stimulus and stress to industry, but setting in motion a great wave of speculation and commerce.

In addition, of course, the longer-run results of exploration brought an economic stimulus of still greater importance. The establishment of colonies in the sixteenth and seventeenth centuries and the subsequent enjoyment of trade with the New World provided a tremendous boost in propelling Europe into a bustling commercial society. The discovery of the New World was, from the beginning, a catalytic and revolutionizing influence on the Old.

The forces of change that we have thus far summarized were actually visible. At any time during the long transition from a nonmarket into a market society we could have witnessed with our own eyes the traveling merchants, the expanding towns, the Crusades, the evidences of a growing national power. Yet these were not the only forces that undermined the feudal system and brought into being its commercial successor. There were, as well, powerful but invisible currents of change, currents which affected the intellectual atmosphere, the beliefs, and attitudes of Europe. One of these, of special importance, was a change in the religious climate of the times.

In our last chapter we saw how deeply the Catholic church was imbued with theological aversions to the principle of gain—and especially to interest taking or usury. An amusing story of the times sums up the position of the Church very well. Humbertus de Romanis, a monk, tells of someone who found a devil in every nook and cranny of a Florentine cloister, although in the marketplace he found but one. The reason, Humbertus explains, was that it took only one to corrupt a marketplace, where every man harbored a devil in his own heart.[5] In such a disapproving climate, it was hard for the commercial side of life to thrive.

To be sure, for all its fulminations against gain and usury, the Church itself grew in time to a position of commanding economic importance. Through its tithes and benefices it was the largest collector and distributor of money in all of Europe; and in an age in which banks and safe deposit boxes did not exist, it was the repository of much feudal wealth. Some of its sub-orders, such as the Knights Templar, became immensely wealthy and served as banking institutions, lending to needy monarchs on stiff terms. Nonetheless, all of this faintly disreputable activity was undertaken despite, and not because of, the Church's deepest convictions. For behind the ecclesiastical disapproval of wealth seeking was a deep-seated theological conviction, a firm belief in the transient nature of this life on earth and the importance of preparing for the Eternal Morrow. The Church lifted its eyes and sought to lift the eyes of others above the daily struggle for existence. It strove to minimize the importance of life on earth and to denigrate the earthly activities to which an all too weak flesh succumbed.

What changed this dampening influence on the zest of wealth making? According to the theories of the German sociologist Max Weber and the English economic historian R. H. Tawney, the underlying cause lay in the rise of a new theological point of view contained in the teachings of the Protestant reformer John Calvin (1509–1564).

Calvinism was a harsh religious philosophy. Its core was a belief in *predestination*, in the idea that from the beginning God had chosen the saved and the damned, and that nothing man could do on earth could alter that inviolable writ. Furthermore, according to Calvin, the number of the damned exceeded by a vast amount the number of the saved, so that for the average person the chances were great that this earthly prelude was but the momentary grace given before eternal Hell and Damnation commenced.

[5] Beard, *A History of the Business Man*, p. 160.

Perhaps only a man of Calvin's iron will could have borne life under such a sentence. For we soon find that in the hands of his followers in the Lowlands and England, the inexorable and inscrutable quality of the original doctrine began to be softened. Although the idea of predestination was still preached, it was now allowed that in the tenor of one's worldly life there was a *hint* of what was to follow. Thus the English and Dutch divines taught that whereas even the saintliest-seeming man might end in Hell, the frivolous or wanton one was certainly headed there. Only in a blameless life lay the slightest chance of demonstrating that Salvation was still a possibility.

And so the Calvinists urged a life of rectitude, severity and, most important of all, diligence. In contrast to the Catholic theologians who tended to look upon worldly activity as vanity, the Calvinists sanctified and approved of endeavor as a kind of index of spiritual worth. Indeed in Calvinist hands there grew up the idea of a man *dedicated* to his work: "called" to it, as it were. Hence the fervid pursuit of one's calling, far from evidencing a distraction from religious ends, came to be taken as evidence of a dedication to a religious life. The energetic merchant was, in Calvinist eyes, a *Godly* man, not an ungodly one; and from this identification of work and worth, it was not long before the notion grew up that the more successful a man, the more worthy he was. Calvinism thus provided a religious atmosphere which, in contrast to Catholicism, encouraged wealth seeking and the temper of a businesslike world.

Perhaps even more important than its encouragement in seeking wealth was the influence of Calvinism on the *use* of wealth. By and large the prevailing attitude of the prosperous Catholic merchants had been that the aim of worldly success was the enjoyment of a life of ease and luxury, while Catholic nobility displayed on occasion a positively grotesque disdain for wealth. In an orgy of gambling that gripped Paris at the end of the seventeenth century, a prince who sent his mistress a diamond worth 5,000 *livres* had it pulverized and strewn over her reply when she rejected it as being too small. The same prince eventually gambled away an income of 600,000 *livres* a year. A *maréchal* whose grandson turned up his nose at a gift of a purse of gold threw it into the street: "Let the street cleaner have it then."[6]

The Calvinist manufacturer or trader had a very different attitude toward wealth. If his religion approved of diligence, it most emphatically did not approve of indulgence. Wealth was to be accumulated and put to good use, not frittered away.

Calvinism promoted an aspect of economic life of which we have hitherto heard very little: *thrift*. It made saving, the conscious abstinence

---

[6] Werner Sombart, *Luxury and Capitalism* (New York: Columbia University Press, 1938), pp. 120ff. Also Thirion, *La Vie Privée des Financiers au XVIIIe Siècle* (Paris: 1895), p. 292.

from the enjoyment of income, a virtue. It made investment, the use of saving for productive purposes, an instrument of piety as well as profit. It even condoned, with various *quids* and *quos,* the payment of interest. In fact, Calvinism fostered a new conception of economic life. In place of the old ideal of social and economic stability, of knowing and keeping one's "place," it brought respectability to an ideal of struggle, of material improvement, of economic growth.

Economic historians still debate the precise degree of influence which may properly be attributed to "the Protestant Ethic" in bringing about the rise of a new gain-centered worldly philosophy. After all, there was nothing much that a Dutch Calvinist would have been able to teach an Italian Catholic banker about the virtues of a businesslike approach to life. Yet, looking back on the subsequent course of economic progress, it is striking that without exception it was the Protestant countries with their "Puritan streak" of work and thrift which forged ahead in the economic race. As one of the powerful winds of change of the sixteenth and seventeenth centuries, the new religious outlook must be counted as a highly favorable stimulus for the evolution of the market society.

The enumeration of all these currents does not exhaust the catalog of forces bearing against the old fixed economic order in Europe. The list could be expanded and greatly refined.* Yet, with all due caution we can now begin to comprehend the immense coalition of events—some as specific as the Crusades, some as diffuse as a change in religious ideals—that jointly cooperated to destroy the medieval framework of economic life and to prepare the way for a new dynamic framework of market transactions.

One important aspect of this profound alteration was the gradual *monetization of feudal obligations.* In locality after locality we can trace the conversion of the old feudal payments in *kind*—the days of labor or chickens or eggs which a lord received from his tenants—into payments of *money* dues and money rents with which they now discharged their obligations to him.

A number of causes lay behind this commutation of feudal payments. One was the growing urban demand for food, as town and city populations began to swell. In concentric circles around the town, money filtered out into the countryside, at one and the same time raising the capacity of the

---

* An extremely important influence (to which we will specifically turn in our next chapter) was the rise of a new interest in technology, founded on scientific inquiry into natural events. Another important causative factor was the development of modern business concepts and techniques. The German economic historian Werner Sombart has even said that if he were forced to give a single date for the "beginning" of modern capitalism he would choose 1202, the year in which appeared the *Liber Abaci,* a primer of commercial arithmetic. Similarly, the historian Oswald Spengler has called the invention of double-entry bookkeeping in 1494 an achievement worthy of being ranked with that of Columbus or Copernicus.

rural sector to buy urban goods and whetting its desire to do so. At the same time, in a search for larger cash incomes to buy a widening variety of goods, the nobility looked with increasing favor on receiving its rents and dues in money rather than in kind. In so doing, however, it unwittingly set into motion a cause for the further serious deterioration of the manorial system. Usually, the old feudal services were converted into *fixed* sums of money payments. This temporarily eased the cash position of the lord, but soon placed him in the squeeze which always hurts the creditor in times of inflation. And even when dues were not fixed, rents and money dues lagged sufficiently behind the growing monetary needs of the nobility, so that still further feudal obligations were monetized to keep the lord in cash. But as prices rose and the monetized style of life expanded still further, these too failed to keep him solvent.

The result was that the rural nobility, which now depended increasingly on rents and dues for its income, steadily lost its economic power.* Indeed, beginning in the sixteenth century we find a new class coming into being— the *impoverished* nobility. In the year 1530 in the Gevaudan district of France, we find that 121 lords had an aggregate income of 21,400 *livres*, but one of these seigneurs accounted for 5,000 *livres* of the sum, another for 2,000—and the rest averaged but a mean 121 *livres* apiece.[7] In fact, the shortage of cash afflicted not only the lesser nobility but even the monarchy itself. Maximilian I, Emperor of the Holy Roman Empire, on occasion lacked the cash to pay for even the overnight lodgings of his entourage on tour; and when two of his grandchildren married children of the King of Hungary, all the trappings of the weddings—2,000 caparisoned horses, jewels, and gold and silver plate—were borrowed from merchant bankers to whom Maximilian had written wheedling letters begging them not to forsake him in his moment of need.

Clearly, the manorial system was incompatible with a cash economy; for while the nobility was pinched between rising prices and costs and static incomes, the merchant classes, to whom cash naturally gravitated, steadily increased their power. In the Gevaudan district, for example, where the richest lord had his income of 5,000 *livres,* the richest town merchants had incomes up to 65,000 *livres.* In Germany, while Maximilian scratched for cash, the great banking families of Augsburg commanded incomes far larger than Maximilian's entire kingly revenue. In Italy, the Gianfigliazzi of Florence, who began as "nobodies" lending money to the Bishop of Fiesole, ended up stripping him of his possessions and leaving him a pauper; while in Tuscany, the lords who looked down their noses at usurers in the tenth

---

* This process of economic decline was considerably enhanced by the ineptitude of the nobility as managers of their estates. The descendants of the Crusaders were not much more businesslike than their ancestors.

[7] *Cambridge Economic History of Europe,* I, 557-58.

century lost their estates to them in the twelfth and thirteenth. All over Europe men of mean social standing turned the monetary economy to good account. One Jean Amici of Toulouse made a fortune in English booty during the Hundred Years War; Guillaume de St-Yon grew rich by selling meat at rapacious prices to Paris; and Jacques Coeur, the most extraordinary figure of all, rose from merchant to King's coiner, then to King's purchasing agent, then to financier not for, but *of*, the King, during the course of which he accumulated a huge fortune estimated at 27 million *écus.**

Appearance of the Economic Aspect of Life

Behind all of these profoundly disturbing events we can discern an immense process of change that literally revolutionized the economic organization of Europe. Whereas in the tenth century, cash and money transactions were only peripheral to the solution of the economic problem, by the sixteenth and seventeenth centuries cash and transactions were already beginning to provide the very molecular force of economic cohesion.

But over and above this general monetization of life, another and perhaps even more profound change was taking place. This was the emergence of a separate *economic* sphere of activity visible within, and separable from, the surrounding matrix of social life. It was the creation of a whole aspect of society which had never previously existed, but which was thenceforth to constitute a commanding facet of human existence.[8]

In antiquity and feudal times, as we have seen, one could not easily separate the economic motivations or even the economic actions of the great mass of men from the normal round of existence itself. The peasant following his immemorial ways was hardly conscious of acting according to "economic" motives; indeed, he did not: he heeded the orders of his lord or the dictates of custom. Nor was the lord himself economically oriented. His interests were military or political or religious, and not basically oriented toward the idea of gain or increase. Even in the towns, as we have seen, the conduct of ordinary business was inextricably mixed with non-economic concerns. The undeniable fact that men were acquisitive, not to say avaricious, did not yet impart its flavor to life in general; the making of money,

* Note, however, that Coeur eventually fell from power, was imprisoned, and died in exile. The counting house was not yet fully master of the castle.

[8] The following section owes much to the insights of Karl Polanyi's famous *The Great Transformation* (Boston: Beacon Press, 1957, paperback ed.), Part II.

as we have been at some pains to indicate, was a tangential rather than a central concern of ancient or medieval existence.

With the ever-widening scope of monetization, however, a genuinely new element of life came slowly to the fore. Labor, for example, emerged as an activity quite different from the past. No longer was "labor" part of an explicit social relationship in which one man (serf or apprentice) worked for another (lord or guildmaster) in return for at least an assurance of subsistence. Labor was now a mere quantum of effort, a "commodity" to be disposed of on the marketplace for the best price it could bring, quite devoid of any reciprocal responsibilities on the part of the buyer, beyond the payment of wages. If those wages were not enough to provide subsistence— well, that was not the buyer's responsibility. He had bought his "labor," and that was that.

This emergence of "pure" labor—labor as a quantity of effort detached from a man's life and bought on the market in fixed amounts—had a parallel in two other main elements of economic life. One of these was land. Formerly conceived as the territory of a great lord, as inviolable as the territory of a modern nation-state, land was now also seen in its economic aspect as something to be bought or leased for the economic return it yielded. An estate which was once the core of political and administrative power became a "property" with a market price, available for any number of uses, even as a site for a factory. The dues, the payments in kind, the intangibles of prestige and power which once flowed from the ownership of land gave way to the single return of *rent;* that is, to a money return derived from putting land to *profitable* use.

The same transformation became true of property. As it was conceived in antiquity and throughout most of the Middle Ages, property was a sum of tangible wealth, a hoard, a treasury of plate, bullion, or jewels. Very logically, it was realized in the form of luxurious homes, in castles and armaments, in costly robes and trappings. But with the monetization and commercialization of society, property, too, became expressible in a monetary equivalent: a man was now "worth" so many *livres,* or *écus,* or pounds, or whatever. Property became *capital,* manifesting itself no longer in specific goods, but as an abstract sum of infinitely flexible use whose "value" was its capacity to earn *interest* or *profits.*

None of these changes, it should be emphasized, was planned, clearly foreseen, or for that matter, welcomed. It was not with equanimity that the feudal hierarchies saw their prerogatives nibbled away by the mercantile classes. Neither did the tradition-preserving guildmaster desire his own enforced metamorphosis into a "capitalist," a man of affairs guided by market signals and beset by competition. But perhaps for no social class was the transition more painful than for the peasant, caught up in a process of history that dispossessed him from his livelihood and made him a landless laborer.

This process, which was particularly important in England, was the *enclosure movement*, a by-product of the monetization of feudal life. Starting as early as the thirteenth century, the landed aristocracy, increasingly squeezed for cash, began to view their estates not merely as the ancestral fiefs, but as potential sources of cash revenue. In order to raise larger cash crops, they therefore began to "enclose" the pasture which had previously been deemed "common land." Communal grazing fields, which had in fact always belonged to the lord despite their communal use, were now claimed for the exclusive benefit of the lord and turned into sheepwalks. Why sheepwalks? Because a rising demand for woolen cloth was making sheep-raising a highly profitable occupation. The medieval historian Eileen Power writes:

The visitor to the House of Lords, looking respectfully upon that august assembly, cannot fail to be struck by a stout and ungainly object facing the throne—an ungainly object upon which in full session of Parliament, he will observe seated the Lord Chancellor of England. The object is a woolsack, and it is stuffed as full of pure history as the office of the Lord Chancellor itself.... The Lord Chancellor of England is seated upon a woolsack because it was upon a woolsack that this fair land rose to prosperity.[9]

The enclosure process in England proceeded at an irregular pace over the long centuries; not until the late eighteenth and early nineteenth centuries did it reach its engulfing climax.* By its end, some ten million acres, nearly *half* the arable land of England, had been "enclosed"—in its early Tudor days by the more or less high-handed conversion of the "commons" to sheep-raising; in the final period, by the forcible consolidation of strips and plots into tracts suitable for commercial farming, for which tenants presumably received "fair compensation."

From a strictly economic point of view, the enclosure movement was unquestionably salutary in that it brought into productive employment land which had hitherto yielded only a pittance. Indeed, particularly in the

[9] *Medieval People* (Garden City, N.Y.: Doubleday, Anchor Books, 1954), p. 125.

* In other European nations an enclosure process also took place, but at a much slower pace. In France, Italy, and southern Germany the small-holder peasant persisted long after he had virtually ceased to exist in England; in northeastern Germany, on the other hand, the small peasant was deprived of his holdings and turned into a landless proletarian.

eighteenth and nineteenth centuries, enclosure was the means by which England "rationalized" its agriculture and finally escaped from the inefficiency of the traditional manorial strip system. But there was another, crueler side to enclosure. As the common fields were enclosed, it became ever more difficult for the tenant to support himself. In the fifteenth and sixteenth centuries, when the initial enclosure of the commons reached its peak, as many as three-fourths to nine-tenths of the tenants of some estates were simply turned off the farm. Whole hamlets were thus wiped out. Sir Thomas More described it savagely in Book I of his *Utopia*.

Your sheep that were wont to be so meek and tame, and so small eaters, now, as I hear say, be become so great devourers and so wild, that they eat up and swallow down the very men themselves. They consume, destroy and devour whole fields, houses and cities. For look in what parts of the realm doth grow the finest, and therefore dearest wool, there noblemen and gentlemen, yea and certain abbots, holy men Got wot, not contenting themselves with the yearly revenues and profits that were wont to grow to their forefathers and predecessors of their land ... leave no ground for tillage, they enclose all into pastures, they throw down houses, they pluck down towns and leave nothing standing, but only the church to make of it a sheep house ...

The enclosure process provided a powerful force for the dissolution of feudal ties and the formation of the new relationships of a market society. By dispossessing the peasant, it "created" a new kind of labor force—landless, without traditional sources of income, however meager, impelled to find work for wages wherever it might be available.

Together with this agricultural proletariat, we begin to see the emergence of an urban proletariat, partly brought about by a gradual transformation of guilds into more "business-like" firms, partly by the immigration into the cities of some of the new landless peasantry. And then to exacerbate the whole situation, from the middle of the eighteenth century a rising population (itself traceable in large measure to the increase in food output resulting from the enclosures) began to pour growing numbers onto the labor market. As a result of this complicated interplay of causes and effects, we find England plagued with the problem of the "wandering poor." One not untypical proposal of the eighteenth century was that they be confined in what a reformer candidly termed "Houses of Terror."

Thus did the emergence of a market-oriented system grind into being a "labor force," and though the process of adjustment for other classes of society was not so brutal, it, too, exacted its social price. Tenaciously the guildmasters fought against the invasion of their protected trades by manufacturers who trespassed on traditional preserves or who upset established modes of production with new machinery. Doggedly the landed nobility sought to protect their ancient privileges against the encroachment of the moneyed *nouveaux riches*.

Yet the process of economic enlargement, breaking down the established routines of the past, rearranging the power and prestige of all social classes, could not be stopped. Ruthlessly it pursued its historic course and impartially it distributed its historic rewards and sacrifices. Although stretched out over a long period, it was not an evolution but a slow revolution which overtook European economic society. Only when that society had run its long gauntlet, suffering one of the most wrenching dislocations of history, would the world of transactions appear "natural" and "normal" and the categories of "land," "labor," and "capital" become so matter-of-fact that it would be difficult to believe they had not always existed.

Yet, as we have seen, it was not at all "natural" and "normal" to have free, wage-earning, contractual labor or rentable, profit-producing land or fluid, investment-seeking capital. They were *creations* of the great transformation of a pre-market into a market society. Economics calls these creations the *factors of production*, and much of economics is concerned with analyzing the manner in which these three basic constituents of the productive process are combined by the market mechanism.

What we must realize at this stage of our inquiry, however, is that "land," "labor," and "capital" do not exist as eternal categories of *social* organization. Admittedly, they are categories of *nature*, but these eternal aspects of the productive process—the soil, human effort, and the artifacts which can be applied to production—do not take on, in every society, the specific separation that distinguishes them in a market society. In pre-market economies, land, labor, and capital are inextricably mixed and mingled in the figure of slave and serf, lord and guildmaster—none of whom enters the production process as the incarnation of a specific economic function offered for a price. The slave is not a "worker," the guildmaster is not a "capitalist," nor is the lord a "landlord." Only when a social system has evolved in which labor is sold, land is rented, and capital is freely invested do we find the categories of economics emerging from the flux of life.

Modern economics thus describes the manner in which a certain kind of society, with a specific history of acculturation and institutional evolution, solves its economic problems. It may well be that in another era there will no longer be "land," "labor," and "capital." If, for example, a pure communist society ever evolves, the method by which the social product will be assured or distributed need not bear any more relation to our present system of wage payments or rental incomes or profit-shares than our own system bears to its feudal predecessor. In that case, "economics" as we know it will have to be revised to correspond to the new social relationships by which the production and distribution problems will be solved.

But the emergence of a market society, with its new factors of production, was not yet the only creation of the forces of change we have examined in this chapter. Along with the new relationships of man to man in the marketplace, there arose a new form of *social control* to take over the guidance of the economy from the former aegis of tradition and command.

What was this new form of control? Essentially, it was a pattern of social behavior, of normal, everyday action that the new market environment imposed on society. And what was this pattern of behavior? In the language of the economist, it was the drive to *maximize one's income* (or to minimize one's expenditures) by concluding the best possible bargains on the marketplace. In ordinary language, it was the drive to buy cheap and sell dear, or in business terminology, the *profit motive*.

The market society had not, of course, invented this motive. Perhaps it did not even intensify it. But it did make it a *ubiquitous* and *necessitous* aspect of social behavior. Although men may have *felt* acquisitive during the Middle Ages or antiquity, they did not enter en masse into market transactions for the basic economic activities of their livelihoods. And even when, for instance, a peasant sold his few eggs at the town market, rarely was the transaction a matter of overriding importance for his continued existence. Market transactions in a fundamentally nonmarket society were thus a subsidiary activity, a means of supplementing a livelihood which, however sparse, was largely independent of buying or selling.

With the monetization of labor, land, and capital, however, transactions became *universal* and *critical* activities. Now everything was for sale, and the terms of transactions were anything but subsidiary to existence itself. To a man who sold his labor on a market, in a society that assumed no responsibility for his upkeep, the price at which he concluded his bargain was all-important. So it was with the landlord and the budding capitalist. For each of these a good bargain could spell riches—and a bad one, ruin. Thus the pattern of economic maximization was generalized throughout society and given an inherent urgency which made it a powerful force for shaping human behavior.

The new market society did more than merely bring about an environment in which men were forced to follow their economic self-interest. It brought into being at the same time a social environment in which men could be *controlled* in their economic activities. With the emergence of a generalized drive to maximize income, it now became possible to steer the application of men's energies in various directions by raising or lowering the rewards offered for different tasks. If more effort was needed in the making of shoes, the market mechanism could attract that effort by raising the rewards for land, labor, and capital employed in shoe manufacture. Or if society wished to diminish the amount of social energy employed in making hats, it had but to lower the market rewards—wages, rents, profits—of hat manufacture, and there would ensue an exodus of the factors of the production from hat-making toward other, more profitable fields. Thus, in the universalized presence of a drive toward income maximization, society possessed a powerful tool for *allocating its resources.*

Note, however, that this regulatory device required more than just the profit motive. Equally necessary was a *mobility of the factors of production.* To the extent that labor was tied to its manorial estates or to its guild establishments, or that guildmasters were forbidden to expand their scales of operation or to venture into new endeavors, the control mechanism would not work. In that case, raising rewards for shoes or lowering rewards for hats could only increase or decrease the incomes of those already engaged in the field, but could not bring about any substantial increase or decrease in the quantity of social effort put into each pursuit.

An essential part of the evolution of the market society was thus not only the monetization of life but the mobilization of life—that is, the dissolution of those ties of place and station which were the very cement of feudal existence. And this essential requirement of mobility leads to a further point. Mobility meant that any job or activity was now open to all comers. *Competition appeared.* The traditional compartmented division of feudal labor had to give way to a universal rivalry among employments. No longer was each employment a protected haven for apprentice and guildmaster alike. Now any worker and any employer could be displaced from his task by a competitor who would do the job more cheaply.

For those who *were* displaced, the institution of competition must have seemed a harsh and unjust one; but for society as a whole, it provided an essential safeguard. Having freed the drive of economic self-interest from the limitations of feudalism, society seemed in danger of being endlessly gouged by profiteering merchants or demanding workmen—the very fear of the medieval social philosopher. What competition did, however, was to *contain* the economic drive. By pitting seller against seller, it made it difficult for any single participant to gain a strategic position for his own advantage. Even though every seller in a competitive market would *like* to charge monopolistic prices, the presence of a crowd of eager competitors at his elbow, each ready to steal away the lucrative business of the next by shading his price, assured society that ultimate selling prices would be no more than the minimum required to make continued production possible.

Competition not only prevented the seller from using his economic power to general social disadvantage, but it also assured a similar restraint on the buyer. No single purchaser could force prices below the cost of production, for other eager buyers would quickly outbid him. And this competitive mechanism worked not only in the market for commodities but in the market for factors, as well. Clearly, no laborer could ask for more than the "going" wage if he wanted to secure employment. But neither would he have to take less from any single wage-cutting employer, for he could always find better wages elsewhere.

Even if all employers in, say, the shoe trade paid lower wages than employers in the hat trade, again competition would provide the remedy. For labor would then leave the shoe trade for the hat trade, thereby bringing about a shortage of workers in the shoe plants and a surplus in hats. Wages would therefore rise in the shoe trade as manufacturers sought to bid labor back into their plants, and they would decline in hats.

Now we begin to see the complex nature of the price control mechanism provided by the competitive struggle. Across the market, buyer and seller faced one another in a contest wherein every buyer sought to pay as little as possible and every seller sought to gain as much as possible. By itself this would be merely a tug of war about the outcome of which one could say very little. But because sellers on one side of the tug of war were themselves engaged in a contest with one another, and because buyers at the other end of the rope were engaged in a similar contest, the outcome of the contest was quite predictable. While prices of goods might sway back and forth in the short run, the interaction of supply and demand operated to bring them always back toward *costs of production* in the long run. And while incomes of factors in different employments might fluctuate temporarily upward or downward, again the competitive mechanism operated always to bring the rewards for similar tasks into a common alignment.

Only one final point remains to be noted. We have seen how a competitive market economy operated to fulfill the wants of society. But who was to say what its wants were?

In pre-market economies, such a question did not pose subtle problems. The "wants" of such societies were either codified by ageless tradition or specifically formulated by its rulers. But in a market society, the specification of wants suddenly takes on a new dimension. It now consists of demands of everyone who has the wherewithal to enter the market. *The "wants" of society are thus expressed by millions of daily orders placed on the market by an entire community.* As these orders enter the marketplace they affect the prices at which goods sell. Thus shifts in prices become, in effect, signals to producers: rising prices betokening an increase in demand and an actual or prospective increase in rewards; falling prices signaling the opposite.

In this way the market society catapults the consumer into a position of extraordinary importance. On his ability and willingness to buy hinges the panoply of demands which confront society's producers. If consumers do not want a good or service, or if they do not wish to buy it at its offered price, that good or service will go unsold. In that case, the production effort needed to supply it will not pay for itself and will soon terminate. *In a market society, the consumer is the ultimate formulator of the pattern of economic activity.* He is now the sovereign of the economic process—sovereign not as an individual, but as a member of an entire society which collectively guides and controls its on-going productive effort through a market mechanism.

Does the market really work as this first introduction to it suggests? Much of the rest of this book will be devoted to that very question—that is, to what extent the outcome of the market process in actuality corresponds with its outcome in a "pure" market system. But we are not yet ready to consider that problem. We have so far traced the market only to its first half-formed appearance when the "theory" of a market was still far from formulated in men's minds. Let us therefore return to our historical narrative as the market system begins to evolve into capitalism itself. For the slow evolution of the market system cannot be considered merely as the rise of a new mechanism of social control. It must also be seen as the evolution of a new socio-economic organization of society, a new structure of law, of political organization, of social institutions, of ideas.

For example, a market society could not coexist with a form of legal organization that did not recognize the freedom of the individual to contract for employment as he wished. Nor could it exist under a code of law that barely recognized "private property" as we know it. Neither could it flourish under a political system in which privilege accrued to birth rather than to achievement, or in which the landed nobility by law and usage possessed the main power to regulate society's affairs. Feudalism as a legal, political, and social organization had to give way to another form of society with a very different set of laws, customs, and political institutions.

We call that other form of society *capitalism,* and the long process of change which we have studied in its economic aspects can be given a wider interpretation as the evolution (and revolution) of feudalism into capitalism. The student of government notes the growth of political representation on the part of the middle classes, a growth most dramatically symbolized in the overthrow of feudal power in the French Revolution, but most fully realized in the long rise of parliamentary power in England. So, too, a student of law notes the rise of the law of contract, or the decline of the legal restrictions of serfdom or in the legal prerogatives of the aristocracy. Without a study of these changes, we cannot fully comprehend the manner in which capitalism arose from feudalism. Yet without an understanding of the deeper-seated economic changes which took place, so to speak, spontaneously and without conscious human intervention, the accompanying legal and political changes cannot themselves be understood.

Many of those necessary changes did not take place until the sixteenth and seventeenth centuries, or even later. After all, serfdom was not formally abolished in France until 1789; and in Germany, not until a half century later. Certainly by 1700, the market society had not yet reached a stage in which capitalism had achieved full legal and political status. Although "land," "labor," and "capital" had come into being, although a highly monetized society characterized France and England and Holland, although the merchant classes were strong and rich, there was still lacking a final achievement of economic "freedom," a final throwing off of traditional bonds and restrictions on labor and capital, a final loosening of controls and commands from above. In England in the late 1700s, for example, no master hatter could employ more than two apprentices, or no master cutler more than one, and these and similar guild regulations did not vanish until the medieval Statute of Artificers was repealed in 1813. Likewise in France, an immense web of regulations bound the would-be capitalist. Rules and edicts, many of them seeking to standardize production, laid down the exact number of threads to be woven into the cloths of the French textile manufacturers, and to disregard these laws was to risk pillorying—first for the cloth, then for the manufacturer.

Thus in the decades before the opening of the eighteenth century—indeed, well into that century—we find the great revolution of the market still incomplete; or rather, we find the nearly complete process of monetization and commercialization contained uncomfortably within a frame of legal and social organization not yet fully adapted to it.

We call this stage of pre-capitalism *mercantilism*, but we must not think of mercantilism solely as a time in which a nascent capitalism was held back by an outmoded social and economic order. On the contrary, it was also a time when the final achievement of capitalism was powerfully stimulated and accelerated. For the policies of mercantilism were devoted to building up national economic strength—in part by highly protectionist foreign trade policies, in part by subsidy; in part by urging the rising manufacturer to expand. Colbert, France's finance minister to Louis XIV, told the butterfly court of Versailles that the greatness of the country depended on its wealth; its wealth, on its work; and its work, on the encouragement of those industrial, commercial, and agricultural producers who were, in the main, regarded with supercilious disdain. Colbert, therefore, struggled to encourage the rising *bourgeoisie* and to promote the interests of manufacture and commerce in general.

He did so in a curiously self-defeating way, with a web of regulations, tariffs, and ordinances which suffocated the entrepreneurial impulse at the same time that it sought to foster it; and the social benefits of his economic policy were largely vitiated by the necessity to abide by a feudal system of taxation which was harsh, iniquitous, and corrupt. Yet, as in no previous period, the seeds for subsequent growth were deliberately sown all through the mercantile era by the royal patronage of shipyards and porcelain factories, tapestry works and arsenals. It is curious that the zest for expansion was often more notable on the part of the monarch than the manufacturer: Frederick the Great complained in the margin of one of his edicts that his commoners had to be dragged to their profits "by their noses and ears."[10]

And one significant anomaly is also to be remarked. Despite the multiplicity of regulations which mercantilism imposed, it was also during these years—perhaps because of the very difficulties of regulation—that the idea of a totally free and unhampered market began to gain acceptance. "Que faut-il faire pour vous aider?" (How may we help you?) wrote Colbert to the merchant Gournay. "Nous laissez faire" (Leave us alone) was the answer. Colbert scarcely heeded the advice, but soon it would become the slogan of the new capitalist world.

A full-scale review of economic history must study European mercantilism at length, for it is a critical era of economic history, an era in which industrial growth was first launched as a deliberate act of national economic policy. Yet it was, so to speak, a position of unstable rest, not fully emancipated from the past, not fully entrant upon the future. The basic elements of capitalism had been created and waited for a full trial. The trial was soon to come, first in England, later throughout Europe and in the United States. We shall soon watch this major chapter of economic history unfold.

KEY CONCEPTS AND KEY WORDS

1. *Powerful forces of change* were operative within European feudalism, and served gradually to introduce the structure of a market society. Primary among these forces were:
   - The role of *the itinerant merchant* in introducing trade, money, and the acquisitive spirit into feudal life.
   - The *process of urbanization* as a source of economic activity, and as the locus of a new, trade-centered seat of power.
   - *The Crusades* as a force for the disruption of feudal life and the introduction of new ideas.
   - The rise of unifying, commerce-supporting *national states*.
   - The stimulus of the *Age of Exploration* and of the *gold* it brought into Europe.
   - The emergence of *new religious ideas* more sympathetic to business activity than Catholicism had been.
   - The *monetization of dues* within the manorial system.

Feudalism

[10] Lowe, *Economics and Sociology* (London: Allen, 1935), p. 23.

2. As a consequence of these forces, we begin to see *the separation of economic from social life.* The processes of production and distribution were no longer indistinguishably melded into the prevailing religious, social, and political customs and practices, but now began to form a sharply distinct area of life in themselves.

Enclosures

3. With the rise of the economic aspect of life, we see *deep-seated transformations* taking place. The peasant-serf is no longer bound to the land, but becomes a free, mobile laborer; the guildmaster is no longer hobbled by guild rules but becomes an independent entrepreneur; the lord of the land becomes (in the modern sense of the word) a landlord. The transformation was a long and often violent one, especially in the complex case of the *enclosures.*

Factors of production

4. The advent of free laborers, capitalists, and landlords, each selling his services on the market for land and capital and labor, made it possible to speak of the *"factors of production."* By this was implied two things: the *physical categories* of land, labor, and capital as distinguishable agents in the production process, and the *social categories* of laborers, landowners, and capitalists as distinct groups or classes entering the marketplace.

Profit motive

5. The emergence of the factors of production signaled the entrance of the full-fledged *market system.* Its earmarks were:
   - The appearance of the *"profit motive"* as a guide for economic behavior.

Mobility
   - The greatly increased legal and social *mobility* of the factors of production.
   - A widespread *competition* among all individuals in their economic activities.

Demand
   - The *appearance of "demand"*—the amounts that consumers were willing and able to spend—as the new regulator of production.
   - The *elevation of the consumer,* en masse, to a new position of economic control.

6. The market system required not alone the economic innovations of the market process, but a whole panoply of *legal and political changes* as well. The freedom and independence of the economic person, an idea quite incompatible with feudalism, was an essential precondition for a fluid market system.

Mercantilism

7. The transformation was not achieved in one bound. The evolution of feudalism into a free market system led to a transitional stage called *mercantilism.* Mercantilism was characterized by an effort to regulate commerce and production in great detail, while at the same time supporting and encouraging it.

Capitalism

Laissez faire

8. The complexities and difficulties of mercantilist regulation gave rise to the slogan that was to be the rallying cry of the new philosophy of *capitalism: laissez faire* (leave us alone).

1. What was so disruptive to feudal life about the activities of the merchant? Are business activities today also the causes of social stress?

2. The underdeveloped nations today often resemble the economies of antiquity or of the Middle Ages, at least insofar as their poverty and stagnation is concerned. Discuss what relevance, if any, the forces of change mentioned in this chapter have on the modernization of these areas. Are there new forces of change?

3. The leading nations in the world, so far as per capita income is concerned, are the U.S., New Zealand and Australia, and the Scandinavian states. Among the less affluent Western nations are Ireland, Spain, Portugal, and Italy. Do you think this proves the validity of the Weber-Tawney thesis as to the importance of the Protestant ethic in economic growth? Does the addition of Latin America change the argument? Japan?

4. The process of monetization and commercialization was often a violent one in Europe. Do you think the Civil War, which ended slavery and displaced the southern semifeudal plantation system, could be considered as part of the same transformation in America?

5. Is economic life distinctly separate from social and political life in America?

6. Do you think most people in the United States obey the profit motive? Are most people mobile in the United States? Do you know anyone who has changed his residence because of economic considerations? His profession?

7. Profit-making is certainly as old as man. Do you think we can speak of the origins of capitalism as being equally old?

8. How would you define *feudalism? Mercantilism? Capitalism?*

9. What legal and political changes were necessary to change feudalism into a market system?

Heretofore, in our survey of economic history, we have concentrated almost entirely on two main currents of economic activity: agriculture and commerce. Yet there was, from earliest days, a third essential source of economic wealth—industry—which we have purposely let slip by unnoticed. For in contrast to agriculture and commerce, industrial manufacture did not leave a major imprint on economic society itself. As a peasant, a serf, a merchant, or a guildsman, the actors in the economic drama directly typified the basic activities of their times, but this would not have been true of someone in industry. Such a person as a "factory worker"—indeed, the very idea of an *industrial* "proletarian"—was singularly absent from the long years before the late seventeenth century.

Let us note as well that the "industrial capitalist" was also lacking. Most of the moneymakers of the past gained their fortunes by trading, or transporting, or lending—not by making. It is amusing—more than amusing: instructive—to mark the best ways of getting rich enumerated by Leon Battista Alberti, a fifteenth-century architect, musician, and courtier. They are: (1) wholesale trade; (2) seeking for treasure trove; (3) ingratiating oneself with a rich man to become his heir; (4) usury; (5) the rental of pastures, horses, and the like. A seventeenth-century commentator adds to this: royal service, soldiering, and alchemy. Manufacturing is conspicuously absent from both lists.[1]

Granted, in ancient Greece, Demosthenes had an armor and a cabinet "factory"; and from long before his time, in ancient Egypt we even have the attendance record of workers in "factories" for the production of cloth. Yet it is clear that this form of production was far less important than either agriculture or commerce in shaping the economic texture of the times. For one thing, the typical scale of manufacture was small. Note that the very word "manufacture" (from the Latin *manus*, hand, and *facere*, to make) implies a system of hand, rather than machine, technology. Demosthenes' enterprises, for example, employed no more than fifty men. It is true that

---

[1] Werner Sombart, *The Quintessence of Capitalism* (New York: Dutton, 1915), pp. 34-35.

CHAPTER

from time to time we do come across quite large manufacturing operations; already in the second century A.D. a Roman brickworks employed forty-six foremen; and by the time we reach the seventeenth century, enterprises with several hundred workers are not unheard of. Yet such operations were the exception rather than the rule. In 1660, for instance, a steelmaker in France needed no more than three tons of pig iron a year for his output of swords or sickle blades or artistic cutlery. Similarly, most guild operations, as we have seen, were small. As late as 1843, a Prussian census showed only sixty-seven working people for every hundred masters.[2] In the past—as today in the East and Near East—most "industry" was carried on in the backs of small shops or the dim cellars of houses, in sheds behind bazaars, or in the scattered homes of workers to whom materials would be supplied by an organizing "capitalist."

In addition to the smallness of the scale of industry, another aspect of the times delayed industrial manufacture from making known its social presence. This was the absence of any sustained interest in the development of an *industrial technology.* Throughout antiquity and the Middle Ages, little of society's creative energy was directed toward a systematic improvement of manufacturing techniques. It is indicative of the disinterest attached to productive technology that so simple and important an invention as the horse collar had to await the Middle Ages for discovery: the Egyptians, Greeks, and Romans, who were capable of a magnificent technology of architecture, were simply not fundamentally concerned with the techniques of everyday production itself.[3] Even well into the Renaissance and Reforma-

PACE OF
TECHNICAL
CHANGE

[2] *Cambridge Economic History of Europe,* II, 34; John U. Nef, *Cultural Foundations of Industrial Civilization* (New York: Harper, Torchbooks, 1960), p. 131; R. H. Tawney, *Equality,* 4th ed. (London: Macmillan, 1952), p. 59.

[3] E. M. Jope, in *History of Technology,* eds. Charles J. Singer *et al.* (New York: Oxford University Press, 1956), II, 553. There was, however, considerable improvement in mining techniques, especially for silver and copper.

tion, the idea of industrial technology hardly attracted serious thought. With the exception of Leonardo da Vinci, whose fecund mind played with inventions of the most varied kind, the serious thinkers of Europe, until well into the seventeenth century, were both ignorant of, and uninterested in, the technology of basic production.

There was good reason for this prevailing indifference: in the societies of the pre-market world, the necessary economic base for any large-scale industrial manufacture was totally lacking. In economies sustained by the labor of peasants, slaves, and serfs, economies in which the stream of money was small and the current of economic life, accidents of war and nature aside, relatively changeless from year to year, who could dream of a process in which avalanches of goods would be turned out? The very idea of industrial production on the large scale was inconceivable in such an unmonetized, static setting.*

For all these reasons, the pace of industrialization was slow. It is a question whether Europe in the year 1200 was significantly more technologically advanced than it had been in the year 200 B.C. The widespread use of waterpower in industry, for instance, did not appear until the fifteenth century, and it would be still another century before windmills provided a common means of tapping the energy of nature. The mechanical clock dates from the thirteenth century, but not for 200 years would significant improvements be made in instruments for navigation, surveying, or measuring. Movable type, that indispensable forerunner of mass communication, did not appear until 1450.

In short, despite important pockets of highly organized production, notably in the thirteenth-century Flanders cloth industry and in Northern Italian towns, not until the late sixteenth century can we discern the first signs of a general ground swell of industrial technology, and even in that day it would have been impossible to foresee that one day industry would be the dominant form of productive organization. As a matter of fact, as late as the eighteenth century, when manufacturing had already begun to reach respectable proportions as a form of social endeavor, it was not generally thought of as inherently possessing any but secondary importance. Agriculture, of course, was the visible foundation of the nation itself. Trading was regarded as useful insofar as it brought a nation gold. But at best, industry was seen as a hand-maiden of the others, providing the trader with the goods to export, or serving the farmer as a secondary market for the products of the earth.†

---

* Even today, one sees the difficulties of the unmonetized, static, underdeveloped societies in finding an industrial-minded, rather than commercial-minded, entrepreneurial group.

† It was in the mid-eighteenth century that the French doctor François Quesnay propounded one of the first systematic explanations of economic production and distribution. It is noteworthy that in his system (called *Physiocracy*) only the farmer was regarded as a producer of net worth; and the manufacturer, while his utility was not ignored, was nonetheless relegated to the "sterile" (i.e., non-wealth-producing) classes.

What finally conspired to bring manufacturing into a position of overwhelming prominence?

It was a complex concatenation of events that finally brought about the eruption we call the industrial revolution. As with the Commercial Revolution and the Mercantile era which preceded it and formed its indispensable preparation, it is impossible in a few pages to do justice to the many currents which contributed to that final outburst of industrial technology. But if we cannot trace the process in detail, we can at least gain an idea of its impetus and of the main forces behind it if we turn now to England around 1750. Here, for the first time, industrial manufacture as a major form of economic activity began to work its immense social transformations. Let us observe the process as it took place.

Why did the industrial revolution originally take place in England and not on the Continent? To answer the question we must look at the background factors which distinguished England from most other European nations in the eighteenth century.

The first of these factors was simply that England was relatively wealthy. In fact, a century of successful exploration, slave trading, piracy, war, and commerce had made her the richest nation in the world. Even more important, her riches had accrued not merely to a few nobles, but to a large upper-middle stratum of commercial *bourgeoisie*. England was thus one of the first nations to develop, albeit on a tiny scale, a prime requisite of an industrial economy: a "mass" consumer market. As a result, a rising pressure of demand inspired a search for new techniques. Very typically, the Society for the Encouragement of Arts and Manufactures (itself a significant child of the age) offered a prize for a machine that would spin six threads of cotton at one time, thus enabling the spinner to keep up with the technologically more advanced weaver. It was this which led, at least in part, to Arkwright's spinning jenny, of which we shall hear more shortly.

Second, England was the scene of the most successful and thoroughgoing transformation of feudal society into commercial society. The process of enclosures was a significant clue to a historic change that sharply marked off England from the Continent. It was that in England alone the aristocracy had made its peace with (and more than that, found its profits in) commerce. Although sharp conflicts of interest remained between the "old" landed power and the "new" monied power, by 1700 the ruling orders in England had decisively opted for adaptation rather than resistance to the demands of the market economy.[4]

Third, England was the locus of a unique enthusiasm for science and engineering. The famous Royal Society, of which Newton was an early

[4] See Barrington Moore, *Social Origins of Dictatorship and Democracy* (Boston: Beacon Press, 1966), Chap. I.

president, was founded in 1660 and was the immediate source of much intellectual excitement. Indeed, a popular interest in gadgets, machines, and devices of all sorts soon became a mild national obsession: *Gentlemen's Magazine,* a kind of *New Yorker* of the period, announced in 1729 that it would henceforth keep its readers "abreast of every invention"—a task which the mounting flow of inventions soon rendered quite impossible. No less important was an enthusiasm of the British landed aristocracy for scientific farming: English landlords displayed an interest in matters of crop rotation and fertilizer which their French counterparts would have found quite beneath their dignity.

Then there were a host of other background causes, some as fortuitous as the immense resources of coal and iron ore on which the British sat; others as purposeful as the development of a national patent system which deliberately sought to stimulate and protect the act of invention itself.* And then, as the Revolution came into being, it fed upon itself. The new techniques (especially in textiles) simply destroyed their handicraft competition around the world and thus enormously increased their own markets. But what finally brought all these factors into operation was the energy of a group of New Men who made of the latent opportunities of history a vehicle for their own rise to fame and fortune.

RISE OF THE NEW MEN

One such, for instance, was John Wilkinson. The son of an old-fashioned small-scale iron producer, Wilkinson was a man possessed by the technological possibilities of his business. He invented a dozen things: a rolling mill and a steam lathe, a process for the manufacture of iron pipes, and a design for machining accurate cylinders. Typically, he decided that the old-fashioned leather bellows used in the making of iron itself were not efficient, and so he determined to make iron ones. "Everybody laughed at me," he later wrote. "I did it and applied the steam engine to blow them and they all cried: 'Who could have thought of it?'"

He followed his success in production with a passion for application: everything must be made of iron: pipes, bridges, even ships. After a ship made of iron plates had been successfully launched, he wrote a friend: "It

---

* Phyllis Deane, in *The First Industrial Revolution* (paperback ed., Cambridge: Cambridge University Press, 1965) ascribes the onset of industrialism in England to a somewhat different set of causes: a rise in population, better food-producing techniques, a boom in foreign trade, and a vast improvement in transportation. There is no doubt that these were also indispensable elements in the process. I mention Miss Deane's book so that a student will not think that there is only one "right" way of accounting for very complex historical transformations. For yet another exceedingly good general account of the process, one might turn to the fascinating chapter by David Landes, "Technological Change and Development in Western Europe" in the *Cambridge Economic History* (Cambridge: Cambridge University Press, 1965), VI, esp. pp. 274-350, where the emphasis is focused on the process of technological advance, and in particular on the strategic inventions of steam power, and textile machinery. Landes' essay has been extended and published as a separate book, *The Unbound Prometheus* (Cambridge: Cambridge University Press, 1969).

answers all my expectations, and has convinced the unbelievers, who were nine hundred and ninety-nine in a thousand. It will be a nine-days wonder, and afterwards, a Columbus' egg."[5]

But Wilkinson was only one of many. The most famous was, of course, James Watt, who, together with Matthew Boulton, formed the first company for the manufacture of steam engines. Watt was the son of an architect, shipbuilder, and maker of nautical instruments. At thirteen he was already making models of machines, and by young manhood he was an accomplished artisan. He planned to settle in Glasgow, but the guild of hammermen objected to his making mathematical instruments—the last remnants of feudalism thus coming into an ironic personal conflict with the man who, more than any other, would create *the* invention that would destroy guild organization. At any rate, Watt found a haven at the university and there, in 1764, had his attention turned to an early and very unsatisfactory steam engine invented by Newcomen. In his careful and systematic way, Watt experimented with steam pressures, cylinder designs, and valves, until by 1796 he had developed a truly radical and (by the standards of those days) extraordinarily powerful and efficient engine. Interestingly, Watt could never have done so well with his engines had not Wilkinson perfected a manner of making good piston-cylinder fits. Previously, cylinders and pistons were made of wood and rapidly wore out. Typically, too, it was Wilkinson who bought the first steam engine to be used for purposes other than pumping: it worked the famous iron bellows.

There was needed, however, more than Watt's skill. The new engines had to be produced and sold, and the factory that made them had to be financed and organized. Watt at first formed a partnership with John Roebuck, another iron magnate, but it shortly failed. Thereafter luck came his way. Matthew Boulton, already a wealthy and highly successful manufacturer of buttons and buckles, took up Roebuck's contract with Watt, and the greatest combination of technical skill and business acumen of the day was born.

Even then the firm did not prosper immediately. Expenses of development were high, and the new firm was not out of debt for twelve years. Yet from the beginning, interest was high. By 1781 Boulton was able to claim that the people of London, Birmingham, and Manchester were all "steam mill mad"; and by 1786, when two steam engines were harnessed to fifty pairs of millstones in the largest flour mill in the world, all of London came to see and marvel.

The steam engine was the greatest single invention, but by no means the sole mainstay, of the industrial revolution. Hardly less important were a group of textile inventions, of which the most famous was Arkwright's

[5] Paul Mantoux, *The Industrial Revolution in the Eighteenth Century,* 2nd ed. (New York: Harcourt, 1928), pp. 313 n., 315.

jenny, or water frame, as it was called to distinguish it from other hand-operated spinning jennies.*

Arkwright's career is, in itself, interesting. A barber, he plied his trade near the weaving districts of Manchester and so heard the crying need for a machine that would enable the cottage spinners to keep up with the technically more advanced weavers. Good fortune threw him into contact with a clockmaker named John Kay, whom he hired to perfect a machine that Kay had already begun with another employer-inventor. What happened thereafter is obscure: Kay left the business accused of theft and embezzlement, and Arkwright appeared as the "sole inventor" of a spinning jenny in 1769.

He now found two rich hosiers, Samuel Need and Jedediah Strutt, who agreed to set up business with him to produce water frames, and in 1771 the firm built its own spinning mill. It was an overnight success; by 1779 it had several thousand spindles, more than 300 workmen, and ran night and day. Within not many years Arkwright had built an immense fortune for himself and founded an even more immense textile industry for England. "O reader," wrote Carlyle, looking back on his career, "what a historical phenomenon is that bag-cheeked, pot-bellied, much enduring, much inventing barber! ... It was this man that had to give England the power of cotton."[6]

THE
INDUSTRIAL
ENTREPRENEUR

It is interesting, as we watch the careers of these New Men to draw a few generalizations concerning them. For these were an entirely new class of economically important persons. Peter Onions, who was one of the inventors of the puddling process, was an obscure foreman; Arkwright was a barber; Benjamin Huntsman, the steel pioneer, was originally a maker of clocks; Maudslay, who invented the automatic screw machine, was a bright young mechanic at the Woolwich Arsenal. None of the great industrial pioneers came of noble lineage; and with few exceptions, such as Matthew Boulton, none even possessed money capital. In agriculture, the new revolutionary methods of scientific farming enjoyed aristocratic patronage and leadership, especially from the famous Sir Jethro Tull and Lord Townshend; but in industry, the lead went to men of humble origin and descent.

Let us note, therefore, that this required a social system flexible enough to permit the rise of such obscure "adventurers." It is not until we see the catalytic effect of unleashing and harnessing the energies of talented men in the lower and middle ranks of the social order that we begin to appreciate the immense liberating effect of the preceding economic and political revolutions. In the medieval hierarchy the meteoric careers of such New Men would have been unthinkable. In addition, the New Men were the product

---

* Essentially what the water frame did was to enable cotton thread of much greater strength to be produced. As a result, for the first time it was possible to use cotton thread instead of linen thread for the warp (the vertical threads that take most of the strain in weaving) as well as for the weft. Not until Arkwright's invention was "cotton cloth" made wholly of cotton. The new cloth was incomparably superior to the old and instantly enjoyed a huge demand.

[6] Mantoux, *The Industrial Revolution in The Eighteenth Century*, p. 225.

of the unique economic preparation of England itself. They were, of course, the beneficiaries of the rising demand and the technical inquisitiveness of the times. Beyond that, many of the small manufacturers were, themselves, former small proprietors who had been bought out during the late period of the enclosure movement and who determined to use their tiny capital in the promising area of manufacture.

Many of these New Men made great sums of money. A few, like Boulton and Watt, were modest in their wants. Despite an iron-clad patent, they charged for their engines only the basic cost of the machine and installation plus one-third the saving in fuel which the customer got. Some, like Josiah Wedgwood, founder of the great china works, actually refused, on principle, to take out patents. But most of them did not display such fine sensibilities. Arkwright retired a multi-millionaire living in ostentatious splendor; Huntsman, Wilkinson, Samuel Walker (who began life as a nail-smith and stole the secret of cast steel)—all went on to roll up huge fortunes.* Indeed, Wilkinson's iron business became a minor industrial state with a credit stronger than many German and Italian principalities. It even coined its own money, and its copper and silver tokens (with a profile and legend of John Wilkinson, Ironmaster) were much in use between 1787 and 1808.

Beyond mere avarice, the manufacturers have been described by the economic historian, Paul Mantoux, as

tyrannical, hard, sometimes cruel: their passions and greeds were those of upstarts. They had the reputation of being heavy drinkers and of having little regard for the honour of their female employees. They were proud of their newly acquired wealth and lived in great style with footmen, carriages and gorgeous town and country houses.[7]

Pleasant or unpleasant, the personal characteristics fade beside one overriding quality. These were all men interested in expansion, in growth, in investment for investment's sake. All of them were identified with technological progress, and none of them disdained the productive process. An employee of Maudslay once remarked, "It was a pleasure to see him handle a tool of any kind, but he was *quite splendid* with an 18-inch file."[8] Watt was tireless in experimenting with his machines; Wedgwood stomped about his factory on his wooden leg scrawling, "This won't do for Jos. Wedgwood," wherever he saw evidence of careless work. Richard Arkwright was a bundle of ceaseless energy in promoting his interests, jouncing about England over execrable roads in a post chaise driven by four horses, pursuing his correspondence as he traveled.

* In contrast to the manufacturers, the inventors did not usually fare successfully. Many of them, who did not have Watt's good fortune in finding a Boulton, died poor and neglected, fruitlessly suing for stolen inventions, unpaid royalties, ignored claims.

[7] Mantoux, *The Industrial Revolution in The Eighteenth Century*, p. 397.

[8] Lewis Mumford, *Technics and Civilization* (New York: Harcourt, 1934), p. 210.

"With us," wrote a French visitor to a calico works in 1788, "a man rich enough to set up and run a factory like this would not care to remain in a position which he would deem unworthy of his wealth."[9] This was an attitude entirely foreign to the rising English industrial capitalist. His work was its own dignity and reward; the wealth it brought was quite aside. Boswell, on being shown Watt and Boulton's great engine works at Soho, declared that he never forgot Boulton's expression as the latter declared, "I sell here, sir, what all the world desires to have—Power."[10]

The New Men were first and last *entrepreneurs*—enterprisers. They brought with them a new energy, as restless as it proved to be inexhaustible. In an economic, if not a political, sense, they deserve the epithet "revolutionaries," for the change they ushered in was nothing short of total, sweeping, and irreversible.

INDUSTRIAL AND SOCIAL REPERCUSSIONS

The first and most striking element of that change was a sharp rise in the output of the newly industrialized industries. The import of raw cotton for spinning weighed 1 million pounds in 1701; 3 million pounds in 1750; 5 million in 1781. That was a respectable rate of increase. But then came the sudden burst in textile technology. By 1784 the figure was over 11 million pounds; by 1789 it was three times greater yet, and still it grew: to 43 million pounds in 1799; 56 million in 1800; 60 million in 1802.[11] So was it with much else where the new technology penetrated. The output of coal increased tenfold in forty years; that of pig iron leaped from 68,000 tons in 1788 to 1,347,000 tons in 1839.[12]

Thus, the first impact of the industrial revolution was an immense quickening of the pace of production in the new industrial sector of the economy, an effect which we find repeated in every nation which goes through an "industrial revolution." In France, for example, the impact of industrial techniques did not make its influence felt until about 1815: between that date and 1845, the French output of pig iron grew fivefold; her coal production, sevenfold; her rate of importation, tenfold.[13]

The industrial revolution, itself, did not immediately exert a comparable leverage on the *over-all* increase of output. The industrial sector, to begin with, was small; and the phenomenal rates of increase in those industries where its leverage was first and most fruitfully applied were by no means mirrored in every industry. What is of crucial importance, however,

---

[9] Mantoux, *The Industrial Revolution in The Eighteenth Century,* p. 404.

[10] H. R. Fox Bourne, *English Merchants* (London: 1866), p. 119.

[11] Mantoux, *The Industrial Revolution in The Eighteenth Century,* p. 258.

[12] J. L. and B. Hammond, *The Rise of Modern Industry* (New York: Harcourt, 1937), p. 160.

[13] A. Dunham, *The Industrial Revolution in France, 1815-48* (New York: Exposition Press, 1955), p. 432.

is that the industrial revolution ushered in the technology by which large-scale, sustained growth was eventually to take place. This is a process into which we must look more carefully at the end of this chapter.

But first we must pay heed to another immediate and visible result of the industrial revolution in England. We can describe it as the transformation of an essentially commercial and agricultural society into one in which industrial manufacture became the dominant mode of organizing economic life. To put it more concretely, the industrial revolution was characterized by *the rise of the factory to the center of social as well as economic life.* After 1850, the factory was not only the key economic institution of England, but it was the economic institution that shaped its politics, its social problems, the character of its daily life, just as decisively as the manor or the guild had done a few centuries earlier.

It is difficult for us today to realize the pace or the quality of change which this rise of factory work brought about. Until the mid-eighteenth century, Glasgow, Newcastle, and the Rhondda Valley were mostly waste or farm land, and Manchester in 1727 was described by Daniel Defoe as "a mere village." Forty years later there were a hundred integrated mills and a whole cluster of machine plants, forges, leather and chemical works in the area. A modern industrial city had been created.

By the 1780s the shape of the new environment was visible. A French mineralogist visiting England in 1784 wrote:

[The] creaking, the piercing noise of the pulleys, the continuous sound of hammering, the ceaseless energy of the men keeping all this machinery in motion, presented a sight as interesting as it was new ... The night is so filled with fire and light that when from a distance we see, here a glowing mass of coal, there darting flames leaping from the blast furnaces, when we hear the heavy hammers striking the echoing anvils and the shrill whistling of the air pumps, we do not know whether we are looking at a volcano in eruption or have been miraculously transported to Vulcan's cave ...[14]

The factory provided not merely a new landscape but a new and uncongenial social habitat. In our day, we have become so used to urban-industrial life that we forget what a wrench is the transition from farm to city. For the peasant, this transfer requires a drastic adjustment. No longer does he work at his own pace, but at the pace of a machine. No longer are slack seasons determined by the weather, but by the state of the market. No longer is the land, however miserable its crop, an eternal source of sustenance close at hand, but only the packed and sterile earth of the industrial site.

It is little wonder that the English laborer, still more used to rural than urban ways, feared and hated the advent of the machine. Throughout the

[14] Mantoux, *The Industrial Revolution in The Eighteenth Century*, p. 313.

early years of the industrial revolution workmen literally attacked the invading army of machinery, burning and wrecking factories. During the late eighteenth century, for instance, when the first textile mills were built, whole hamlets rose in revolt rather than work in the mills. Headed by a mythical General Ludd, the Luddites constituted a fierce but fruitless opposition to industrialism. In 1813, in a mass trial which ended in many hangings and transportations, the movement came to an end.*

Distasteful as was the advent of the factory itself, even more distasteful were the conditions within it. Child labor, for instance, was commonplace and sometimes began at age four; hours of work were generally dawn to dusk; abuses of every kind were all too frequent. A Committee of Parliament appointed in 1832 to look into conditions gives this testimony from a factory overseer.

Q. At what time in the morning, in the brisk time, did these girls go to the mills?

A. In the brisk time, for about six weeks, they have gone at three o'clock in the morning and ended at ten or nearly half past at night.

Q. What intervals were allowed for rest and refreshment during those nineteen hours of labour?

A. Breakfast a quarter of an hour, and dinner half an hour, and drinking a quarter of an hour.

Q. Was any of that time taken up in cleaning the machinery?

A. They generally had to do what they call dry down; sometimes this took the whole time at breakfast or drinking.

Q. Had you not great difficulty in awakening your children to the excessive labour?

A. Yes, in the early time we had to take them up asleep and shake them.

Q. Had any of them any accident in consequence of this labour?

A. Yes, my eldest daughter ... the cog caught her forefinger nail and screwed it off below the knuckle.

Q. Has she lost that finger?

A. It is cut off at the second joint.

Q. Were her wages paid during that time?

A. As soon as the accident happened the wages were totally stopped.[15]

---

* Even in our day, however, we use the word "Luddite" to describe an attempt to "fight back" at the threat of machinery.

[15] Tawney, Bland, and Brown, *English Economic History, Selected Documents* (London: Bell, 1914), p. 510.

It was a grim age. The long hours of work, the general dirt and clangor of the factories, the lack of even the most elementary safety precautions, all combined to give early industrial capitalism a reputation from which, in the minds of many people of the world, it has never recovered. Worse yet were the slums to which the majority of workers returned after their travail. A government commissioner reports in 1839 on one such workers' quarter in Glasgow called "the wynds."

The wynds ... house a fluctuating population of between 15,000 and 30,000 persons. This district is composed of many narrow streets and square courts and in the middle of each court there is a dunghill. Although the outward appearance of these places was revolting, I was nevertheless quite unprepared for the filth and misery that were to be found inside. In some bedrooms we visited at night we found a whole mass of humanity stretched on the floor. There were often 15 to 20 men and women huddled together, some being clothed and others naked. There was hardly any furniture there and the only thing which gave these holes the appearance of a dwelling was fire burning on the hearth. Thieving and prostitution are the main sources of income of these people.[16]

Without question, the times were marked by tremendous social suffering. But it is well, in looking back on the birth years of industrial capitalism, to bear several facts in mind:

1. *It is doubtful if the poverty represented a deterioration in life for the masses in general.*

In at least some sections of England, industrialism brought immediate benefits. Wedgwood (an exceptionally good employer, it is true) used to tell his employees to ask their parents for a description of the country as *they* first knew it and to compare their present state. So, too, the twelve-hour day in Arkwright's mills was a two-hour *improvement* over previous Manchester standards. Furthermore, the existing poverty was not by any means new. As we know from Hogarth's etchings, long before the industrial revolution, "Gin Lane" already sported its pitiful types. As one reformer of the mid-nineteenth century wrote, those whose sensibilities were revolted by the sight of suffering factory children thought "how much more delightful would have been the gambol of free limbs on the hillside; the sight of the green mead with its spangles of buttercups and daisies; the song of the bird and the humming of the bee ... [but] we have seen children perishing from sheer hunger in the mud hovel or in the ditch by the wayside."[17]

---

[16] Quoted in F. Engels, *The Condition of the Working Class in England* (New York: Macmillan, 1958), p. 46

[17] Friedrich Hayek, ed., *Capitalism and the Historians* (Chicago: University of Chicago Press, 1954), p. 180.

2. *Much of the harsh criticism to which early industrial capitalism was subjected derived not so much from its economic but from its political accompaniments.*

For coincident with the rise of capitalism, and indeed contributory to it, was a deep-seated change in the vantage point of political criticism. New ideas of democracy, of social justice, of the "rights" of the individual charged the times with a critical temper of mind before which *any* economic system would have suffered censure.

To be sure, the political movements by which capitalism was carried to its heights were not working-class movements, but middle-class, bourgeois movements: the rising manufacturers in England and France had little "social conscience" beyond a concern for their own rights and privileges. But the movement of political liberalism which they set into motion had a momentum beyond the narrow limits for which it was intended. By the first quarter of the nineteenth century, the condition of the working classes, now so exposed to public view in the new factory-slum environment, had begun to curry public sympathy.

Thus, one of the unexpected consequences of the industrial revolution was a sharp reorientation of political ideas. In the creation of an industrial working class and an industrial environment, the revolution bequeathed a new economic framework to politics. Karl Marx and Friedrich Engels were to write in 1848 that "all history" was the history of class struggle, but never did that struggle emerge so nakedly into the open as after the industrial environment had been brought into being.

Equally important was that the rise of political liberalism not only roused feelings of hostility toward the prevailing order, but initiated the slow process of amelioration. *From the outset, a reform movement coincided with capitalism.* In 1802, pauper apprentices were legally limited to a twelve-hour day and barred from night work. In 1819, the employment of children under nine was prohibited in cotton mills; in 1833, a 48- to 69-hour week was decreed for workers under eighteen (who comprised about 75 per cent of all cotton mill workers), and a system of government inspection of factories was inaugurated; in 1842, children under ten were barred from the coal mines; in 1847 a 10-hour daily limit (later raised to $10\frac{1}{2}$) was set for children and women.

The nature of the reforms is itself eloquent testimony to the conditions of the times, and the fact that the reforms were bitterly opposed and often observed in the breach is testimony to the prevailing spirit. Yet capitalism, unlike feudalism, was from the beginning subject to the corrective force of democracy. Karl Marx, drawing on the material of the 1830s, drew a mordant picture of the capitalist process in all its economic squalor, but he overlooked (or shrugged off) this countervailing force whose power was steadily to grow.

3. *The most important effect of the industrial revolution we have left for last: its long-term leverage on economic well-being.*

The ultimate impact of the industrial revolution was to usher in a rise of living standards on a mass scale unlike anything that the world had ever known before.

This did not happen overnight. In 1840, according to the calculations of Arnold Toynbee, Sr., the wage of an ordinary laborer came to eight shillings a week, which were six shillings less than he needed to buy the bare necessities of life.[18] He made up the deficit by sending his children or his wife, or both, to work in the mills. If, as we have noted, some sections of the working class gained from the early impact of industrialization, others suffered a *decline* from the standard of living enjoyed in 1795 or thereabouts. A Committee of Parliament in the 1830s, for example, discovered that a hand weaver at that earlier date could have bought more than three times as many provisions with his wages as at the later date. Although not every trade suffered equally, the first flush of the industrial revolution brought its hardships to bear full force, while its benefits were not as immediately noticeable.

By 1870, however, the long-run effects of the industrial revolution were beginning to make themselves felt. The price of necessaries had by then risen to fifteen shillings, but weekly earnings had crept up to meet and even exceed that sum. Hours were shorter, too. At the Jarrow Shipyards and the New Castle Chemical Works, the workweek had fallen from 61 to 54 hours; and even in the notoriously long-worked textile mills, the stint was down to "only" 57 hours. It was still a far cry from an abundant society, much less an "affluent" one, but the corner had been turned.

The Industrial Revolution in the Perspective of Theory

We have reviewed very briefly the salient historic features of the rise of industrial capitalism. Now we must reflect back on the great economic and social changes we have witnessed and ask a pertinent economic question: *How did the process of industrialization raise material well-being?* To answer the question, we must turn to economic theory to elucidate systematically what we have thus far only described.

Let us begin by asking what is necessary for a rise in the economic well-being of a society. The answer is not difficult. If we are to enjoy a greater material well-being, generally speaking, we must produce more. This

[18] *The Industrial Revolution* (Boston: Beacon Press, 1956), p. 113.

is particularly true when we begin at the stage of scarcely-better-than-subsistence which characterized so much of Europe before the industrial revolution. For such a society to raise the standard of living of its masses, the first necessity is unquestionably higher production. Despite all the inequities of distribution which attended the society of serf and lord, capitalist and child-employee, underlying the meanness of the times was one overriding reality: the sheer inadequacy of output. There was simply not enough to go around, and if somewhat less lopsided distributive arrangements might have lessened the moral indignity of the times, they would not have contributed much to a massive improvement in basic economic well-being. Even assuming that the wage of the city laborer and the income of the peasant could have been doubled had the rich been deprived of their share—and this is a wildly extravagant assumption—still, the characteristic of rural and urban life would have been its poverty.

We must add only one important qualification to this emphasis on increased output as the prerequisite of economic improvement. Over-all living standards will not improve if a country's population is growing even faster than its increased output. The production of goods and services must rise *faster* than population if individual well-being is to improve.

How does a society raise its *per capita* output?

We cannot fully analyze this problem here. But our study of the industrial revolution in England enables us to understand a great deal about the problem. For clearly, *the key to higher output lies in enhancing the human energies of the community with the leverage of industrial capital.* Our analytic understanding of the growth must begin by looking further into this extraordinary power which capital possesses.

CAPITAL AND
PRODUCTIVITY

We have already frequently used the word "capital," but we have not yet defined it. We can see that in a fundamental sense, capital consists of anything which can enhance man's power to perform economically useful work. An unshaped stone is capital to the cave man who can use it as a hunting implement. A hoe is capital to a peasant; a road system is capital to the inhabitants of a modern industrial society. Knowledge is capital, too—indeed, perhaps the most precious part of society's stock of capital.

When economists talk of capital, however, they usually confine their meaning to *capital goods*—the stock of tools, equipment, machines, and buildings which society produces in order to expedite the production process.* All these capital goods have one effect in common on the productive

* Is money capital? It certainly is to the individual who possesses it. But it is not capital for society as a whole. For money only represents *claims* to society's real wealth, which is its goods and services. If an individual's money disappears, he loses his claim on those goods and services, and we can indeed say that he has lost his "capital." But if *all* money disappeared, we could not say that society had lost its claim on its own wealth. It would only have to devise another system of tickets.

process: they all operate to make human labor more productive. They make it possible for a worker to produce more goods in an hour (or a week, or a year) than he could produce without the aid of that capital. Capital is therefore a method of raising per capita *productivity,* which is an individual's output in a given span of time. For example, in a forty-hour week a typical modern worker using power-driven mechanical equipment can physically outproduce three men working seventy hours a week with the simpler tools of a half-century ago. To put it differently, in one day a modern worker will turn out as much output as his counterpart of 1900 in a full week—not because the modern worker works harder, but because he has at his command thousands of dollars worth of capital equipment rather than the few hundred dollars worth available to a worker in 1900.

Why does capital make labor so much more productive?

The most important reason is that capital goods enable man to use principles and devices such as the lever and the wheel, heat and cold, combustion and expansion in ways that the unaided body cannot. *Capital gives men mechanical and physicochemical powers of literally transhuman dimensions.* They magnify enormously his muscular strength; they refine his powers of control; they endow him with endurance and resilience far beyond those of the flesh and bone. In using capital, man utilizes the natural world as a supplement to his own feeble capacities.

Another reason for the augmentation of production lies in the fact that capital facilitates the *specialization of man's labor.* A team of men working together, each man tending to one job alone in which he is expert, can usually far outproduce the same number of men, each of whom does a variety of jobs. The prime example is, of course, the auto production line in which a thousand men cooperate to produce an immensely larger output of cars than could be achieved if each man built a car by himself. Auto assembly lines, of course, use prodigious quantities of capital in the overhead conveyor belts, the inventories of parts on hand, the huge factory with its power system, and so on. And while not all specialization of labor depends on capital, capital is usually necessary for the large-scale industrial operations in which specialization becomes most effective.

In our next chapter we will return to these important matters in the context of the development of modern industry. But while we are still discussing the basic question of the rise of industry itself, there is a fundamental problem to be disposed of. This is the question of how capital is made in the first place, of how a society generates the capital equipment it needs in order to grow.

This brings us for the first time to a relationship that we will encounter many more times in our study of economics, both in a perspective of history and from a later vantage point of theory. The relationship is between the creation of those physical artifacts we call capital, and the inescapable prior act that we call *saving*.

When we think of saving, we ordinarily picture it in financial terms; that is, as a decision not to spend part of our income. Behind this financial act, however, lies a "real" act that we must now clearly understand. *When we save money we also abstain from using a certain quantity of goods and services we might have bought.* To be sure, our money savings represent a claim on goods and services, a claim that we may later exercise. Until we do, however, we have freed resources which would otherwise have been used to satisfy our immediate wants. From these freed resources, society builds its capital or, in more technical language, carries out the act of *investment*.

In the simplest example, we can see this real meaning of saving in the case of a primitive hunter who abstains from a full meal today, so that he will not have to hunt tomorrow. By saving half of today's kill, he frees the resource of (his own) labor: instead of hunting, tomorrow, he will make a better spear. In a much more indirect and complex fashion, when we save money we are also giving up a potential meal (or some other consumption good), so that society can then make capital out of the goods and services we would otherwise have consumed.

Thus the acts of saving and investment are inextricably linked: saving is the releasing of resources from consumption; investment is the employment of these resources in making capital. Indeed, from society's point of view, saving and investment are only two sides of the same coin. Why do we then separate them in economic discourse? The reason is that different people may perform the saving and investing functions, especially in modern societies. We are no longer hunters and spear makers. Those who release the resources of society are usually not the same individuals as those who gather up those resources for investment purposes. Nonetheless, we can see that every act of investment, no matter who performs it, requires the presence of released resources.*

This does not mean that investment necessarily entails a *diminution* of consumption. A rich society does not feel its normal, recurrent saving as a "pinch" on its spending. A society with unemployed factors can put its idle resources to work building capital without diminishing its expenditure on consumption. (It is still saving, of course, insofar as it is not using those newly employed resources to make consumption goods.) But—and this is a crucial point—when a *fully employed* society builds more capital, it *must* curtail its consumption. In this case, there is nowhere whence the needed

---

* Note, however, that an act of saving—i.e., an abstention from consumption—does not *automatically* bring about an act of purposive investment. This leads to serious problems to which we shall turn in Chapter 8.

capital-building resources can come but from their erstwhile consumption employments.

Let us go on still further. We can now see that the *rate* at which an economy can invest—that is, the size of the yearly addition it can make to its stock of capital goods—depends on its capacity to save. If its living standards are already close to the margin of existence, it will not be able to transfer much labor from consumption effort to capital-building effort. However badly it may wish for more tools, however productive those tools would prove to be, it cannot invest beyond the point at which its remaining consumption activity would no longer be adequate to maintain subsistence. At the other extreme, if a society is well-to-do, it may be able to abstain from a great deal of current consumption effort to provide for the future. Accordingly, its growth will be fast. *It is a hard economic reality that the amount of construction for the future can never exceed the amount of resources and effort which are unused, or which can be released from consumption in the present.*

This seems to imply that the process of economic growth must perforce be very slow in a poor economy. And so it is. In England, as we have already seen, nearly three-quarters of a century elapsed before the new process of industrialization brought about an increase in productivity sufficiently large to be felt as a general improvement in the lot of the workingman. In the underdeveloped nations, as we shall see in Chapter 11, the prospect is equally or even more sluggish. At its best, growth is a gradual and cumulative, rather than an "instant" phenomenon; and where the initial level of savings is low because of poverty, the rate of advance is correspondingly slower.

Perhaps we can better appreciate this over-all determinant of the pace of growth if we now examine the actual social circumstances under which saving arose in early nineteenth-century England.

For who did the saving? Who abstained from consumption? Well-to-do agriculturalists and manufacturers (for all their ostentatious ways) were certainly important savers who plowed substantial sums into more new capital investments. Yet the savers were not just the manufacturers or the gentry but also another class—the industrial workers. Here, in the low level of industrial wages, a great sacrifice was made—not voluntarily, by any matter of means, but made just the same. From the resources the workers could have consumed was built the industrial foundation for the future.

We can also see something which is perhaps even more significant. This is the fact that England *had* to hold down the level of its working class consumption in order to free productive effort for the accumulation of capital goods. In point of historic actuality, the "holding-down" was accomplished largely by the forces of the market place—with a liberal assist, to be sure, from the capitalists and from a government quick to oppose the demands of labor in the interests of its upper classes. But social inequities aside, the hard fact remains that had industrial wages risen very much, a vast demand for consumers' goods would have turned the direction of the English economy away from capital-building, toward the satisfaction of current wants. This would certainly have redounded to the immediate welfare of the English worker (although the increase in per capita consumption would have been small). At the same time, however, it would have *postponed* the day when society's overall productive powers were capable of generating an aggregate output of very large size.

This bitter choice must be confronted by every industrializing society, capitalist or socialist, democratic or totalitarian. To assuage the needs of today or to build for tomorrow is *the* decision which a developing society must make. As we shall see in Chapter 11, it is a decision which lies behind much of the political and economic agony of a large part of the world today.

INCENTIVES
FOR GROWTH

There remains but one last question. We have gained some insight into the mechanics of growth, but we have not yet answered the question: how are these mechanics brought about? How does society arrange the reallocation of its factors of production to bring about the creation of the capital it needs?

This query brings us again to a consideration of our original division of economic societies into three types: traditional, command, and market. It also leads to some very important conclusions.

The first of these is obvious: it is that tradition-bound societies are not apt to grow. In such societies there is *no* direct social means of inducing the needed reallocation of factors. Worse yet, there are often strong social and religious barriers which create obstacles to the needed shifts in employment.

The situation is very different, however, when we turn to command societies. We have seen a striking use of command as the industrializing-agency in modern times. In at least one country, the Soviet Union, command has been the principal mechanism for a dramatic transition from peasanthood into industrialization, and in many other collectivist economies, command is now trying to bring into effect such a transition.

In Chapter 10 we shall return to the Russian experience. Meanwhile, let us not forget that command was also one of the principal ways by which Europe began its industrialization. In the state-directed establishment of shipyards and armories, the construction of royal palaces and estates, tapestry works and chinaware factories, a very important organizing impetus was given to the creation of an industrial sector in the mercantilist era. True, of course, that in those days, command was never so ruthlessly applied nor so widely directed as with the Communist states. But however much milder the dosage, the medicine was in essence the same: the *initial* transfer of labor from the traditional pursuits of the land to the new tasks of the factory depended on a commanding authority which ordered the new pattern into being.*

But command was by no means the main agency for the final industrialization of the West. Rather, the organizing force which put men to work in making capital equipment was the market.

How did the market bring about this remarkable transformation? It achieved its purposes by the lure of monetary rewards. It was the hope of *profits* that lured manufacturers into turning out more capital goods. It was the attraction of better *wages* (or sometimes of *any* wages) that directed workers into the new plants. It was the signal of rising prices that encouraged, and falling prices that discouraged, the production of this or that particular capital good.

And what, we may next ask, opened the prospect of profits large enough to induce entrepreneurs to risk their savings in new capital goods? The answer brings us full circle to the focal point of this chapter. For the answer is to be found primarily in the body of technological advance constituting the core of the industrial revolution.

Not that every new invention brought with it a fortune for its pioneering promoters, or that every new product found a market waiting for it. The path of technical advance is littered with inventions born "too soon" and with enterprises founded with great hopes and closed down six months later. But looking back over the vast process of capital accumulation which, beginning in the late eighteenth century, lifted first England and then America into the long flight of industrial development, there is little doubt that the impelling force was the succession of inventions and innovations that successively opened new aspects of nature to human control. Steam power, the cheap and efficient spinning and weaving of cloth, the first mass production of iron, and later steel—these were the great breakthroughs of industrial science that opened the way for the massive accumulation of capital. And once the great inventions had marked out the channel of advance, secondary improvements and subsidiary inventions took on an important supporting role. To the enterpriser with a cost-cutting innovation went the prize of a market advantage in costs and a correspondingly higher profit. More than that, once one pioneer in a field had gained a technical

* As Barbara Ward has written in *India and the West:* "A developing society must at some point begin to save, even though it is still poor. This is the tough early stage of growth which Marx encountered in Victorian England and unfortunately took to be permanent. It is a difficult phase in any economy—so difficult that most societies got through it by *force majeure* ... No one asked the British laborers moving into the Manchester slums whether they wanted to save.... The Soviet workers who came to Sverdlovsk and Magnitogorsk from the primitive steppes had no say in the scale or the condition of their work. Nor have the Chinese in their communes today."

advantage, competition quickly forced everyone else in the field to catch up as quickly as they could. Most of the cost-cutting innovations involved adding machinery to the production process—and this in turn boosted the formation of capital.

Capitalism as a whole proved an unparalleled machine for the accumulation of capital. In its development we find the first economic system in history in which economic growth became an *integral* part of daily life. As Marx and Engels were to write in the *Communist Manifesto:* "The bourgeoisie, during its scarce one hundred years, has created more massive and more colossal productive forces than have all preceding generations together." And the compliment, all the more meaningful coming from the two archenemies of its social order, was true.

KEY CONCEPTS AND KEY WORDS

Industrial revolution

1. The industrial revolution *is a* great *turning period* in history, during which manufacturing and industrial activity become primary forms of social production.

2. The industrial revolution began in England in the mid- to late eighteenth century (although its roots are far deeper). There are numerous reasons why it occurred there and then:
   - England was *a wealthy trading nation* with a well-developed middle class.
   - England's *aristocracy was much more commerce-minded* than the aristocracies of the Continent.
   - England was the home of a widespread vogue of *scientific investigation* and of "gentlemen farmers" interested in *agricultural innovation.*
   - England's relatively *open social structure* permitted the rise of New Men, such as Watt or Wilkinson, who brought to manufacturing a burst of new social energies.
   - Many other causes could be cited as well. The industrial revolution was a *many-sided, complex chain* of events.

Output

3. The revolution brought with it changes of the greatest importance in society.
   - It ushered in a slow, but cumulative *rise in output* that was eventually to lift the industrial world out of an age-old poverty.
   - It brought the *factory* (and the *industrial slum*) as a new environment for work and life.
   - It gave rise to new kinds of *social abuses* and greatly sharpened the general *awareness of economic conditions.*

Capital-building

4. The industrial revolution was essentially a *capital-building process* (machines, buildings, canals, railways), as a result of which the productivity of labor was greatly increased.

Productivity

5. *Capital generally enhances productivity* because it gives man for greater physical and chemical capabilities than he enjoys with unaided labor alone. It also enables men to combine and *specialize* their labor, as in modern factory production lines.

Saving

6. *Capital-building requires saving.* Capital can be built only if society has the use of resources normally used for filling its consumption needs. Saving releases these resources; investing puts them to use.

7. Society cannot devote more resources or energies to capital-building than those it releases from other uses (or those it has available as unemployed resources). Hence, by and large, *saving regulates the pace at which investment can proceed.* Poor societies, in which it is difficult to give up consumption, accordingly have great problems in amassing enough resources for investment.

Investment

Consumption

8. The saving necessary for investment can come from agriculture, manufacturing enterprises, and many other sources. In poor nations, it must also often be wrung from workers or peasants by denying them the use of all the nation's economic potential to fill their consumption needs.

9. Hence *saving in poor nations is usually an involuntary process.* Capital-building in many developing nations today, particularly those under collectivist regimes, is accomplished by the agency of command. In the industrial revolution, it was accomplished in part by command, but mainly by the market system. The remarkable inventions of the industrial revolution served as sources of profits that resulted in great accumulations of capital.

Q U E S T I O N S

1. It is interesting to note that technical improvements in agriculture or manufacturing have generally been slow to arise in countries that have relied on slave labor. Can you think of a reason why this might be so?

2. What forces do you think would be necessary to bring a new "industrial revolution" to the underdeveloped world today? Is an industrial revolution there apt to resemble that in England in the eighteenth century?

3. Industrialization in England was marked by a sharp growth of bitter political feeling on the part of the new factory proletariat. Do you think this must be an accompaniment of industrialization everywhere, or was it a particular product of early capitalism?

4. How does capital help human productivity? Discuss this in relation to the following kinds of labor: farm labor, office help, teaching, government administration.

5. When General Motors devotes a billion dollars to new investment (building new factories, warehouses, offices, etc.), who does the saving that is required? Stockholders? Workers? The public? Buyers of cars?

6. It is estimated that the value of the capital structures and equipment in the U.S. is some $2 trillion. Assume that half of it were wiped out in some catastrophe. What would happen to U.S. productivity? To average U.S. well-being? How could the damage be repaired?

7. Does all investment require saving? Why?

8. Is capital-building in the U.S. today directed by the market alone? Does the government accumulate capital? Does public capital improve productivity as well as private capital?

9. Is building a school "investment"? Is building a hospital? A sports stadium? A housing project? A research lab? What do you think distinguishes investment, in general, from consumption?

With this chapter, we enter a new major period of economic history. Formerly we have dealt largely with the past, giving only an occasional glance to later echoes of the problems we have encountered. Commencing with this chapter, our focus turns toward and into the actual present. We have reached the stage of economic history whose nearest boundary is our own time. Simultaneously, our point of geographic focus shifts. As economic history enters the mid-nineteenth century, the dynamic center of events comes increasingly to be located in the United States. Not only do we now begin to enter the modern world, but the economic trends in which we will be interested take us directly into our own society.

What will be the theme of this chapter? Essentially it will be a continuation of a motif we began with the industrial revolution—the impact of technology on economic society. Looking back, we can see that the burst of inventions which marked "the" revolution was not in any sense the completion of an historic event. Rather, it was merely the inception of a process of technological change which would continually accelerate down to the present time.

We can distinguish three or even four stages of this continuous process. The "first" industrial revolution was largely concentrated in new textile machinery, improved methods of coal production and iron manufacture, revolutionary agricultural techniques, and steam power. It was succeeded in the middle years of the nineteenth century by a "second" industrial revolution: a clustering of industrial inventions centering on steel, railroad and steamship transportation, agricultural machinery, and chemicals. By the early years of the twentieth century there was a third wave of inventions: electrical power, automobiles, the gasoline engine. In our own time there is a fourth: the revolution of electronics, air travel, automation, and, of course, nuclear energy.

It is difficult, perhaps impossible, to exaggerate the impact of this continuing industrial revolution. Now advancing rapidly, now slowly; now on a broad front, now on a narrow salient; now in the most practical of inventions, again in the purest of theoretical discoveries, the cumulative application of science and technology to the productive process was *the* great change of the nineteenth and twentieth centuries. The initial industrial revolution was thus in retrospect a kind of discontinuous leap in human history; a leap as important as that which had lifted the first pastoral settlements above the earlier hunting communities. We have already noted that in the factory the new technology brought a new working place for man, but its impact was vastly greater than that alone. The enormously heightened powers of transportation and communication, the far more effective means of wresting a crop from the soil, the hugely enhanced ability to apply power for lifting, hauling, shaping, binding, cutting—all this conspired to bring about a literal remaking of the human environment, and by no means an entirely benign one.

In this book we cannot do more than inquire into some of the economic consequences of the incursion of industrial technology into modern society, but it may help us gain some insight into the dimensions of that penetrative process if we follow for a short distance the repercussions of a single invention.

IMPACT
OF ONE
INVENTION

Let us therefore look in on the Paris Exposition of 1867, where curious visitors are gathered around an interesting exhibit: a small engine in which illuminating gas and air are introduced into a combustion chamber and ignited by a spark. The resulting explosion pushes a piston; the piston turns a wheel. There is but one working stroke in every four, and the machine requires a large flywheel to regularize its movement, but as the historian Allan Nevins writes, the effect of the machine "was comparable to the sudden snapping on of an electric globe in a room men had been trying to light with smoky candles."[1] It was the world's first internal combustion engine.

It was not long before the engine, invented by Dr. N. A. Otto of Germany, was a regular feature of the American landscape. Adapted to run on gasoline, a hitherto uninteresting by-product of kerosene manufacture, it was an ideal stationary power plant. Writes Nevins, "Soon every progressive farm, shop, and feed-mill had its one-cylinder engine chugging away, pumping water, sawing wood, grinding meal, and doing other small jobs."[2] By 1900 there were more than 18,500 internal combustion engines in the United

---

[1] *Ford, the Times, the Man, the Company* (New York: Scribner's, 1954), I, 96.
[2] *Study in Power, John D. Rockefeller* (New York: Scribner's, 1953), II, 109.

States; and whereas the most powerful model in the Chicago World's Fair in 1893 was 35 horsepower, at the Paris Exposition seven years later it was 1,000 horsepower.

The internal combustion engine was an extraordinary means of increasing, diffusing, and giving mobility to a basic requirement of material progress: power. And soon the new engine opened the way for a yet more startling advance. In 1886, Charles E. Duryea of Chicopee, Massachusetts had already decided that the gasoline engine was a far more promising power source than steam for a self-propelling road vehicle. By 1892 he and his brother had produced the first gas-powered "automobile," a weak and fragile toy. The next model in 1893 was a better one, and by 1896 the Duryea brothers actually sold thirteen cars. In that same year, a thirty-two-year-old mechanic called Henry Ford sold his first "quadricycle." The history of the automobile industry had begun.

Its growth was phenomenal. By 1905 there were 121 establishments making automobiles, and 10,000 wage earners were employed in the industry. By 1923 the number of plants had risen to 2,471, making the industry the largest in the country. In 1960 its annual payroll was as large as the national income of the United States in 1890. Not only that, but the automobile industry had become the single greatest customer for sheet steel, zinc, lead, rubber, leather. It was the buyer of one out of every three radios produced in the nation. It absorbed twenty-five billion pounds of chemicals a year. It was the second largest user of engineering talent in the country, bowing only to national defense. It was the source of one-sixth of all the patents issued in the nation and the object of one-tenth of all consumer spending in the country. In fact, it has been estimated that no less than one job out of every seven and one business out of every six owed their existences directly or indirectly to the car.

Even this impressive array of figures by no means exhausts the impact of the internal combustion engine and its vehicular mounting. Roughly eight out of every ten families today own a car; nearly six out of ten own two or more cars. As a result, some fifty thousand towns managed to flourish without rail or water connections, an erstwhile impossibility; and seven out of ten workers no longer live within walking distance of their places of employment but drive to work. To an extraordinary extent, in other words, our entire economy has become "mobilized"—which is to say, dependent for its very functioning on the existence of wheeled, self-propelled transportation. If by some strange occurrence our automotive fleet were put out of commission—say by a spontaneous change in the nature of the gasoline molecule, rendering it incombustible—the effect would be as grave and as socially disastrous as a catastrophic famine in the Middle Ages.*

* I believe it was the economist Kenneth Boulding who suggested that if the United States were to be visited by intelligent beings from another part of the universe, their initial impression would likely be that the dominant form of life here consists of hard-shelled creatures with soft pulpy insides, who are propelled by wheels, although the creatures are capable of sluggish motion on their own when not encased in their natural exoskeletons.

We dwell on the impact of the car, not because it is the most significant of technological changes. Before the car, there was the startling economic transformation caused by the train, and after it came the no less totally transforming effects of electrical communication. Rather, we touch on the profound economic implications of the automobile to illustrate the diffuse effects of all industrial technology—effects which economics often cannot measure and which exceed its normal area of study but which must, nonetheless, be borne in mind as the ever-present and primary reality of the technological revolution itself. Let us mention a few of these general effects on the society in which we live.

The first has been a *vast increase in the degree of urbanization of society*. To an extraordinary extent (as we shall see in our next chapters) technology has enhanced the ability of the farmer to support the nonfarmer. As a result, society has more and more taken on the aspects and problems of the city rather than the country. In 1790 only 24 towns and cities in all of the United States had a population of more than 2,500, and together they accounted for only 6 percent of the total population. By 1860 the 392 biggest cities held 20 percent of the population; by the late 1960s almost two-thirds of the nation's people lived in 212 great "standard metropolitan areas," and the belt from Boston to Washington was in fact, if not in government, one vast sprawling "city." Industrial technology has literally refashioned the human environment, bringing with it all the gains—and all the terrible problems—of city life on a mass scale.

Second, *the steady growth of industrial technology has radically lessened the degree of economic independence of the average citizen*. In our opening chapter we noted the extreme vulnerability of the "unsupported" inhabitant of a modern society, dependent on the work of a thousand others to sustain his own existence. This, too, we can now trace to the effect of the continuing industrial revolution. Technology has not only moved men off the soil and into the city, but has vastly increased the specialized nature of work. Unlike the "man of all trades" of the early nineteenth century—the farmer who could perform so many of his necessary tasks himself—the typical factory worker or office worker is trained and employed to do only one small part of a social operation which now achieves staggering complexity. Technology has vastly increased the degree of economic interdependence of the modern community and has made the solution of the economic problem hinge on the smooth coordination of an ever-widening network of delicately connected activities.

Third, *the expansion of industrial technology has radically altered the character of work*. For the greater part of man's history, work has been a strenuous physical activity, largely carried on alone or in small groups in the open air, requiring considerable dexterity to match human strength to the infinite variations of the natural environment, and culminating in an end product as unambiguously identifiable as the grain in the field or the cloth on a loom.

The industrial revolution profoundly altered these attributes of work.

Work now consisted more and more of repetitive movements which, however exhausting after a full day, rarely involved more than a fraction of a man's full muscular ability. In place of the judgments and aptitudes required to meet the variations of nature, it demanded only the ability to repeat a single task adapted to a changeless work surface. No longer alone in nature, the worker performed his job in vast sheds with regiments like himself. And most wrenching of all, in place of "his" product, what he saw emerging from the factory was an object in which he could no longer locate, much less appreciate, his own contribution.

A worker in an automobile plant reports:

I work on a small conveyor which goes around in a circle. We call it a "merry-go-round." I make up zigzag springs for front seats. Every couple of feet on the conveyor there is a form for the pieces that make up the seat springs. As the form goes by me, I clip several pieces together, using a clip gun. I then put the pieces on the form, and it goes around to where other men clip more pieces together.... The only operation I do is work the clip gun. It takes just a couple of seconds to shoot six or eight clips into the spring and I do it as I walk a few steps. Then I start right over again....[3]

What has been the effect on workers of this basic alteration in the pace and pattern of labor? Looking around us at factories (and offices), we find that industrial technology often subjects men to a stultifying and enervating discipline—that it makes work a singularly joyless and meaningless process to which they must subordinate their individual personalities. This is an aspect of technology that has disturbed observers since Adam Smith commented, two hundred years ago, that a man who endlessly performed the same task "generally becomes as stupid and ignorant as it is possible for a human creature to become."[4] Later, Karl Marx wrote with passion and perception about the terrible effects of industrial capitalism in divorcing the worker from the fruits of his own toil; and since Marx, writers in socialist as well as in capitalist nations have articulated the feelings of impotence and estrangement experienced in a vast, mechanized environment.

Is industrial technology in fact the cause of a pervasive "alienation" of man? We do not really know. Man today is certainly as much the servant as the master of his industrial apparatus. Yet we must guard against too easy an indictment of technology as the great dehumanizer. Let us not forget the terrible toll on the human personality of preindustrial labor, with its exhausted peasants and its brutalized common laborers. Further, let us bear in mind that if the repressive and disciplinary aspects of technology predominate in our time, it may be because we are still only in the inception of the industrial history of humankind. In a longer perspective, this same technology holds forth at least the promise of an eventual emancipation of man, as machinery gradually takes over his onerous, monotonous tasks.

[3] Charles R. Walker and Robert H. Guest, *The Man on the Assembly Line* (Cambridge: Harvard University Press, 1952), p. 46.
[4] *The Wealth of Nations* (New York: Modern Library, 1937), p. 734.

We will return again to some of these problems of technology. But meanwhile we must pay heed to another important aspect of the technological invasion. This is the striking alteration it has brought about in the tasks of social provisioning. It is obvious that the inventory of work-skills that we possessed in 1800 would never suffice to operate the social machine of the 1960s. But even in the much shorter span since 1900, the required distribution of skills has significantly changed, as Table 6-1 shows.

Note how different is our profile of occupations today from the not too distant past. We have already commented on the sharp drop in the number of people needed to feed the nation, but we can also see a shift within the "blue collar" group from unskilled to skilled and semiskilled jobs, as more people labor with capital equipment than with their hands. In addition, as the sharp increase in the number of managers and clerical workers indicates, a swifter and more complex production process requires ever more people to coordinate and oversee the actual making of goods. In 1899 there was one nonproduction worker for every thirteen production workers in manufacturing; in 1964, one for three.

Before we leave this discussion of the general impact of technology on economic society, we must briefly look into one last attribute of industrialism—the rise of labor unions within the market system during the late nineteenth and early twentieth centuries.

TABLE 6 • 1

OCCUPATIONAL
DISTRIBUTION
OF THE
LABOR FORCE
1900–1968

	Percent of labor force	
	1900	1968
Managerial and professional		
Professional and technical workers	4.1	14.4
Managers, officials, and proprietors (nonfarm)	5.9	10.5
White-collar		
Clerical workers	3.1	17.9
Sales workers	4.8	6.0
Blue-collar		
Skilled workers and foremen	10.3	12.7
Semiskilled workers	12.8	17.6
Unskilled workers	12.4	4.6
Household and other service workers	8.9	12.4
Farm		
Farmers and farm managers	20.0	2.2
Farm laborers	17.6	1.9

Source: 1900 figures calculated from *Historical Statistics of the United States*, Series D 72–122, p. 74; 1968 figures from *Statistical Abstract*, 1970, p. 225. Totals do not add to 100 percent, owing to rounding. Farmers and farm laborers partly estimated (*Statistical Abstract*, p. 228).

Actually we can trace the origins of trade unionism back to early Roman times, when some workmen joined into semifraternal orders. But unionism as an important social institution obviously had to await the creation of a free labor force, and that, as we know, did not occur un relatively recent times. Even after labor had been pried loose from its feuda status and thrown upon the market for survival, unionism still awaited as a final stimulus the advent of an industrial technology that brought masses of men together in the insecure and impersonal environment of the factory.

Thus, all through the nineteenth century, as industrial technology entered nation after nation, we also find a strong impetus toward union organization. In nearly every nation, it should also be noted, these movements were met at first with determined and often ferocious resistance: under the so-called Conspiracy Doctrine and the Combination Laws (1800) of Great Britain, for example, thousands of workmen were punished for combining to raise wages—although in no case were employers punished for combining to lower them. Indeed, for a quarter of a century, British unionists were treated as rebels or common criminals, as they also were, for that matter, in France or Germany.

In America, trade union progress was also slow. The strong American belief in "rugged individualism"—a belief shared by many workers as well as by their bosses—a reliance on docile immigrant labor in the heavy industries, and the use of every legal and many illegal weapons on the part of employers kept American unionism largely limited to the skilled crafts long after the union movement had finally gained acceptance and some measure of power in Europe.

During the 1920s, for example, union membership *dropped* some 30 percent, partly as a result of an all-out attack by the National Association of Manufacturers; partly as a consequence of labor's own indifference to unionism. By 1929 less than one nonagricultural worker in five belonged to a union, and not a single industrial union of consequence had yet organized a mass production industry.*

Industrial unionism came to America in a few dramatic years in the mid-1930s. The New Deal, the newly-formed Committee for Industrial Organization—later Congress of Industrial Organizations (CIO)—and long pent-up pressures on labor frustration combined to break corporate resistance. In a "sit-down strike," forerunner of the "sit-in," the CIO occupied buildings and won formal recognition with a union contract from General Motors. Shortly after, U.S. Steel voluntarily recognized the Steelworkers. Other companies held out longer; but in 1941 the National War Labor Board ordered recognition from Bethlehem Steel and Ford, and the long battle for industrial unionism was over.

* Craft unions seek to organize the workers of a particular skill (regardless of where they work) into one union; examples are the Newspaper Guild and the carpenters' or the plumbers' unions. Industrial unions, on the other hand, join all the members of a given industry (regardless of their craft or level of skill); examples are the Steelworkers and the United Auto Workers.

It is difficult today to reconstruct that era, not so very long past, when Walter Reuther, the great organizer of the United Auto Workers, was thrown down a flight of concrete stairs and kicked by the hired strongmen of the Ford Motor Company, when coal miners carried rifles to fight the local police, or when strikers actually seized and occupied General Motors and Chrysler plants. The tumultuous history of this turning point in labor history has today given way to a much calmer era, in which tensions and conflicts continue to mark the relations of business and labor (as they always will in a market society), but the attitudes and actions of the antilabor past already seem to be ancient history.

We cannot trace here the full story of American unionism (including the very important and checkered history of its efforts at self-government), but one point seems worth making before we return to our main narrative. It is that a high point in union membership seems to have been reached in the late 1950s when just over 18 million workers, or about 32 percent of all nonagricultural employment, belonged to affiliates of the AFL-CIO or to independent unions. Since then there has been a stagnation in union growth, all the more noticeable against a rising total labor force. Today only about 23 percent of the total labor force is unionized, and less than 28 percent of all workers in nonagricultural establishments belong to unions.

Why has the union movement ceased to grow? The single, most cogent reason seems to lie in the very shift in the job spectrum we have already examined. Blue-collar jobs, where trade unionism has traditionally been strongest, are now a static or perhaps slowly declining fraction of the work force. Conversely, the fastest growing area of employment is in the service and white-collar sectors, where the antipathy to unionism has traditionally been greatest.

Out of this shift in occupations may come a new era in labor relations—and in labor problems. It is unlikely, as we have seen, that industrial unionism will experience much further dynamic growth. But this does not mean that the power of organized labor is therefore on the wane. For the stability or shrinkage in industrial unionism has been compensated in recent years by a sudden rise of union activity in the service and white-collar areas, particularly in the public sector. Strikes of sanitation workers and teachers can be very disruptive and, more important, may be difficult to settle without large wage increases. Unlike the case of a union dealing with a corporation, a union dealing with a municipality or a state does not have to temper its demands to the ability of its adversary to pay wages out of its *sales*. Instead, wage increases are ultimately limited only by the amount of additional *tax revenues* that the union can force the public authority to allocate to its members. Thus, restraints on public wages are very hard to impose.

There is a second and even more cogent reason for labor's gain in the balance of power between employer and worker. Traditionally, the employer has held the whip hand over the union, because in all labor disputes, sooner or later, the pressure of sheer need would compel the union to agree to the employer's offer. But this inherent inequality is changing as technology increases the general affluence of the economy. When workers' bank balances and union treasuries are full, and when it is easy for strikers to find temporary employment, the traditional pressures on the union to "settle" lose much of their effect.

All this implies that considerable labor problems may lie ahead, for which there are no simple solutions. What is necessary is to recognize that these problems, which we tend to blame on this union leader or on that company or public official, have their roots in a much deeper change of situation—indeed, that they ultimately spring, as we have said, from the power of technology to increase productivity and to alter the occupational mix. Another way of putting it is that technology has rearranged the priorities of society, lessening the pressing nature of the production problem and exacerbating that of the distribution problem; and while such reflections do not solve our problems, they help us to understand them better.

ECONOMIES OF LARGE-SCALE PRODUCTION

Thus far we have examined some of the diffuse effects of industrial technology on the life-ways of society. Now we must turn back to a more technical aspect of the industrial process—but one that in many ways underlies the larger and more general effects we have been studying. This is the development of a new method of industrial production first visible after the 1860s, although not fully realized until the turn of the twentieth century. This is the method of *mass production*.

Allan Nevins has described what mass production techniques looked like in the early Ford assembly lines.

Just how were the main assembly lines and lines of component production and supply kept in harmony? For the chassis alone, from 1,000 to 4,000 pieces of each component had to be furnished each day at just the right point and right minute; a single failure, and the whole mechanism would come to a jarring standstill . . . . Superintendents had to know every hour just how many components were being produced and how many were in stock. Whenever danger of shortage appeared, the shortage chaser—a familiar figure in all automobile factories—flung himself into the breach. Counters and checkers reported to him. Verifying in person any ominous news, he mobilized the foreman concerned to repair deficiencies. Three times a day he made typed reports in manifold to the factory clearing-house, at the same time chalking on blackboards in the clearing-house office a statement of results in each factory-production department and each assembling department.[5]

Such systematizing in itself resulted in astonishing increases in productivity. With each operation analyzed and subdivided into its simplest components, with a steady stream of work passing before stationary men, with a relentless but manageable pace of work, the total time required to assemble

[5] *Ford, the Times, the Man, the Company*, I, 507.

a car dropped astonishingly. Within a single year, the time required to assemble a motor fell from 600 minutes to 226 minutes; to build a chassis, from 12 hours and 28 minutes to 1 hour and 33 minutes. A stopwatch man was told to observe a 3-minute assembly in which men assembled rods and piston, a simple operation. The job was divided into three jobs, and half the men turned out the same output as before.[6]

But what interests us in the context of our study are not the technical achievements of mass production as much as its economic results. For increases in productivity bring reductions in cost. Even though the machinery needed for mass production is extremely expensive, output increases so fast that costs *per unit* of output drop dramatically.

Imagine, for instance, a small plant turning out 1,000 items a day with the labor of ten men and a small amount of equipment. Suppose each man is paid $10, each item before manufacture costs 10¢, and the daily amount of "overhead"—that is, the daily share of costs such as rent, plant maintenance, office salaries, and wear-and-tear on equipment—comes to $100. Then our total daily cost of production is $300 per day ($100 of payroll, $100 of raw material costs, and $100 of overhead). Divided among 1,000 items of output, our cost per item is 30¢.

Now imagine that our product lends itself to mass production techniques. Our payroll may then jump to $1,000 and with our much larger plant and equipment, our daily overhead to $5,000. Nevertheless, mass production may have boosted output as much as 100 times. Then our total daily cost of production will be $16,000 ($1,000 of payroll, $5,000 of overhead, and $10,000 of raw material costs). Divided among our 100,000 items of output, our cost per item has fallen to 16¢. Despite a quintupling of over-all expense, our cost per unit has almost halved.

This is not a far-fetched example of what economists call *the economies of large-scale production*. A glance at Table 6-2 shows how mass production

TABLE 6·2

Year	Unit sales, Ford cars	Price of typical model (touring)	
1907–1908	6,398	$2,800 (Model K)	
1908–1909	10,607	850	
1909–1910	18,664	950	
1910–1911	34,528	780	
1911–1912	78,440	690	
1912–1913	168,304	600	Model T
1913–1914	248,307	550	
1914–1915	221,805 (10 mos.)	490	
1915–1916	472,350	440	
1916–1917	730,041	360	

Compiled from Nevins, *Ford, the Times, the Man, the Company*, pp. 644, 646–47.

[6] *Ibid*, pp. 504, 506.

techniques did, in fact, boost output of Ford cars by more than one hundred times while reducing their cost by seven-eighths.

Nor do the dynamics of the industrial process come to a halt with these formidable economies of large-scale production. For this technological achievement brings into the market system itself a new element of primary importance. That element is *size*.

It is not difficult to see why. Once a firm—by virtue of adroit management, improved product, advantages of location, or whatever other reason—steps out decisively in front of its competitors in size, *economies of large-scale production operate to push it out still further in front*. Bigger size usually means lower cost, at least for a young expanding industry. Lower cost means bigger profits. Bigger profits mean the ability to grow to still larger size. Thus the techniques of large-scale manufacture bring about a situation threatening to alter the whole meaning of competition. From a mechanism that prevents any single firm from dominating the market, competition now becomes a force that may drive an ever-larger share of the market into the hands of the largest and most efficient producer.

THE GREAT ENTREPRENEURS

We shall have much more to say about the economics of the drive to bigness when we study the market system in Chapter 7. Yet, it may be helpful if we look once again at the actual historic scene in which this internal growth took place. For the processes of economic change described in this chapter did not occur in a vacuum. They were brought about by a social "type" and a business milieu which powerfully accelerated and abetted the process of industrial enlargement, much as the New Men had speeded along the initial industrializing process in England in the late eighteenth century.

The agents of change during the late nineteenth century in America were very much the descendants of their industrial forebears a century earlier. Like Arkwright and Watt, many of the greatest American entrepreneurs were men of humble origin endowed with an indomitable drive for business success. There was Carnegie in steel, Harriman in railroads, Rockefeller in oil, Frick in coke, Armour and Swift in meat packing, McCormick in agricultural machinery—to mention but a few. To be sure, the *typical* businessman was very different from these Horatio Alger stereotypes of the business hero. Economic historians, such as F. W. Taussig, looking back over the careers of the business leaders of the late nineteenth century, have discovered that the average entrepreneur was not a poor, industrious immigrant lad, but the son of well-circumstanced people often in business affairs themselves. Nor was the average businessman nearly so successful as a Carnegie or a Rockefeller.

Yet in nearly every line of business, at least *one* "captain of industry" appeared who dominated the field by his personality and ability. Though few achieved their supreme degree of pecuniary success, the number who climbed into the "millionaire class" was impressive. In 1880 it had been estimated that there were 100 millionaires in the country. By 1916 the number had grown to 40,000.

Interesting and significant differences distinguish these nineteenth century business leaders from those of a century earlier. The American captains of industry were not typically men whose leadership rested on inventive or engineering skills. With the growth of large-scale production, the engineering functions became the province of salaried production experts, of second-echelon plant managers. What was required now was the master touch in guiding industrial strategy, in making or breaking alliances, choosing salients for advance, or overseeing the logistics of the whole operation. More and more the great entrepreneurs were concerned with the strategy of finance, of competition, of sales, rather than with the cold technics of production itself.

Then, too, we must make note of the entrepreneurial tactics and tone of the period. In a phrase that has stuck, Matthew Josephson once called the great men of business in this era "the robber barons." In many ways, they did indeed resemble the predatory lords of the medieval era. For example, in the 1860s a small group of California entrepreneurs under the guiding hand of Collis Huntington performed the astonishing feat of building a railroad across the hitherto impassable Rockies and Sierras. Aware that Huntington and his associates would thereby have a monopolistic control of all rail traffic to California, the Congress authorized the construction of three competing lines. But the legislators had not taken the measure of the wily pioneers. Before their own line was completed, they secretly bought the charter of one competitive line; and when the second proved somewhat harder to buy out, they simply built it out, recklessly flinging their lines into its territory until it, too, was forced to surrender. Thereafter it was no great trick to buy out the third, having first blocked it at a critical mountain pass. Only one competitive source of transportation remained: the Pacific Mail Steamship Company. Fortunately, this was owned by the obliging Jay Gould, a famous robber baron in his own right; and for the payment of a proper tribute, he agreed to eliminate San Francisco as a cargo port. There was now *no* way of bringing goods across the nation into southern California except those which the Huntington group controlled. Counting the smaller lines and subsidiaries which passed into their grasp, *nineteen* rail systems, in all, came under their domain. It was not surprising that to the residents of California the resulting unified system was known as "the Octopus" and that its average freight rate was the highest in the nation.

And it was not just the railroad industry that used economic power to create a monopoly position. In whisky and in sugar, in tobacco and cattle-feed, in wire nails, steel hoops, electrical appliances, tin plate, in matches and meat there was an octopus similar to that which fastened itself on

California. One commentator of the late 1890s pictured the American citizen born to the profit of the Milk Trust and dying to that of the Coffin Trust.

If the robber barons milked the public as consumers (and to an even greater extent bilked them as stockholders), they also had no compunctions about cutting each other down to size. In the struggle for financial control of the Albany and Susquehanna Railroad, for instance, James Fisk and J. P. Morgan found themselves in the uncomfortable position of each owning a terminal at the end of a single line. Like their feudal prototypes, they resolved the controversy by combat, mounting locomotives at each end and running them full tilt into each other—after which the losers still did not give up, but retired, ripping up the line and tearing down trestles as they went. In similar spirit, the Huntington group that built the Central Pacific hired General David Colton to run a subsidiary enterprise for them, and the General wrote to his employers:

I have learned one thing. We have got *no true* friends outside of us five. We cannot depend upon a human soul outside of ourselves, and hence we must all be good-natured, stick together, and keep to our own counsels.

whereupon he proceeded to swindle his friends out of several millions.

With this buccaneering went as well another identifying mark of the times: what the economist Thorstein Veblen was to call Conspicuous Consumption. One repentant member of the gilded age recalled in his memoirs parties at which cigarettes were wrapped in money for the sheer pleasure of inhaling wealth; a dog that was presented with a $15,000 diamond collar; an infant, resting in a $10,000 cradle, attended by four doctors who posted regular bulletins on the baby's (excellent) health; the parade of fabulous chateaux stuffed with fabulous and not-so-fabulous works of art on New York's Fifth Avenue; and the collection of impecunious European royalty as sons-in-law of the rich.

The age was a rollicking, sometimes cruel, but always dynamic one. Yet what interests us here is not to recount its colorful social history as much as to understand its deeper economic consequences. It is impossible to consider the period with which we have been concerned without taking into account the social type of the robber baron and the milieu in which he operated. Bold, aggressive, acquisitive, competitive, the great entrepreneur was the natural agent to speed along the process for which the technology of the day prepared the way. But as yet we have only begun to sketch out the changes wrought by the joint impact of strong men and ever-more complex machinery. Now we must look more carefully into the effect that this combination produced.

1. The industrial revolution brought not one but *successive waves of technical progress* and economic advance.

Technical progress

2. In studying the impact of these industrial discoveries, we must broaden our lens to look beyond the effect on productivity alone (although that was no doubt the single most important result). Industrialization brought:
   - A vast increase in *urbanization.*

   Urbanization

   - A cumulative rise in the degree of *economic interdependence* of individuals within society.
   - A new climate for and character of work, including *the disturbing problems of monotonous industrial work* (alienation).

   Alienation

   - A *sweeping redistribution of occupations* away from unskilled toward semiskilled, technical, and managerial labor.
   - The rise of *unionism.*

   Unions

3. The new technology brought as well a change in the character of both production and competition. Production became more and more a process of highly intergrated subassemblies, making possible the *mass production* of goods. The large amounts of capital required for mass production led to very great *economies of scale.*

Mass production
Economies of scale

4. With the advent of mass production, *the nature of competition also changed into a destructive force.* Economies of scale led to situations in which a leading firm could undersell all competitors and thus dominate a market.

Destructive competition

5. The dynamic potential of the new technology was given further impetus by the *aggressive "Robber baron" era* of business leadership.

"Robber baron"

Q   U   E   S   T   I   O   N   S

1. Describe the social, as well as economic, repercussions of the following inventions: the typewriter, the jet airplane, television, penicillin. Which do you think is greater in each case—the social or economic impact?

2. The philosopher Karl Jaspers has claimed that modern technology brings an "immense joylessness." Do you agree? Is factory work unpleasant, to your mind? Office work, in a very large organization such as an insurance company? Do you think the nature of industrial work can be basically changed?

3. White-collar jobs have always proved harder to unionize than so-called blue-collar (factory floor) jobs. Why do you think this is so? Do you think it might change?

4. Suppose that you have a business in which you hire five men, to whom you pay $2 an hour; suppose further that you have overhead costs of $100 a day and that you pay $1 in materials cost for each item that your business manufactures. Assuming that you keep all five men, what is your average cost per unit of output if your plant turns out 10 items per 8-hour day? 100 items? 1,000?

5. Which is more economical, a plant with a payroll of $400 a week, with $100 of overhead a week, and with an output of 100 units per week, or a plant with a payroll of $80,000 a week, an overhead of $100,000 a week, and with an output of 50,000 units per week?

6. How do you explain economies of large-scale production? Why do certain businesses, such as cigarette manufacture, seem to enjoy them, whereas other businesses, such as barbering, do not?

So far we have investigated the impact of the new technology of mass production mainly insofar as it exerted its pervasive influence on "social" life, and we have only glanced at its effects on the workings of the economic system proper. Now we must look more carefully into this latter problem. For under the joint impetus of the drive of bold entrepreneurs and the self-feeding tendencies of economies of large-scale production dramatic changes began to appear in many sectors of the economy by the end of the nineteenth century. A system originally characterized by large numbers of small enterprises was starting to give way to one in which production was increasingly concentrated in the hands of a relatively few, very big and very powerful business units.

By 1900, for example, the number of textile mills, although still large, had dropped by a third from the 1880s; over the same period, the number of manufacturers of agricultural implements had fallen by 60 percent, and the number of leather manufacturers by three-quarters. In the locomotive industry, two companies ruled the roost in 1900, contrasted with nineteen in 1860. The biscuit and cracker industry changed from a scatter of small companies to a market in which one producer had 90 percent of the industry's capacity by the turn of the century. Meanwhile in steel there was the colossal U.S. Steel Corporation, which alone turned out over half the steel production of the nation. In oil, the Standard Oil Company tied up between 80 to 90 percent of the nation's output. In tobacco, the American Tobacco Company controlled 75 percent of the output of cigarettes and 25 percent of cigars. Similar control rested with the American Sugar Company, the American Smelting and Refining Company, the United Shoe Machinery Company, and dozens more.

From an overall view, the change was even more impressive. In the early 1800s, according to the calculations of Myron W. Watkins, no single plant controlled as much as 10 percent of the output of a manufacturing industry. By 1904, 78 enterprises controlled over half the output of their industries, 57 controlled 60 percent or more, and 28 controlled 80 percent or more. From industry to industry, this degree of "concentration" varied—from no significant concentration at all in printing and publishing, for instance, to the highly concentrated market structure of industries like copper or rubber. But there was no mistaking the overall change. In 1896, railroads excepted, there were not a dozen $10 million companies in the nation. By 1904, there were over 300 of them with a combined capitalization of over $7 billion. Together, these giants controlled more than two-fifths of the industrial capital of the nation and affected four-fifths of its important industries.[1]

Clearly something akin to a major revolution in market structure had taken place. Let us examine more closely the course of events which led up to it.

The initial impact of the trend to big business was an unexpected one. Rather than diminishing the degree of competitiveness of the market structure, it extended and intensified it. In the largely agricultural, handicraft, and small factory economy of the early nineteenth century, "the" market consisted mainly of small, localized markets, each insulated from the next by the high cost of transportation and each supplied by local producers who had neither the means nor the motivation to invade the market on anything resembling a national scale.

CHANGE IN COMPETITION

The rise of mass production radically changed this fragmented market structure and, with it, the type of competition within the market. As canals and railroads opened the country and as new manufacturing techniques vastly increased output, the parochial quality of the market system changed. More and more, one unified and interconnected market bound together the entire nation, and the petty semimonopolies of local suppliers were invaded by products from large factories in distant cities.

Quickly, a second development followed. As the new production techniques gained momentum, aggressive businessmen typically not only built, but overbuilt. "As confident entrepreneurs raced to take advantage of every ephemeral rise in prices, of every advance in tariff schedules, of every new market opened by the railroads and puffed up immigration," write Thomas Cochran and William Miller in a history of these industrializing times, "they

---

[1] John Moody, *The Truth about Trusts* (Chicago: Moody, 1904). See also Ralph Nelson, *Merger Movements in American Industry, 1895-1956* (Princeton, N.J.: National Bureau of Economic Research, 1959).

recklessly expanded and mechanized their plants, each seeking the greatest share of the new melon."[2]

The result was a phenomenal burst in output but, simultaneously, a serious change in the nature of competition. Competition now became not only more extensive, but more *expensive*. As the size of the plant and the complexity of equipment grew, so did the "fixed charges" of a business enterprise—the interest on borrowed capital, the depreciation of capital assets, the cost of administrative staff, the rent of land, and "overhead," generally. These costs tended to remain fairly constant, regardless of whether sales were good or bad. Unlike the payment of wages to a working force, which dropped when men were fired, there was no easy way to cut down the steady drain of payments for these fixed expenditures. The result was that the bigger the business, the more vulnerable was its economic health when competition cut into its sales.

The ebullience of the age, plus the steady growth of a technology that required massive investments, made competition increasingly drastic. As growing giant businesses locked horns, railroad against railroad, steel mill against steel mill, each sought to assure the coverage of its fixed expenses by gaining for itself as much of the market as it could. The outcome was the emergence of "cutthroat competition" among massive producers, replacing the more restricted, local competition of the small business, small market world. In 1869, for example, the New York-Chicago railway freight rate on a hundredweight of grain crashed from $1.80, on February 4, to 40¢ twenty days later, climbed back to $1.88 in July, and then plummeted to 25¢ in August when another "war" broke out. In the oil fields, the coal fields, among the steel and copper producers, similar price wars repeatedly occurred as producers sought to capture the markets they needed to achieve a profitable level of production. All this was unquestionably favorable to the consumer, as indeed competitive situations always are, but it threatened literal bankruptcy for the competing enterprises themselves—and furthermore, bankruptcy on a multimillion dollar scale.

LIMITATION OF COMPETITION

In these circumstances, it is not difficult to understand the next phase of economic development. The giants decided not to compete.

But how were they to avoid competition? Since common law invalidated any contract binding a competitor to fixed prices or production schedules, there seemed no alternative but voluntary cooperation: trade associations, "gentleman's agreements," or "pools," informal treaties to divide the market. By the 1800s there were a cordage pool and a whiskey pool, a coal pool, a salt pool, and endless rail pools, all calculated to relieve the individual producers from the mutually suicidal game of all-out competition. But to little avail. The division of the market worked well during

[2] *The Age of Enterprise,* rev. ed. (New York: Harper, Torchbooks, 1961), p. 139.

good times; but when bad times approached, the pools broke down. As sales fell, the temptation to cut prices was irresistible, and thus began again the old, ruinous game of competition.

The robber baron ethics of the day contributed to the difficulties. "A starving man will usually get bread if it is to be had," said James J. Hill, a great railway magnate, "and a starving railway will not maintain rates."[3] Typically, at a meeting of rail heads called to agree upon a common freight schedule, the president of one road slipped out, during a brief recess, to wire the new rates to his road, so that it might be the first to undercut them. (By chance, his wire was intercepted, so that when the group next met it was forced to recognize that even among thieves there is not always honor.)

During the 1880s, a more effective device for control became available. In 1879, Samuel Dodd, lawyer for the new Standard Oil Company, had a brilliant idea for regulating the murderous competition that regularly wracked the oil industry. He devised the idea of a trust. Stockholders of companies that wished to join in the Standard Oil Trust were asked to surrender their actual shares to the board of directors of the new trust. Thereby they would give up working control over their companies, but in return they would get "trust certificates" which entitled them to the same share in the profits as their shares earned. In this way, the Standard Oil directors wielded control over all the associated companies, while the former stockholders shared fully in the profits.

Eventually, as we shall see, the trusts were declared to be illegal. But by that time, still more effective devices were created. In 1888 the New Jersey legislature passed a law allowing a corporation chartered in the state to buy stock in another corporation. This was a privilege that had not previously been available to corporations chartered anywhere in the United States. The result was the rapid appearance of the corporate merger, the coming together of two corporations to form a new, bigger one. In manufacturing and mining, alone, there were 43 mergers in 1895 (affecting $41 million dollars worth of corporate assets); 26 mergers in 1896, 69 mergers in 1897. Then in 1898 there were 303—and finally in 1899 a climactic *1,208 mergers combined some $2.26 billion in corporate assets.*[4] Another great wave of mergers occurred in the 1920s. In all, from 1895 to 1929, some $20 billion of industrial corporate wealth were merged into larger units.*

[3] Cochran and Miller, *The Age of Enterprise*, p. 141.

[4] *Historical Statistics of the United States*, Series V, pp. 30-31.

* We must take a footnote to call attention to a development that deserves a chapter in itself. This is the importance of the *corporation*, as a marvelously adaptive legal form of organizing production, in spurring on the growth of the economy. Unlike the personal proprietorship or partnership, the corporation existed quite independently of its owners, survived their deaths, and could enter into binding contracts in "its" own name. Further, by limiting the liability of its owners to the value of the stock they had bought, it protected a capitalist against limitless loss. Much has been written, quite rightly, about the abuses of corporations, but it is important to recognize how valuable was this ingenious legal innovation in encouraging the accumulation of capital and in creating the organizational means to supervise and direct that capital into production.

Another effective means of limiting competition was the *holding company*. Having passed a law permitting its corporations to buy stock in one another, New Jersey now allowed its corporations to do business in any state. Thus the legal foundation was laid for a central corporation which could control subsidiary enterprises by the simple means of buying a controlling share of their stock. By 1911, when the Standard Oil combine was finally dissolved, Standard Oil of New Jersey had used this device to acquire direct control over seventy companies and indirect control over thirty more.

Yet we must not think that it was only the movement toward trustification and merger that brought about the emergence of the giant firm with its ability to limit—or eliminate—competition. Equally, perhaps more, important was simply the process of internal growth. Ford and General Motors, General Electric and A.T.&T., DuPont and Carnegie Steel (later to be the core of U.S. Steel) grew essentially because their market was expanding and they were quick, able, efficient, and aggressive enough to grow faster than any of their competitors. All of them gobbled up some small businesses along the way, and most of them benefited from agreements not to compete. But their gradual emergence to a position of dominance within their industries was not, in the last analysis, attributable to these facts. It was the dynamism of their own business leadership, coupled with a production technique which made enormous size both possible and profitable.

THREAT OF ECONOMIC FEUDALISM

Certainly, size became enormous. By the end of the nineteenth century, some business units were already considerably larger than the states in which they were located. Charles William Eliot pointed out in 1888 that a single railway with headquarters in Boston not only employed three times as many people as the entire government of the Commonwealth of Massachusetts, but enjoyed gross receipts nearly six times that of the state government which had created it. But by comparison with the findings of the Pujo Committee of the U.S. Senate, not quite twenty-five years later, the railway was still small. The committee pointed out that the Morgan banking interests held 341 directorships in 112 corporations whose aggregate wealth exceeded by three times the value of *all* the real and personal property of New England. And not only was the process of trustification eating away at the competitive structure of the market, but the emergence of enormous financially controlled empires posed as well a political problem of ominous portent. As Woodrow Wilson declared: "If monopoly persists, monopoly will always sit at the helm of government. I do not expect to see monopoly restrain itself. If there are men in this country big enough to own the government of the United States, they are going to own it."[5]

[5] Richard Hofstadter, *The Age of Reform* (New York: Knopf, 1955), p. 231.

Not surprisingly, from many quarters the trend to bigness was vehemently opposed. From the 1880s on, a series of state laws strove to undo the trusts which squeezed their citizens. Louisiana sued the Cottonseed Oil Trust; New York, the Sugar Trust; Ohio, the Oil Trust—but to little avail. When one state, like New York, clamped down on its trusts, other states, seeing the revenue available from a change in corporate headquarters, virtually invited the trust to set up business there. When the Supreme Court ruled that corporations, as "persons," could not be deprived of property without "due process of law," state regulation became almost totally useless.

It was soon clear that if something further were to be done, the federal government would have to do it. "Congress alone can deal with the trusts," said Senator Sherman in 1890, "and if we are unwilling or unable, there will soon be a trust for every production and a master to fix the price for every necessity of life."[6]

The result was the Sherman Antitrust Act, an act which, on its surface, was an effective remedy for the problem. "Every contract, combination . . . or conspiracy, in restraint of trade" was declared to be illegal. Violators were subject to heavy fines and jail sentences, and triple damages could be obtained by persons who proved economic injury because of unfair price rigging.

Indeed, under the Sherman Act a number of trusts were prosecuted; and in a famous action in 1911, the great Standard Oil Trust was ordered dissolved. Yet, despite the break-up of a few trusts, the act was singularly weak. Fines for violations were too small to be effective, and in any case, few were levied: not until Franklin Roosevelt's time would the Antitrust Division of the Department of Justice have as much as a million dollars with which to investigate and control the affairs of a multi-billion dollar economy. In fact, during the first fifty years of its existence, only 252 criminal actions were instituted under the Sherman law. And then too, the prevailing judicial opinion of the 1890s and early 1900s was not much in sympathy with the act. The Supreme Court early dealt it a severe blow by finding, in the American Sugar Refining case, that manufacturing was not "commerce," and therefore the American Sugar Refining Company, which had bought controlling stock interests in its four largest competitors, was not to be considered as acting "in restraint of trade." It is not surprising that the concentration of business was hardly slowed in such a climate of opinion. As a humorist of the times put it: "What looks like a stone wall to a layman is a triumphal arch to a corporation lawyer."

These weaknesses led to further acts in 1914: primarily, the Clayton Antitrust Act, prohibiting specific kinds of price discrimination and mergers by the acquisition of stock in competing corporations; and the Federal Trade Commission, which sought to define and prevent "unfair" business

[6] Cochran and Miller, *The Age of Enterprise,* p. 171.

practices. As we shall see later, these acts were not without their effect. Yet, undermining the entire antitrust movement there remained one critical and vitiating fact. The purpose of antitrust was essentially to restore competitive conditions to markets which were in danger of becoming "monopolized" by giant firms. Against this tendency, antitrust legislation could pose a deterrent only insofar as the monopolization process resulted from the outright *combination* of erstwhile competitors. Against a much more fundamental condition—the ability of large businesses to enjoy decisive advantages in finance, merchandising, and research over small businesses—it could offer no remedy. While antitrust effort concentrated its fire against collusion or amalgamation, it was powerless against the fact of spontaneous internal growth.

And therefore growth continued. Through most of the first quarter of the twentieth century, the biggest corporations not only grew, but grew much *faster* than their smaller competitors. As Adolf Berle and Gardiner Means pointed out in a famous study in 1932, between 1909 and 1928 the 200 largest nonfinancial corporations increased their gross assets over 40 percent more rapidly than all nonfinancial corporations.[7] Looking into the future, Berle and Means concluded:

Just what does this rapid growth of the big companies promise for the future? Let us project the trend of the growth of recent years. If the wealth of the large corporations and that of all corporations should each continue to increase for the next twenty years at its average annual rate for the twenty years from 1909 to 1929, 70 percent of all corporate activity would be carried on by two hundred corporations in 1950. If the more rapid rates of growth from 1924 to 1929 were maintained for the next twenty years 85 percent of corporate wealth would be held by two hundred huge units. ... If the indicated growth of the large corporations and of the national wealth were to be effective from now until 1950, half of the national wealth would be under the control of big companies at the end of that period.[8]

Indeed, warned the authors, if the trend of the past continued unchecked, it was predictable that in 360 years all the corporate wealth in the nation would have become fused into one gigantic enterprise, which would then have an expected life span equal to that of the Roman Empire.

STRUCTURE OF THE NATIONAL MARKET: PERIPHERY AND CENTER

Has the Berle and Means projection come true? The question brings to a climax our long survey of the changing market structure. We have been concerned with gathering up the various forces that created and shaped the market as a great system of economic control. Now we must see what the outcome of that process has been.

[7] *The Modern Corporation and Private Property* (New York: Macmillan, 1948), p. 36.
[8] *Ibid.*, pp. 40-41.

Let us begin by looking at the market system in the United States today. Immediately, we notice one thing: there is not one market system in America, but two. One of them, with which we are all familiar at firsthand, consists of the millions of small enterprises that make up the large stratum of the population known as "small-business men." Here are the stores we pass every day on the avenues, the columns of names in the yellow pages of the phone books.

There are roughly 12 million "small" businesses in America, counting every one from the newsstand through the farm (2.9 million farms) up to enterprises that employ several hundred people and count their dollar volume in tens of millions.* Among these 12 million business units, corporations number only about 1.5 million, but these 1.5 million corporations do nearly *five times* as much business as all the small proprietorships and partnerships. In turn, however, most of the 1.5 million corporations are small, even when measured by a small-business yardstick. Over half do less than $100,000 a year in sales, with the result that the whole group of little corporations accounts for only 2 percent of all corporate sales.

Thus, in terms of sales (or assets), little business is little indeed. Yet, by virtue of its numbers, the small businesses of America are by no means unimportant in the national economic picture. Small business collectively employs roughly 40 percent of the American labor force. (This compares with 35 percent of the labor force that works for the "not-for-profit" sector—state, local, and federal government, hospitals, social services agencies, clubs, etc.—and with 25 percent that works for big business.) Millions of small entrepreneurs constitute the very core of the American "middle class," and thus give a characteristic small-business view to much of American political and social life.

Yet it must be emphasized that even as a collectivity, the 12 million minibusinesses do not begin to match the economic power of a tiny number of giant enterprises at the other end of the scale. In the apt phrase of Robert Averitt, small business constitutes the Periphery, but the giants constitute the Center.[9] For here, in a few hundred large industrial corporations, is an economy within an economy, a "system" unto itself. All by itself, this very small core of corporations—500 at the most—accounts for a third of all industrial sales, and within that core there is an inner core that by itself produces the main flow of industrial production on which the economy rests.

* Just to get an idea of scale: the 500th largest American industrial firm in 1969 (in terms of sales) was Montfort of Colorado, a meatpacking firm with sales of $161 million. The 500th biggest in terms of *assets* was another meatpacker, Missouri Beef Packers, worth $19.8 million. At the other end of the list, the largest industrial corporation in terms of sales was General Motors, with a sales volume of $24 *billion*. Biggest in terms of assets was Standard Oil (N.J.) with assets of almost $15 billion. This does not count A.T.&T., which is not classified as an "industrial" company, but which is the largest enterprise in the nation, by far, in terms of assets—$49.6 billion in 1970.

[9] Robert T. Averitt, *The Dual Economy* (New York: Norton, 1968).

Table 7-1 gives us a first overview of the strategic position of the giant corporation within various divisions of the economy.

TABLE 7 • 1

GIANT
CORPORATIONS

RELATIVE SHARES OF LARGE CORPORATIONS IN VARIOUS SECTORS, 1967

Sector	All corporations		Corporations with assets of $250 million or more	
	Number	Total assets ($ billion)	Number	Percent of assets in that sector
Mining	14,441	$ 18.1	12	31
Manufacturing	197,023	448.0	243	58
Transportation, communication, utilities	66,045	221.1	95	79
Finance, insurance, real estate	388,115	1,097.3	517	55
Wholesale and retail trade	465,841	144.1	29	20
All industrial divisions a	1,534,360	2,010.7	958	53

Source: *Statistical Abstract*, 1970, p. 475. (Data calculated from tax returns.)
a Including divisions not shown in table.

The table speaks for itself. Note that the giant corporation is much more dominant in some sectors, such as transportation and communication, than in others, such as retail and wholesale trade. The Center and the Periphery stand out particularly in the latter sector where we find nearly a half-million corporate enterprises (note that we are not even counting the millions of proprietorships and partnerships), but where 29 giant companies, such as Sears Roebuck, A&P, Safeway, and others, nonetheless control almost 30 percent of the total assets.

These figures, however, do not give us a sense of the movement toward corporate concentration that is still going on. For in recent years there has been a burst of merger activity comparable to the great merger movement of the late nineteenth century. Between 1951 and 1960, one-fifth of the top 1,000 corporations disappeared—absorbed within the remaining four fifths. As a result of this and other growth, by 1968 the *100* largest manufacturing corporations owned 49.3 percent of the assets of all manufacturing corporations—*a larger percentage than the top 200 corporations had held in 1948!*

Moreover, the pace of this centralizing activity has been steadily growing. Between 1963 and 1966 the value of assets acquired by the big mining and manufacturing companies averaged $4 billion to $5 billion a year. This rate rose to $10 billion in 1967, then to $15 billion in 1968, and reached an all-time peak *rate* of $20 billion in the first quarter of 1969. The subsequent break in the stock market thereupon brought mergers to an abrupt halt, but the total for 1969 was nonetheless almost at the 1968 level.[10]

Here is a trend that seems to confirm the worst fears of Berle and Means. Does the conclusion they feared also follow? For in *The Modern Corporation and Private Property* (p. 46), they wrote: "a society in which production is governed by blind market forces is being replaced by one in which production is carried on under the ultimate control of a handful of individuals." In the light of our historical study, we can rephrase that conclusion very simply. It meant that the market as the basic control mechanism within capitalism was about to be replaced by another system, akin to a new economic feudalism. Is that the conclusion to which the statistics on corporate size now force us?

CONGLOMERATES AND THE MARKETPLACE

The answer is not a simple one. There is no question that a massive concentration of corporate power exists in America and that the degree of concentration within business as a whole is increasing. At the same time, rather surprisingly, the degree of concentration in the *marketplace*—an area of critical importance for the control mechanism of the capitalist society—does not seem to be getting significantly worse.

How can that seemingly contradictory state of affairs exist? How can corporations be getting bigger and not be increasingly monopolistic? The answer is that the merger wave that has so dramatically boosted the figures for the national concentration of business wealth has taken place largely by the rise of so-called *conglomerates*—corporations that have grown by merging with other corporations not *within* a given market but in a *different* market. Consider the case of International Telephone and Telegraph. Originally a much smaller company wholly engaged in running foreign communications systems, ITT determined in 1961 to embark on a major acquisition and diversification program. During the next 7 years it acquired 52 domestic and 55 foreign companies with combined assets of 1.5 billion. In 1969 alone, the directors approved an additional 22 domestic and 11 foreign acquisitions. As a result it has jumped from 34th to 9th in industrial size, with sales and assets of $5 billion each and 353,000 employees—the 5th largest private

[10] *Statistical Abstract,* 1970, pp. 476, 483. See also Federal Trade Commission, *Staff Report on Corporate Mergers,* October 1969, esp. pp. 184-98.

employer in the world. More important, whereas it had once been a "one-product" company, selling and operating telecommunications systems, by 1970 ITT rented cars (Avis), operated motels and hotels (Sheraton), built homes (Levitt), baked bread (Continental), sold insurance, produced glass, made consumer loans, managed a mutual fund and processed data—among other things.

We do not yet know what may be the long-term consequences of the rise of such giant, diversified companies. Many of them have been put together more with an eye to realizing the profits that could be had from exchanges of shares than with any careful consideration of operating efficiencies, and some have already come unglued in the 1969-1970 stock market decline. Others may indeed prove to be efficient combinations of diverse activities that will enjoy the advantages of access to a central pool of capital and a topflight supermanagement. Still others may run afoul of antitrust laws and may be forced to dissolve.

STABILITY OF MARKET SHARES

But as matters now stand, it seems unlikely that the conglomerates will be adding to their size by buying up *competitors*. Hence it is likely that the structure of the individual markets in which they operate will show no more change than they have in the past. And here, in the critical area of the marketplace, we discover a truly surprising long-run stability. For more than half a century, now, there has been no substantial increase in "monopoly" in the nation's markets, considered as a whole. Going back to 1901, we find some industries—tobacco, chemicals, stone, clay and glass, transportation equipment—where industrial concentration has risen; but in others, no less important—food, textiles, pulp and paper, petroleum and coal products, rubber, machinery—concentration has fallen since 1901.

The same conclusion holds for more recent years. If we take the four largest companies in any industry between 1947 and 1966 (the latest year for which figures are available) and compare the value of their total shipments to the value of all shipments in the industry, we find a similar mixed trend. In a few instances, such as the automobile industry, where some early postwar competitors were shaken out, the concentration ratio has increased appreciably: in the case of autos, from 56 percent in 1947 to 79 percent in 1966. In the majority of industries, however, the movement toward concentration was insubstantial; and in a considerable number, concentration actually declined.

Perhaps most convincing of all is a recent government study that shows the degree of concentration within 213 industrial markets to be virtually unchanged between 1947 and 1966. In 1947, the average share of all markets going to the top four firms was 41.2 percent; in 1966 it was 41.9 percent. Moreover, the number of highly concentrated industries—where the top four firms did three-quarters or more of all sales—showed a sharp drop during the period.[11]

[11] *The New York Times,* January 26, 1969.

What has produced this stabilization of concentration within industry? Two reasons suggest themselves.

The first is the *restraining effect of antitrust legislation*. At the point at which we left our historical narrative, we had seen only the ineffectiveness of early antitrust legislation. But beginning in the 1930s under Franklin Roosevelt, a much stronger enforcement of the various antitrust laws began to gain favor. A vigorous campaign to block the drift toward concentration resulted in a number of suits brought against major corporations for restraint of trade. No less important was a change in the prevailing judicial view, which now construed much less narrowly the powers of the Constitution to impose social controls over business enterprise. In more recent years, new amendments to the antitrust acts and a growing stringency of Justice Department rulings have made the marriage of competitive firms increasingly difficult.

One result of these obstacles in the way of direct "concentration-affecting" mergers is that corporations have been forced to seek acquisitions in fields considerably removed from their original base of operations. This is one source of that trend toward conglomerates we noted above. What interests us here is that this process of diversification has put many large corporations into fields in which they are not the dominant companies by any means. One study shows that in a thousand different product markets, the 100 biggest firms are not even among the four biggest sellers in almost half these markets.[12] By way of illustration, in 1965 the Radio Corporation of America acquired Random House, a book publisher. In its manufacturing activities, RCA is a large producer in a moderately concentrated field (the top four companies make just under half of all radios); in its broadcasting activities, as the owner of NBC, it is one of three great broadcasting networks; but as a book publisher it sails in a highly competitive race.

A second reason for the stabilization within markets is more diffuse, but no less significant. It lies in a decisive *change in the character of business management*.

We have already noticed a certain change in the evolution of the great entrepreneur, from the production-oriented industrialist of the early nineteenth century to the sales and strategy-oriented "captain of industry" of the late nineteenth. Yet throughout the first century of rapid corporate expansion, one characteristic marked both types of business leaders. Both were the direct owners of their enterprises. The men who ran the corporations were themselves the men who had put up the capital or who owned large blocks of stock in the enterprises. The Carnegie Steel Company, the Standard Oil Company, the Ford Motor Company were all extensions of the personalities of Carnegie, Rockefeller, and Ford. This personal direction of affairs was

---

[12] A. D. H. Kaplan, *Big Enterprise in a Competitive System* (Washington, D.C.: Brookings, 1964), p. 286.

the case in the overwhelming majority of the other large and small enterprises of the day.

But with time, a significant change set in. As the original founders of the great businesses died, their stock was inherited by heirs who often did not have business ability and who receded into the background. In addition, the widening dispersion of stock ownership among more and more small investors made it unnecessary for any group to own an actual majority of the stock to exercise control over a company. In 1928, for example, the board of directors of U.S. Steel (which included two of the largest stockholders in the company) held only 1.4 percent of the company's stock. In that year, the biggest stockholder in A.T.&T. held but seven-tenths of 1 percent of the company's total stock and the biggest shareowners of the Pennsylvania Railroad held less than 3 percent of the firm's stock.

The result was that the active direction of the big firms passed from owner-capitalists to a new group of "managers" who ruled the corporation by virtue of their *expertise* rather than because they owned it. The new management was different in many ways from its predecessors. In 1900, for example, half the top executives of the biggest corporations had followed paths to the top that could be described as "entrepreneurial" or "capitalist"—that is, half had built their own businesses or had risked their own capital as the means to business preeminence. By 1925 only a third of the top corporate executives had followed this path, and in 1960 *less than 3 percent* had done so. More and more, the route to success lay through professional skills, whether in law or engineering or science, or in the patient ascent of the corporate hierarchical ladder. Significantly there was a visible change as well as a marked change in the educational background of the top corporate officials. As recently as the 1920s, a majority of the topmost corporate leaders had not gone to college; today over 90 percent have college degrees and a third hold graduate degrees.[13]

The new management brought important changes in its wake. The affairs of big companies increasingly became matters to be handled in systematized, "professional" ways, rather than in the often highly personal, Haroun-al-Raschid mode of the founders. A certain bureaucratization thus crept into the conduct of business life, at the very time that the business community was waxing most vocal about the dangers of bureaucracy in government. More important, the new management now adopted a new strategy for corporate growth—or rather, abandoned an older one. Advances in technology, changes in product design, vigorous advertising, the wooing of businesses to be acquired in other fields—all these provided ample outlets for the managerial impulse toward expansion. But one mode of growth—the mode that the founders of the great enterprises had never hesitated to use—was now ruled out: growth was no longer to be sought by the direct head-on competition of one firm against another in terms of *price*.

[13] Mabel Newcomer, *The Big Business Executive* (New York: Columbia University Press, 1955), pp. 61-63; and Jay Gould, *The Technical Elite* (New York: Augustus Kelley, 1966), pp. 160-71.

Thus, the evolution of a more "statesmanlike" attitude in business affairs brought a significant change in business tactics. But the change cannot be ascribed solely to a new outlook on the part of big-business men. Behind that new outlook was *a change in the market environment.*

We call this new kind of market situation *oligopoly,* meaning a market shared by a few sellers. Note that it is not *monopoly,* which is a market entirely served by one seller. Neither is it "pure competition," such as we envisaged when we first looked into the theory of a market economy.

What is the essential difference? We cannot investigate it thoroughly in this book, but the main points of the contrast are not difficult to grasp. Classical competition implies a situation in which there are so many firms (of roughly the same order of size) that no one of them by itself can directly influence market prices. This is the case—more or less—within much of the Periphery. In oligopoly, by way of contrast, the numbers of firms are few enough (or the disparity in size among the few large ones and the host of smaller ones is so great) that the large firms cannot help affecting the market situation. Here is the typical situation at the Center. As a result, whereas in classical competition firms must accept whatever prices the market thrusts upon them, in oligopolistic markets, prices can be "set," at least within limits, by the direct action of the leading firms.

In many of the most important industrial markets, as we have seen, it is oligopoly rather than pure competition that is the order of things today. In industry after industry, economies of large-scale production have brought about a situation in which a few large producers divide the market among themselves. Often these markets are dominated by one very large firm that serves as "price leader," raising or lowering its prices as general economic conditions warrant, and being followed up or down by everyone else in the field. U.S. Steel in the steel industry, General Motors in the auto field, Corn Products Refining in the cornstarch industry have more or less consistently "led" their industries in this fashion. By and large, as we would expect, these prices are considerably higher than the prices that a pure competitive market would enforce. General Motors, for instance, "targets" its prices to attain a 15 to 20 percent return after taxes, *calculating its costs on the assumption that it will use only 60 to 70 percent of its total plant capacity.* U.S. Steel sets its prices high enough so that it can earn a small profit *even if it operates only two days out of five.* In fact "target pricing" has come to be the established procedure for many leading manufacturing firms.[14]

Prices set by leading firms, rather than by the interplay of competition among many firms, are called *administered prices.* This does not mean that in each of these industries firms do not vie with one another. On the contrary, if you ask a General Motors or a U.S. Steel executive, he will tell you of vigorous competition. He may show you that Ford had edged out General Motors in such-and-such a line, or that Bethlehem Steel has cap-

---

[14] *Study of Administered Prices in the Steel Industry* and *Study of Administered Prices in the Automobile Industry,* Senate Report 1387, 85th Cong., 2nd sess.; see also R. F. Lanzillotti, "Pricing Objectives of Large Companies," *American Economic Review,* December 1958, pp. 921–40.

tured some of U.S. Steel's business. The point, however, is *that the competition among oligopolists typically utilizes every means except one: price cutting.* The tactics of lowering price to secure a rival's business is not regarded as "fair play," although once in a while it breaks out, just as it did in the days of cutthroat competition of the 1880s.* But what was common practice then is rare now. Competition among oligopolists today means winning business away from another by advertising, customer service, or product design—but not by "chiseling" on price. Everyone recognizes that it is to his advantage not to disturb the market. There have been few instances in steel, or oil, or automobiles, or chemicals, or cigarettes when out-and-out price "warfare" has taken the place of nonprice "competition."

CHALLENGE
TO CONSUMER
SOVEREIGNTY

Our inquiry has led us from the emergence of the giant corporation—a process that we have seen to be still going on—to a consideration of the change in corporate tactics within industrial markets. Now we must stand back a pace and once again look at the operation of the market system as a whole, seeking an answer to the questions we posed at the outset. What is the consequence of the giant corporation for American society? What are its effects on the operation of a market economy?

The second question is easier to cope with than the first. We will remember that a distinguishing feature of the market system was that the *power of control was vested in the consumer.* There were two aspects of this power. First, a market society enabled consumers to have the ultimate decision as to the allocation of the factors of production. *Their* desires arranged the productive pattern of society, not the desires of society's rulers, its keepers of traditions, or its producers. Second, the market society assured the consumer that he would be able to buy the output of society at the lowest price compatible with a continued flow of production. While producers might wish to make exorbitant profits from consumers, they would be prevented from doing so by the pressure of competition from other producers.

Does the consumer still exercise this economic sovereignty? In a general sense he does. If the consumer does not choose to buy the goods produced by giant concerns, those concerns have no choice but to curtail the production of those goods. For example, in the mid-1950s the Ford Motor Company poured nearly a quarter of a billion dollars into the production of a new car, the Edsel. The car was rejected by consumers, and after a few years its production was quietly discontinued. Familiar, too, is the effect of a swing in consumer tastes. From the mid-1950s on, imports of foreign

---

* On occasion, the administered prices in an oligopoly are maintained by out-and-out collusive agreement, which is strictly illegal. This was the case when General Electric, Westinghouse, and a number of smaller manufacturers were discovered in 1959 to be rigging prices and sharing the market for heavy electrical equipment. A number of top executives in the main concerns were sent to jail, heavy fines were imposed, and the purchasers of the equipment sued for triple damages. More frequently, however, oligopolistic prices are maintained simply by tacit consent.

sports and small cars rose steadily—from 57,000 vehicles in 1955 to 668,000 in 1959. With the exception of American Motors, the major car manufacturers insisted that the trend to compacts was only a fad and that Americans "wanted" bigger cars. But there was no brooking the contrary opinion of consumers themselves. Eventually, all the major manufacturers were *forced* into the production of small cars.

What then is the difference between this state of affairs and that of the "ideal" market system? One major difference lies in the fact that the great corporations today do not merely "fill" the wants of consumers. They themselves help to *create* these wants by massive efforts to interest the public in buying the products they manufacture. In 1969, for example, business spent some $20 billion on advertising its products—an expenditure two-thirds as large as our total expenditures for public elementary and secondary education. By way of contrast, in 1867 we spent only $50 million on advertising; and in 1900, only $542 million. So it is that while consumers still move the factors of production to satisfy their "wants," these wants are themselves increasingly influenced by the producers. In contrast to the ideal market where producers hasten at the beck of an imperious consumer demand, in the new market, consumers are to some extent themselves at the beck of an imperious producer demand.

We might note, for instance, that no sooner was the first small Ford placed on the market than the company announced a "luxury" small car, and this example was quickly followed by other producers. It may very well be that consumers prefer a large spectrum of sizes and shapes of automobiles. But it is difficult to square the original image of serving the consumers' uninfluenced wants with the process by which new models are designed and touted. We shall have a further word to say about this at the conclusion of our chapter.

The second main attribute of the ideal market was that consumers' interests were satisfied as cheaply as possible because prices were forced down to the average cost of producing goods. Is this still true?

We have already seen that prices in oligopolistic industries are considerably higher than they would be under competitive conditions. Yet they are not wholly without controls. If a direct price struggle is conspicuously lacking within oligopolistic industries, there are other pressures that nonetheless enforce a certain degree of price discipline.

One of these pressures has been called by John Kenneth Galbraith "countervailing power."[15] By this, Galbraith means that in an oligopolistic world the opposition of interests across the market provides some compensation for the absence of a contest of interests on each side of the market. Today, powerful corporate sellers often face equally powerful corporate

[15] See John K. Galbraith, *American Capitalism, the Concept of Countervailing Power* (Boston: Houghton Mifflin, 1952), pp. 115ff.

buyers. The giant raw materials producer who faces little or no competition within his industry must sell to the giant chemical or other processing plant; the giant steel mill to the giant auto firm; the giant canner to the giant supermarket chain. Not least important, the large firm no longer bargains with the individual employee, but with large and powerful unions. This kind of neutralization of economic power does not hold true in every market nor in every situation, but, Galbraith contends, it is true in enough markets and in enough situations to constitute a powerful restraining force on the unhindered exercise of oligopolistic power.

A second restraining force is the competition among different *products.* Even if all steel prices are kept at "administered" levels, steel as a whole must compete with aluminum. Nor does the competition end here. What we find, indeed, is an immense chain of interproduct competition—steel against aluminum, aluminum against glass, glass against plastics, plastics against wood, wood against concrete, concrete against steel. And this competition is without doubt effective. Note that automobile engines are now made of cast aluminum as well as of steel; that buildings are now sheathed in glass as well as brick or concrete; that cooking utensils are made of glass as well as of aluminum; that drinking "glasses" are often made of plastic.

Thus prices are not *wholly* free from control. That does not mean that they are therefore adequately controlled. Oligopoly does not mean *arbitrarily* high prices, but it does mean a price structure considerably higher than those which a more competitive system might enjoy. "What few will question," writes Gardiner Means in a study of steel pricing, "is that the after-tax target rates of 16 and 20 percent and the actual earnings in excess of these targets are well above a competitive rate of return. Prices set to achieve these targets must involve substantial premiums over costs, taxes and a legitimate rate of return. To this extent, the public interest is not served. . . ."[16]

POWER AND RESPONSIBILITY

What can be done about the fortresses of power that have emerged in modern capitalism? Is there a way of imposing public responsibility on the labor union, the government office, the big corporation? As we shall see, the question is exceedingly difficult. Let us discover this for ourselves by examining four frequently encountered proposals for increasing the social responsibility of the giant corporation.

1. *Profit as social responsibility.*

The first suggestion is most prominently associated with the name of Professor Milton Friedman, whose views we have previously encountered in our study of inflation. Professor Friedman is a philosophic conservative whose response to the question of what a corporation should do to discharge its social responsibility is very simple: *make money.*

[16] *Pricing Power and the Public Interest* (New York: Harper, 1962), p. 268.

The function of a business organization in society, argues Friedman, is to serve as an efficient agent of production, not as a locus of social improvement. It serves that productive function best by striving after profit—conforming, while doing so, to the basic rules and ethical norms of society. It is not up to business to "do good"; it is up to government to prevent it from doing bad.

Moreover, as soon as a businessman tries to apply any rules other than money-making, he takes into his own hands powers that rightfully belong to other parts of society, such as its political authorities. Friedman would even forbid corporations to give money to charities or universities. Their business, their responsibility to society, he insists, is *production.* Let the dividend-receivers give away the money the corporations pay them, but do not let corporations become the active social welfare agencies of society.[17]

The counterarguments to Friedman's position are not difficult to frame. They are two:

(1) Friedman assumes that stockholders' moral claims to the earnings of the vast semimonopolies they "own" are superior to claims of the consumers or workers from whose pockets these profits are plucked. This is at least a debatable point: since the stockholders are *not* active entrepreneurs, they make little or no contribution to the profits of the corporation. Why, then, should their claim exceed a reasonable compensation for the risk of their money?

(2) Friedman assumes that the government, whose purpose is to set the rules and oversee the operations of business, acts *independently* of the corporations they regulate. But many studies show that the so-called regulatory agencies of the government usually act on *behalf of the big corporations* they "regulate," rather than on behalf of the consumer. For example, the Food and Drug Administration banned cyclamates as a dangerous food additive in 1969, *nineteen years* after the first warnings of their dangerous effects had been brought to its attention! In the long interim, it failed to act, largely because of its reluctance to incur the wrath (and political counterattack) of the industry it was supposedly "regulating."[18]

2. *The corporation as social arbiter.*

Quite a different approach to the problem of social responsibility has been widely espoused by many concerned corporate executives. This view recog-

[17] Friedman, *Capitalism and Freedom,* Chap. 8. Professor Frank Knight, a distinguished predecessor of Friedman's at the University of Chicago, would agree with the proposal and carry it even further: force corporations, he urges, to pay out to stockholders *all* their earnings every year! That would deprive them of the market power that stems from the very large "retained earnings" they do not distribute as dividends. Under Knight's proposal, a corporation would be under constant economic scrutiny from its stockholders who would have to be persuaded to reinvest their earnings with the company if it were to grow.

[18] See James S. Turner, "The Chemical Feast," in *The Report on the Food and Drug Administration,* eds. Ralph Nader and Summer Study Group (New York: Grossman, 1970), pp. 5–30. See also John C. Esposito, "Vanishing Air," in *The Ralph Nader Study Group Report on Air Pollution* (New York: Grossman, 1970); and Grant McConnell, *Private Power and American Democracy* (New York: Knopf, 1966).

nizes that the corporation, by virtue of its immense size and strength, has power thrust upon it, whether it wishes to have it or not. The solution to this problem, as these men see it, is for corporate executives to act "professionally" as the arbiters of this power, doing their best to adjudicate equitably among the claims of the many constituencies to which they are responsible: labor, stockholders, customers, and the public at large. The executive of one of the largest enterprises in the nation said, two decades ago, "The manager is becoming a professional in the sense that like all professional men he has a responsibility to society as a whole."[19]

There is no doubt that many top corporate executives think of themselves as the referees among contending groups, and no doubt many of them use caution and forethought in exercising the power of decision. But the weaknesses of this argument are also not difficult to see. Unlike other professions, there are neither criteria for "qualifying" as a corporate executive nor penalties for failing to accept social responsibilities. The executive of a corporation who fails to act responsibly may incur the opprobrium of the public, but the public has no way of removing him from office or reducing his salary.

Nor is there any clear guideline, even for the most scrupulous executive, defining the manner in which he is *supposed* to exercise his responsibility. Is his concern for the prevention of pollution to take precedence over his concern for turning in a good profit statement at the end of the year or giving wage increases or reducing the price of his product? Is the contribution of "his" company to charity or education supposed to represent *his* preferences or those of his customers or workers? Has Xerox a right to help the cause of public broadcasting; Standard Oil of New Jersey, to help finance Harlem Academy (a private school aimed at assisting Harlem youths to go on to college); the makers of firearms, to help support the National Rifle Association?

These are questions to which there are no answers. But they begin to indicate the complexity of the issue of "social responsibility" and the problems implicit in allowing these extremely important *social* decisions to be made by private individuals who are in no way publicly accountable for their actions.

3. *Dissolution of monopoly.*

A third approach to the problem of responsibility takes yet another tack. It suggests that the power of big business be curbed dividing large corporations into several much smaller units. A number of studies have shown that the largest *plant* size needed for industrial efficiency is far smaller (in terms of financial assets) than the giant firms typical of the *Fortune* list of the top 500 industrial corporations (or for that matter of the next 500). Hence a

---

[19] R. W. Davenport and *Fortune* editors, *U.S.A.: The Permanent Revolution* (Englewood Cliffs, N.J.: Prentice-Hall, 1951), p. 79. (The executive is Frank Abrams of Standard Oil, N.J.)

number of economists have suggested that a very strict application of antitrust legislation should be applied, not only to prohibit mergers but to separate a huge enterprise such as General Motors into its natural constituent units: a Buick Company, an Oldsmobile Company, a Chevrolet Company, and so on.

One major problem stands in the way of this frontal attack on corporate power. It is that size and social responsibility are by no means clearly correlated. Professor Galbraith has wryly remarked that the showpiece firms of the economy are the very ones that the Department of Justice suspects of antitrust practices. The other side of that coin is that small competitive industry is typically beset by low research and development programs, antilabor practices, and a general absence of the kinds of amenities we associate with "big business."

Moreover, there is no reason to believe that smaller firms would be more pollution-conscious (indeed, owing to competitive pressures, they might be less inclined to minimize pollution) or that they would be more conscientious in advertising, racial nondiscrimination, and other practices. In other words, the loss of *political* power, which might well accompany the fractioning of the largest firms, is apt to be offset by a rise in certain forms of economic ruthlessness or even antisocial behavior.

Competition, it has been remarked more than once, is a social condition to which all parties in an enterprise economy pay homage, but which only economists take seriously. Business and labor both spend much of their energies trying to avoid competition or to minimize it, and the attempt to intensify competition by breaking up large firms into smaller ones might bring about worse problems than it alleviates.

4. *Nationalization.*

Then why not nationalize the large firms? The thought comes as rank heresy to a nation that has been accustomed to equating nationalization with socialism. Yet Germany, France, England, Sweden, Italy, and a host of other capitalistic nations have nationalized industries ranging from oil refineries to airlines, from automobile production to the output of coal and electricity. Hence, Professor Galbraith has suggested that we should nationalize the giant armaments producers who are wholly dependent on the Pentagon, in order to bring such firms under public control.

But would nationalization achieve its purpose of assuring social responsibility? We have seen the Pentagon prevent one of its "ward" companies, Lockheed Aircraft, from suffering the fate of an ordinary inefficient firm by rescuing it from bankruptcy with special contracts and "loans." Outright nationalization would only cement this union of political and economic power, by making Lockheed a part of the Pentagon and thus making it even more difficult to put pressure on it to perform responsibly.

Or take the Tennessee Valley Authority, perhaps the most famous American public enterprise: it is currently being sued for the environmental devastation it has wrought by its strip-mining operations. So, too, the Atomic Energy Commission, which operates "nationalized" plants, has been severely criticized for its careless supervision of radioactive processes, and the Post Office has been converted into a semi-autonomous agency, having proved a disaster as a "nationalized" industry.

The problem is that nationalization not only removes the affected enterprise *entirely* from the pressures of the market, but almost inevitably brings it under the political shelter of the government, which further removes the venture from any effective criticism. Experience in the socialist world (to which we will turn in Chapter 10) as well as in Europe, where a number of industries have been nationalized, suggests that nationalization may be a necessary step to rescue a sick industry, but that it is no guarantee of the good operation of a potentially healthy one.

REMAINING
POSSIBILITIES

All these difficulties make it clear that the problem of social responsibility will not be easy to solve (or for that matter, even to *define*), no matter what step we choose, from Professor Friedman's laissez faire to Galbraith's nationalization. And for each of these problems with regard to the corporation, we could easily construct counterparts that have to do with the control over labor unions or over the government itself.

What, then, is to be done? A number of lines of action suggest themselves. One is the widening of the *legal responsibility* of the corporation to include areas of responsibility for which it now has little or no accountability. Environmental damage is one of these; consumer protection is another. (The suits filed against the Chevron Oil Company for its oil spills and against the producers of the thalidomide sleeping pills are important first steps in this direction.) Ralph Nader has further suggested that a top corporate official be legally charged with seeing to it that his company complies with the law in full, and that the top officers of noncomplying companies be suspended, as is the case in certain violations of SEC regulations. He also strongly advocates the federal, rather than state, incorporation of big companies—a step that would greatly facilitate the establishment of tough national standards of corporate responsibility.

A second step would be a widening of *public accountability through disclosure*—the so-called fishbowl method of regulation. Corporations could be required to report to public agencies their expenditures for pollution control, for political lobbying, and so on. Corporate tax returns could be opened to public scrutiny. Unions and corporations both could be required to make public disclosure of their race practices, with regard to hiring or admission, advancement, and rates of pay. Public responsibility for advertising, with formal proofs submitted to back all claims, is yet another means of securing better accountability to the public.

Still another course of action would be to appoint *public members* to boards of directors of large companies or to executive organs of large unions and to charge these members with protecting the consumers' interest and with reporting behavior that seemed contrary to the public interest. Worker-members of boards of directors might also serve such a useful purpose (there are such members in Germany). The mobilization of the votes of concerned stockholders (nonprofit institutions own $26 billion of corporate securities) is still another way of bringing social pressure to bear.

Finally, there is the corrective action of dedicated private individuals such as Ralph Nader, who rose to fame on his exposé of the safety practices of the auto industry, and who has since turned his guns on pollution, and other irresponsibilities of big business, and on poor performance in the federal bureaucracy. Such public pressure is necessarily sporadic and usually short-lived, but it has been a powerful source of social change.

It would be a mistake to conclude this recital with the implication that corporate (or union or government) power can be easily brought under control through a few legal remedies or by the power of public opinion. Certainly, many abuses can be curbed, and much better levels of social performance achieved.

But it is a sober fact that mass organizations seem an inescapable concomitant of our age of high technology and increasing social interdependence. The roots of this fact were discussed earlier, and its broader consequences will be seen later. Here we should note that, depending on our interests, we stress different aspects of this universal phenomenon. To some, who fear the continued growth of very large-scale business, the most significant aspect is that we have not managed to control business power. To others, concerned over the emergence of large labor unions, it is labor power that most dangerously eludes effective control. And to still others who are most worried by the growth of big government, it is the growth of public power that is the main problem.

What is common among these concerns is the awareness that very large, only half-controlled organizations have come to dominate much of the market system. But the problem is bigger than that. For if we look to the nonmarket systems, we see the growth of socialist ministries of production and administration that display much the same bureaucratic indifference and mixed political and economic power as do our corporations, unions, and government agencies, together with the same uncertainty about how to reconcile their power with their conception of the public good.

This is a problem that we will examine in Chapter 12. But there we will also see that the market system, for all its problems, has certain advantages that go a long way toward redressing the balance in historical perspective. The market system has huge strengths in bringing about the *efficient operation* of an economic society, and these strengths may be more important *at certain stages of historical development* than the weaknesses into which we have been looking.

In other words, in a final appraisal of the market system—and of capitalist society that depends on a market mechanism—it is a historical perspective that we require more than any narrow calculus of pluses and minuses. For that, let us return to our narrative.

KEY CONCEPTS AND KEY WORDS

Concentration

1. A combination of aggressive entrepreneurship and the economies of scale typical of industrial technology brought about a *concentration of economic power* in many markets in the late nineteenth and early twentieth centuries.

Merger

2. The emergence of large firms with massive capital structures led to "cutthroat" competition that was exceedingly dangerous for the firms concerned. Hence there were *many attempts to stabilize the competitive struggle* by means of pools, trusts, holding companies, and mergers.

Antitrust

3. As the great trusts and combines rose to power, there was a "countervailing" thrust of political *antitrust legislation,* culminating in the Sherman Antitrust Act (1890), later in the Clayton Antitrust Act (1914), and in subsequent amendments designed to make mergers more difficult.

Internal growth

4. None of these laws prohibited or interfered with *internal growth.* As a result, large businesses continued to expand. A famous survey by Berle and Means in 1933 predicted that if the rate of growth of the top 200 nonfinancial corporations continued, they would soon own virtually the entire economy.

Conglomerates

5. This prediction has been partly borne out, especially in the recent rise of the *conglomerates*—enormous diversified corporations—that have dramatically increased the concentration of all manufacturing wealth held by the top 100 corporations. At the same time, the very diversification of these enterprises has precluded any marked change in concentration within industrial markets.

Monopoly

6. This stability within markets can be traced to several causes:
   • More effective *antitrust* legislation.
   • The *diffusion of corporate growth* into new, competitive markets.

Bureaucratization
   • The *bureaucratization* of business management.
   • The rise of *more stable market structures.*

Oligopoly

7. We call the new market structures *oligopoly,* meaning few sellers. *The outstanding difference between oligopoly and traditional competition is that oligopolistic firms can set the levels of their prices more or less at their own discretion, whereas competitive firms have no alternative but to meet the "going" price of the market.*

Stability of market structures

8. The effect of oligopoly is twofold. First, it greatly *reduces the role of price competition.* Second, it opens the consumer to the *influence of advertising.*

9. The shift of power from consumer to producer is not total. Consumer tastes, however influenced, cannot be shaped at will or ignored. And *competition among products* still exercises an important restraint on firms.

Power

10. Power is a difficult problem of modern society. A market system finds an important rationale in the idea of *consumer sovereignty,* in which power is fragmented into the households who constitute the sources of demand (and of factor supply). But it is clear

Consumer sovereignty

that in modern society, huge units of business, labor, and government have greatly reduced, although not entirely eliminated, consumer sovereignty.

11. A number of proposals have been advanced for assuring the responsible social conduct of large corporations. These include: (1) strict attention to *profit-making only;*

Corporate responsibility

(2) *"professional" standards* of conduct and self-conscious attention to social needs; (3) *break-up of big business;* and (4) *nationalization.*

12. Each of these proposals has its weaknesses. (1) The abdication of social responsibility by business assumes that stockholders have a "right" to profits and that government will in fact supervise, and not protect, big business. (2) The professionalization of corporate management ignores the absence of any professional standards for management and the essential arbitrariness of corporate decisions in the social area. (3) The breakup of big business assumes that smaller, more competitive business is also more socially responsible, which is doubtful; and (4) nationalization ignores the sorry record of many state-owned enterprises.

13. There remain as means of improving corporate (or union or government) performance the development of new *legal responsibilities* for business and labor, new areas of *public accountability, public representation* on executive boards, and the important power of *private investigation and publicity.*

14. The overall problem of power remains recalcitrant, not only in a market society but in all societies. This is a problem to which we will return in our subsequent investigation of the historical trajectory of the market system itself.

Q U E S T I O N S

1. Can you name the chief corporate executives of the top ten industrial firms in the U.S. (General Motors, Standard Oil of New Jersey, Ford, General Electric, Socony, U.S. Steel, Chrysler, Texaco, Gulf, Western Electric)? How many names of leading businessmen do you know? What does this suggest as to the character of business leadership today contrasted with the 1890s?

2. Why does heavy overhead cost lead to "cutthroat competition"? Why is this kind of competition dangerous?

3. Suppose Congress decided to foster a return to classical competition in the United States. What changes would have to be wrought in the American business scene? Do you think this is a practical possibility?

4. Compare the situation of a farmer selling fruit on a roadside stand and an executive of a large auto company selling a new model. How much latitude does each have in pricing his product?

5. Do you believe that tastes are ever created by advertising? Have your own been?

6. What do you consider to be the most desirable characteristic of bigness in business? The most undesirable?

7. Suppose you wanted to measure concentration in an industry. What attributes of the firms in that industry would interest you: their respective sales? their assets? their number of employees? Might different measures give different concentration ratios?

8. What are the important differences between "pure" competition and oligopoly as regards the position of the consumer? The producer? On net balance which do you think is preferable? Why?

9. Do you think businessmen should be more socially responsible? How would you go about achieving a higher level of social responsibility in the following areas: (1) truth in advertising, (2) absence of political interference with government, (3) colorblind hiring and promotion, (4) high levels of antipollution performance? What measures would you propose for numbers 2 and 3 with regard to labor unions? How would you bring government agencies to a higher level of social responsibility?

10. Do you think corporations have a right to back right-wing groups? Left-wing groups? Center-wing groups? Modern art? Old-fashioned art? Universities? Sports groups? Political parties? How do you justify your answers?

11. Do you think it would help to nationalize the big arms companies? Could you imagine a situation in which you would favor the nationalization of any company? How about the railroads, if they were about to go bankrupt and leave the nation stranded? How about GM if it defied a government regulation with regard to producing a pollution-free vehicle? How about a textile company that admitted to racial discrimination in its advancement policies?

12. What relation do you see between the growth of power in all areas of the society and the development of modern technology? Discuss with relation to the automobile, the airplane, nuclear power, the computer.

In the preceding chapter we concentrated on important aspects of the developing industrial economy—the swift rise in productivity, the impact of mass production, the thickening texture of the market. But we purposely ignored one effect of technology which, in retrospect, towers over the others. This effect was the tremendous impetus that technology gave to the process of economic growth.

In Chapter 5, "The Industrial Revolution," we commented on the importance of technology for growth. Prior to that time, a chart of the well-being of the average person in Europe would have shown a distressingly horizontal profile, rising in some years or even centuries, falling in others, perhaps tilted slightly upward as a whole, but certainly displaying nothing like a steady year-by-year increase in the output of goods and services available per capita. Even with the initial introduction of the new technology we noted that the standard of living did not immediately improve. But starting in the third quarter of the nineteenth century, the accumulations of capital and the accretion of *expertise* began to display their hidden powers. In nearly every industrializing country, and most dramatically in the United States, the profile of economic well-being now began to show that steady and regular improvement that has become the very hallmark of modern economic times.

Figure 8-1 shows us the general path of this growth in the United States from the 1870s, when the process was in full swing, to 1929 when it reached a dramatic peak, to which we will shortly return. If we draw a line through the irregularly upward-moving graph to express the average rate of growth taking good years and bad together, we find it to be about 3.5 percent (with all price changes eliminated), which means that the total volume of output was doubling about every 22 years. Since the number of mouths was also doubling, although more slowly, *per capita* shares in this mounting volume of goods obviously grew more slowly. Roughly, we can estimate that individuals improved their lot at a rate of about $1\frac{1}{2}$ to 2 percent a year, doubling their real incomes every 40 years on the average. There is no doubt that the period as a whole was one of unprecedented progress and improvement. How strange then that it should have ended in the greatest disaster in the history of the market system—one that very nearly spelled the end of capitalism and that permanently altered the system in ways that we must now learn about.

We in America today are nearer to the final triumph over poverty than ever before in the history of any land. The poorhouse is vanishing from among us. We have not yet reached the goal, but, given a chance ... we shall soon with the help of God be in sight of the day when poverty will be banished from this nation.

AMERICA
IN 1929

Thus spoke Herbert Hoover in November 1928, and indeed by 1929 the American economy had shown extraordinary progress. Population had grown from 76 million in 1900 to over 121 million, while ten years had been added to the expectation of life at birth for whites and thirteen for non-whites. To hold and feed and sustain its growing numbers, the nation had built up two new cities to a million each, five to over half a million, nearly 1,500 from rural to urban classification; $75 billion worth of homes, $9 billion worth of new farm structures; over $30 billion worth of new indus-trial equipment. Meanwhile, there were jobs for 48 million people—all save 3.2 percent of the labor force in 1929. Furthermore, these job holders had

FIG. 8•1   REAL GNP (1929 PRICES) AGGREGATE AND PER HEAD

seen average weekly hours of work in manufacturing drop from nearly 60 in 1900 to 44. Average hourly earnings rose from 20 cents in 1909 to 56 cents, while consumer prices lagged sufficiently behind to allow a rise in real wages of some 10 to 20 percent. It was not surprising, then, that an atmosphere of optimism gripped America in 1929 and that President Hoover's official words only reflected an informal sentiment throughout the nation.

Certainly few Americans suspected that a major economic calamity might be just around the corner. On the contrary, most people were concerned with quite another prospect of the American economy, and a highly attractive one. This was the great stock market boom—a boom which by 1929 had pulled perhaps 10,000,000 people into "the market," where they had the pleasure of watching their money painlessly and effortlessly grow. As Frederick Lewis Allen, the social historian of the Twenties, described it:

The rich man's chauffeur drove with his ears laid back to catch the news of an impending move in Bethlehem Steel; he held fifty shares himself on a twenty point margin. The window cleaner at the broker's office paused to watch the ticker, for he was thinking of converting his laboriously accumulated savings into a few shares of Simmons. Edwin Lefevre (an articulate reporter on the market at this time who could claim considerable personal experience) told of a broker's valet who made nearly a quarter of a million in the market, of a trained nurse who cleaned up thirty thousand following the tips given her by her grateful patients; and of a Wyoming cattleman, thirty miles from the nearest railroad, who bought or sold a thousand shares a day.[1]

It was, of course, admittedly speculative, and yet the risks seemed eminently justified. Someone who had put $1,000 each year, from 1921 on, into a group of representative stocks would have found himself worth over $6,000 in 1925, almost $9,000 in 1926, well over $11,000 in 1927, and an incredible $20,000 in 1928. And that was just the beginning: during June and July of 1929 industrial stock averages went up nearly as much as they had during the entire year of 1928, which had been, in its time, a year of unprecedented rise. By August 1929, the three-months' summer spurt had already outdistanced the entire 1928 rise. In those three months alone, an investor who had bought 100 shares of Westinghouse would have almost doubled his money; even a buyer of staid A.T.&T. would have been richer by a third. It seemed that everyone had but to beg or borrow money to buy shares in order to get rich.

THE
GREAT
CRASH

What pricked the bubble? No one knows exactly what final event was to blame. But when the boom did break, it was as if an enormous dam had suddenly crumbled. All the frenzy that had stretched out over two years in

[1] *Only Yesterday* (New York: Bantam, 1946), p. 349.

sending stocks up was concentrated in a few incredible weeks beating them down. On Tuesday, October 29, 1929 an avalanche of selling crushed the exchanges. On occasion there were *no* offers to buy stock at all—just to sell it. Goldman Sachs, a much sought-after investment trust, lost almost half its quoted value on this single day. By the end of the trading session (the ticker, lagging behind, stretched out the agony two-and-a-half hours longer than the actual market transactions) 16,410,000 shares of stock had been dumped. In a single day, the rise in values of the entire preceding year had been wiped out. A few weeks later, $30 billion of "wealth" had vanished in thin air. Millions who had counted their paper gains and thought themselves well off discovered they were poor.

The great crash is in itself a fascinating chapter in the "madness of crowds." At first it seemed unconnected with anything bigger. In fact, the early weeks after the crash were regularly marked with expressions of confidence: the general cliché of the day was that things were "fundamentally sound." Yet things were *not* fundamentally sound. The terrifying Crash ushered in the much more terrifying Depression.

Frederick Lewis Allen wrote:

It was an oddly invisible phenomenon, this Great Depression. If one observed closely, one might note that there were fewer people on the streets than in former years, that there were many untenanted shops, that beggars and panhandlers were much in evidence; one might see breadlines here and there, and "Hoovervilles" in vacant lots at the edge of town (groups of tar-paper shacks inhabited by homeless people); railroad trains were shorter, with fewer Pullmans; and there were many factory chimneys out of which no smoke was coming. But otherwise there was little to see. Great numbers of people were sitting home, trying to keep warm.[2]

However invisible to the casual observer, the Depression was far from being a mere figment of the imagination. To begin with, gross national product—the measure of the nation's total output—fell precipitously from $104 billion in 1929 to $56 billion in 1933. Almost one dollar's worth of final output out of every two simply disappeared. As a result, unemployment soared. In 1929, the unemployed had numbered 1.5 million. By 1933 the number had risen eightfold until *one person out of every four in the entire labor force was without a job.* In the nation as a whole, residential construction fell by 90 percent: there were virtually no houses built. Nine million savings accounts were lost as banks closed their doors. Eighty-five thousand businesses failed. In Pennsylvania in 1932, it was reported by the State Department of Labor that wages had fallen to 5 cents an hour in sawmills, 6 cents in brick and tile manufacturing, 7.5 cents in general contracting. In Tennessee, women in mills were paid as little as $2.39 for a 50-hour week. In Kentucky, miners ate the weeds that cows ate; in West Virginia, people

[2] *The Big Change* (New York: Harper, 1952), p. 248.

began to rob stores for food. In California, a child starved to death and was discovered to have been living on refuse.[3]

CAUSES OF THE
DEPRESSION:
SPECULATION

How did this tragedy come about?

An immediate, precipitating cause was, of course, the speculative fever that had engulfed the economy by 1929. The mania was not just confined to Wall Street. Throughout the nation, a get-rich-quick philosophy had destroyed normal business and banking caution. Foreign bonds of the most dubious validity were eagerly (and sometimes ruthlessly) pushed by the banks into investors' hands or, worse folly, put into their own portfolios.* In addition, huge pyramided structures of investment trusts and holding companies erected a house of cards atop the operating base of enterprise. For instance, Georgia Power & Light Company was controlled by the Seaboard Public Service Corporation, which was controlled by the Middle West Utilities Company, which was controlled by Insull Utility Investments, Inc., which was controlled by the Corporation Securities Company of Chicago (which was controlled, in turn, by Insull Utility Investments, which presumably *it* controlled). Of these companies, only one—Georgia Power—actually produced electricity. The rest produced only profits and speculative opportunities. And the Insull empire was only one of *twelve* holding companies that owned 75 percent of all the utility operating plants in the country.

All these manipulative activities helped to pave the way for the Depression. When the stock market finally crashed, it brought down with it an immense flimsy structure of credit. Individual investors who had borrowed to the hilt to buy securities had their stock sold out from under them to meet their indebtedness to brokers. Banks and financial institutions, loaded with dubious foreign bonds, were suddenly insolvent. Meanwhile, to compound the terrible panic, the monetary authorities pursued policies that unwittingly weakened the banking system still further.[4]

WEAKNESS
ON THE FARM

In the vulnerability of an economy bound up with a rickety and speculative financial superstructure we have located one reason for the Great Depression—or, more specifically, one reason why the Wall Street Crash pulled down with it so much business activity. But we have far from exhausted the explanations for the Depression itself. For the Crash, after all,

[3] Arthur Schlesinger, Jr., *The Crisis of the Old Order* (Boston: Houghton Mifflin, 1957), pp. 249–50.

* Many of these deals were unsavory to the point of malfeasance. The son of the President of Peru, for instance, was paid $450,000 by the securities affiliate of the National City Bank for his services in connection with a $50 million bond issue which the bank's affiliate then floated for Peru. The President's son's "services" consisted almost entirely of an agreement not to block the deal. Eventually, of course, the bonds went into default. (John K. Galbraith, *The Great Crash, 1929*. Boston: Houghton Mifflin, 1955, p. 186.)

[4] See Milton Friedman and Anna Schwartz, *The Great Contraction* (Princeton, N.J.: Princeton University Press, 1965).

might have been no worse than many previous speculative disasters. Why was it protracted into a chronic and deep-rooted ailment?

The question turns our attention away from the spectacular misfortunes of 1929 to a consideration of the state of the economy as a whole in the years preceding the collapse. We have already characterized the first quarter of the twentieth century as a time of unprecedented expansion. Could it be, however, that behind the overall figures of rising output and incomes there were concealed pockets of trouble?

There was no question that one such worrisome sector existed. This was the farm sector, especially the all-important grains. All through the 1920s, the farmer was the "sick man" of the American economy. Each year saw more farmers going into tenantry, until by 1929 four out of ten farmers in the nation were no longer independent operators. Each year the farmer seemed to fall further behind the city dweller in terms of relative well-being. In 1910 the income per worker on the farm had been not quite 40 percent of the nonfarm worker; by 1930, it was just under 30 percent.

Part of this trouble on the farm, without question, stemmed from the difficult heritage of the past. Beset now by drought, now by the exploitation of powerful railroad and storage combines, now by his own penchant for land speculation, the farmer was proverbially an ailing member of the economy. In addition, the American farmers had been traditionally careless of the earth, indifferent to the technology of agriculture. Looking at the average individual farmer, one would have said that he was poor because he was unproductive. Between 1910 and 1920, for instance, while nonfarm output per worker rose by nearly 20 percent, output per farm worker actually fell. Between 1920 and 1930, farm productivity improved somewhat, but not nearly so fast as productivity off the farm. For the great majority of the nation's agricultural producers the trouble appeared to be that they could not grow or raise enough to make a decent living.

If we had looked at farming as a whole, however, a very different answer would have suggested itself. Suppose that farm productivity *had* kept pace with that of the nation. Would farm income as a whole have risen? The answer is disconcerting. The *demand* for farm products was quite unlike that for manufactured products generally. In the manufacturing sector, when productivity rose and costs accordingly fell, the cheaper prices of manufactured goods attracted vast new markets, as with the Ford car. Not so with farm products, however. When food prices fell, people did not tend to increase their actual consumption very greatly. Increases in over-all farm output resulted in much lower prices but not in larger cash receipts for the farmer. Faced with what is called an *inelastic demand*—a demand that does not respond in proportion to price changes, sellers are *worse* off than they were before a flood of output.

That is very much what happened during the 1920s. From 1915 to 1920, the farmer prospered because World War I greatly increased the demand for his product. Prices for farm output rose, and his cash receipts rose as well; in fact, they more than doubled. But when European farms resumed their output following the war, the American farmers' crops simply glutted the market. Although prices fell precipitously (40 percent in the single year 1920-1921), the purchases of farm products did not respond in anything like equal measure. As a result, the cash receipts of the farmer toppled almost as fast as prices. Meanwhile, his taxes were up by some 70 percent, and his mortgage payments and his cost of living in general had approximately doubled. Matters improved somewhat during the later 1920s but not enough to bring the crop farmers back to substantial prosperity.

There is a lesson here in economics as well as history. Had farmers constituted an oligopolistic market, the decline in farm income might have been limited. A few producers, facing an inelastic demand for their products, can see the sense in mutually curtailing output. Rather than flooding a market which does not want their product, they can agree, tacitly or otherwise, to hold back production to some amount which the market will absorb at a reasonable price. But the individual farmer is about as far from an oligopolist as one can imagine. When the price for his crop falls, it gains the individual farmer nothing to decrease his output. On the contrary, in his highly competitive situation, the best that he can do is to rush to sell as much as he can before things get worse—thereby unwittingly *making* things worse.

As its core, the trouble with the farm sector was that the market mechanism in this particular case did not yield a satisfactory result.* That might not have been so serious, had it not been for another development: while agriculture remained static and stagnant, the manufacturing sector was growing by leaps and bounds. Yet its growth was undermined because a fifth of the nation—the agricultural sector—was unable to match the growing volume of production with a growing volume of purchasing power. As the farmers' buying power lagged, it pulled down the demand for tractors, cars, gasoline and electric motors, and manufactured consumers' goods, generally. Weakness on the farm was thus symptomatic of a weakness throughout the economy, a failure of purchasing power across the whole lower stratum of the nation to keep up with the tempo of national industrial production.

WEAKNESS IN THE FACTORY

Most economists of the 1920s, as we have said, would have agreed that there was a source of potential trouble on the farm. Had we suggested that there might be another potential breeding ground for trouble in the factory

---

* In theory, we will remember (pp. 71-73) there was a cure for situations in which the producers of one commodity were undercompensated relative to other pursuits: producers would leave the undercompensated field for more lucrative occupations. Indeed, the American farmer tried this cure. It has been estimated that 20 farmers left the soil to seek city work for every urban worker who came to the land. Unfortunately, the cure did not work fast enough. While the agricultural sector steadily diminished in relative size, it could not shrink its absolute numbers significantly. From 1910 to 1930 approximately 10 million farmers remained "locked" on the farm, perhaps half of them barely contributing to national output beyond their own meager livelihoods.

or the mine, however, few would have given their assent. Most people's eyes, during the 1920s, were fixed on only one aspect of the industrial sector—production—and here there was surely little reason for complaint.

Yet had scrutiny penetrated a bit deeper, very serious signs might well have been spotted in this presumably most buoyant section of the economy. For while production was steadily rising, *employment* was not. In manufacturing, for example, physical output in 1929 was up 49 percent over 1920, while employment was precisely unchanged. In mining, output was up 43 percent, while employment had shrunk some 12 percent. In transportation and in the utility industry again output was higher—slightly in transportation, spectacularly in utility's electrical output—and again employment had actually declined.

Overall employment had not, of course, declined. It was significantly up in construction, in trade and finance, in the service industries, and in government. But note that all these employment-absorbing industries were characterized by one common denominator: they were all relatively devoid of technological advance. Or to put it the other way around, all the employment-static or declining industries were singularly characterized by rapid technological advance. In other words, pressing against the overall upward tendency of the economy was an undertow of *technological displacement.*

Heretofore in our frequent consideration of technology, we have never stopped to inquire what its effects might be on employment. Rather, we have implicitly assumed those effects to be positive, as we dwelt on the capacity of industrial technology to increase output. Yet it is not difficult to see that technology need not always be favorable for employment. When a new invention creates a new industry, such as the automobile, it is clear that its employment-creating effect can be enormous. Yet, even in such an instance there is an undertow, albeit a small one, as the growing automobile industry crowds out the old carriage industry. When we turn to inventions that do not create new *demands* but merely make an established industry more productive, it is clear that the initial impact of technical change can generate serious unemployment.

Technologically displaced workers may be reabsorbed eventually, particularly if the economy is growing rapidly. We will return to this problem later on in the chapter, but now we want to examine still further the effect of rapid technological change in the "displacing industries" themselves, during the 1920s. And here we see an interesting fact. As production soared and employment sagged, the output per man-hour rose rapidly; in fact, between 1920 and 1929 it increased over 30 percent in transportation, over 40 percent in mining, and over 60 percent in manufacturing.* This much larger flow of production per hour meant that wages *could have* been raised substantially or prices cut sharply. But this is not what we find to have been the case. Only on the unionized railroads did wage rates rise (by about 5 percent). In mining, hourly earnings fell by nearly 20 percent, and in

* These productivity indexes cannot be computed from our previous output and employment figures, since weekly hours changed. For the original figures, see *Historical Statistics,* Series W.

manufacturing they remained steady. Since the hours of work per week were also declining, the average annual earnings of employees in these industries were far from keeping pace with the rise in their productivity. In mining, average yearly earnings fell from $1,700 to $1,481. In transportation and manufacturing, yearly earnings fell from 1920 through 1922 and did not regain 1920 levels until 1928 and 1929.

Thus the gains from higher productivity were not passed along to the industrial worker in terms of higher wages. Were they passed along via lower prices? Yes, to some extent. The overall cost of living between 1920 and 1929 fell by about 15 percent. Part of this reduction, as we have seen, was due to falling food prices. Nonfood goods fell sharply in price from 1920 postwar peaks to 1921; thereafter they, too, declined about about 15 percent up to 1929, but the fall was not enough to distribute all the gains from industrial technology. How do we know this? Because the *profits* of large manufacturing corporations soared between 1920 and 1929. From 1916 through 1925, profits for these companies had averaged around $730-odd million a year; from 1926 through 1929, they averaged $1,400 million. Indeed, in the year 1929, profits were triple those of 1920.[5]

MALDISTRIBUTION OF INCOME

Now we can generalize from what we have just discovered about the trend of wages and profits, to state one further reason for the sudden weakness which overcame the economy, beginning in 1929. Income was distributed in such a way as to make the system vulnerable to economic shocks.

This does *not* mean that somehow the American economy was failing to generate "enough" purchasing power to buy its own output. An economy always creates enough *potential* buying power to purchase what it has produced.

There can, however, be a very serious *maldistribution* of the income payments arising from production. For not all the proceeds arising from production may be placed in the hands of people who will *exercise* their purchasing power. Incomes paid out to the lower-paid strata of the labor force do, indeed, return to the stream of purchasing power, for the working-man tends to spend his wages quickly. But incomes which take the form of profits, or business accruals, or as very high individual compensations may not quickly turn over as purchasing power. Profits or high incomes may be saved. They may eventually return to the great stream of purchasing demand, but income which is saved does not "automatically" return via the route of consumption expenditure. Instead, it must find a different route—the route of investment, of capital-building.

Returning to the economy in 1929, we can now see as well what was perhaps the deepest-seated reason for its vulnerability: the fact that its income payments were not going in sufficient volume to those who would

[5] *Historical Statistics,* V, 236.

surely spend them. We have already understood why farmers and working men, who were indeed possessed of a "limitless" desire to consume, were pinched in their *ability* to buy. Now we must complete the picture by seeing how the failure to distribute the gains of productivity to the lower-income groups swelled the incomes of those who were potential *non*spenders.

TABLE 8 • 1

TOP INCOMES

PERCENTAGE SHARES OF TOTAL INCOME RECEIVED BY THE TOP 1 PERCENT AND TOP 5 PERCENT OF TOTAL POPULATION *		
Year	Top 1 percent	Top 5 percent
1919	12.2	24.3
1923	13.1	27.1
1929	18.9	33.5

* The table shows the "disposable income variant": i.e., income after payment of taxes and receipt of capital gains.
Source: *Historical Statistics*, G135-6.

What we see here is an extraordinary, and steadily worsening, concentration of incomes. By 1929, the 15,000 families or individuals at the apex of the national pyramid, with incomes of $100,000 or more each, probably received as much income as 5 to 6 million families at the bottom of the pyramid. And more was involved here than just a matter of moral equity. It meant that the prosperity of the Twenties—and for the majority of the nation it *was* a prosperity of hitherto unequalled extent—in fact covered over an economic situation of grave potential weakness. For *if* the nation's on-going momentum should be checked, in this lopsided distribution of purchasing power lay a serious problem. So long as the high profits and salaries and dividends continued to be returned to the income stream, all was well. But what if they should not be?

CRITICAL ROLE OF CAPITAL FORMATION

The question brings us to a critical relationship that has gradually been emerging throughout these pages as the central dynamic process in determining the level of activity in a market society. The relationship is that between the savings that a society desires to make on the one hand, and its opportunities for profitable investment, on the other. We cannot explain the main events of the Great Depression unless we have a general grasp of the central economic problem of a market society.

Actually we have already understood half the saving-investment relationship. In our chapter on the industrial revolution we saw that saving was an indispensable prerequisite for capital formation. Now we must complete our understanding by adding the next step in the growth process. *Unless we make large enough capital expenditures to absorb our saving, we will not be able to keep the economy moving forward.* If saving is essential for investment, investment is essential for prosperity.

Indeed, because investment expenditure is the way we return savings to the income flow, we can see that the rate at which we add to our stock of capital equipment will have a deep effect on our over-all economic well-being. When spending for investment is sluggish, bad times are upon us. When spending for capital formation quickens, good times are again at hand. In other words, *the rate of capital formation is really the key to prosperity or recession.*

That does not yet tell us why the rate of capital expenditure should fluctuate. But a moment's reflection makes the answer clear enough. Spending for consumption purposes tends to be a reliable and steady process. Most consumer goods are quickly used up and must be replaced. The desire to maintain a given standard of living is not subject to sudden shifts or changes. As consumers, we are all to a considerable extent creatures of habit.

Not so with capital expenditures. Unlike consumer goods, most capital goods are durable and their replacement can therefore easily be postponed. Again in contrast to consumer goods, capital goods are not bought out of habit or for personal enjoyment. They are bought only because they are expected to yield a *profit* when put to use. We commonly hear it said that a new store, a new machine, or an additional stock of inventory must "pay for itself." And so it must. New investment increases output and that additional output must have a profitable sale. If for any reason a profit is not anticipated, the investment will not be made.

This enables us to see that the *expectation* of profit (which may be greater or less than profits actually being realized at the moment) plays a crucial role in the rate of capital formation. But why—and this is the last and obviously the key question—should a profit not be expected from a new investment good?

The answers all bring us back to our point of departure in the early 1930s. One answer may be that a speculative collapse, such as the Great Crash, destroys "confidence" or impairs financial integrity and leads to a period of retrenchment while financial affairs are put in order. Another reason may be that costs shoot up and monetary troubles impede the boom: the banks may become loaned up and money for new capital projects may suddenly become "tight" and dear. Still another reason may be that consumption expenditures are sluggish, owing perhaps to a maldistribution of income, such as that of the late 1920s, thereby discouraging plant expansion. Or the rate of population growth or of family formation may decline, bringing a slowdown in the demand for housing. Or the boom may simply die a "natural death"—that is, the wave of technological advance on which it rode may peter out, the great investments needed to build up a tremendous industry may be completed, and no second wave of equal capital-attracting magnitude may immediately rise to take its place.

Many of these reasons, as we have seen, served to bring capital formation to a halt in the Great Depression. The Crash itself, with its terrible blow to confidence and to the solvency of banks and holding companies, the weakness of the agricultural sector, the drag of technological displacement, and the maldistribution of income, all combined to bring about a virtual cessation of economic growth. The figures in Table 8-2 for gross private domestic investment—the proper nomenclature for private capital formation—tell their own grim story.

TABLE 8•2

GROSS PRIVATE DOMESTIC INVESTMENT

	BILLIONS OF CURRENT DOLLARS			
Year	Residential nonfarm construction	Other construction	Producers' durable equipment	Change in inventories
1929	$3.6	$5.1	$5.9	$+1.7
1932	.6	1.2	1.6	−2.6

Thus the Great Depression can be characterized essentially as a tremendous and long-lasting collapse in the rate of capital formation. In housing, in manufacturing plant and equipment, in commercial building, in the accumulation of inventories, a paralysis afflicted the economy. Between 1929 and 1933 investment goods output shrank by 88 percent in real terms—that is, after allowances for price changes. Although the capital goods industries employed only one-tenth of the total labor force in 1929, by 1933 one-third of total unemployment had been caused by the shrinkage of these critical industries.

Here is a major key to the Depression. But the trouble did not end there. When savings are not returned to active purchasing power because of inadequate investment, the fall in buying begins to spread. Let us say that a steelworker is laid off because of the slump in building. He will certainly pare his family's budget to the bone. But this in turn will create a further loss in income for the businesses where the steelworker's family ordinarily spent its income. Others will lose their jobs or have their wages reduced. In this way a kind of snowball effect, or to use the proper term, a *multiplier effect,* is brought about.

This helps us understand the mechanism of the Great Depression. As capital expenditures fell during the early 1930s, they pulled down consumption expenditures with them; and because of the multiplier effect, by an even larger amount than the fall in investment. From 1929 to 1933, consumption declined from $79 to $49 billion, nearly twice as large a drop as the absolute fall in investment. And the fall of consumption, in turn, pulled down still further the flow of capital expenditures.

To be sure, the process works the other way around, as well. When capital expenditures again begin to mount, consumption expenditures typically climb by an even larger amount. For example, President Truman pointed out in a radio address in 1949 that $1 billion of new public expenditures, which gave initial income to some 315,000 people, also added to the incomes of some 700,000 more. In expansion as well as in contraction, there is a typical *cumulative* pattern to economic activity, as success breeds further success, and failure breeds further failure.

Our brief excursion into the theory of economic fluctuations comes to an end at this point. But the understanding we have gained enables us to see the Great Depression not only as an historical phenomenon, but as an instance of a more endemic problem of a market society. We have seen how that society paved the way for the Great Depression by its malfunctions in the 1920s. Now let us follow the struggles of the economy in the 1930s as it sought to escape from the deepest and most destructive depression it had ever known.

KEY CONCEPTS AND KEY WORDS

Growth

1. The outstanding economic fact of the hundred years prior to 1929 was the long trend of *economic growth*—a trend that doubled per capita incomes in the United States roughly every forty years and that brought U.S. prosperity in 1929 to unprecedented heights.

Depression

2. The long trend of growth came to a disastrous stop—for nearly a decade—with the advent of the *Great Depression.* The causes of the Depression were many:

Credit structure

   • A *speculative and shaky credit structure* that was demolished by the *stock market crash* of 1929, and by *inept monetary policy.*

Technological unemployment

   • A *steady deterioration of farm purchasing power* aggravated by the inelastic demand for farm products.

   • A considerable undertow of *technological unemployment.*

Distribution of income

   • A bad and *worsening distribution of income.*

Capital formation

3. The joint effect of these causes was a tremendous *collapse in capital formation.* Between 1929 and 1933 investment (in real terms) declined by 88 percent.

National income

4. A *fall in investment is a prime cause of a fall in national income,* because investment is the route over which savings return to the flow of national spending. When investment fails to return savings, recession begins.

5. Investment is thus a critical element in determining the level of prosperity. It is, however, a highly volatile element, since *investment spending depends on expected profits.* When expectations are not optimistic, new capital will not be built.

6. A relatively small decline in investment spending can spread through the economy. This is called the *multiplier effect.*

Q U E S T I O N S

1. Discuss the causes of the Great Depression in terms of what you know about the economy today. Do you think another Great Depression is possible? Another stock market crash?

2. Among the families you know, how many work for companies that provide goods or services for capital formation—that is, for investment purposes rather than for consumption?

3. Suppose that you were a businessman who intended to build a plant to turn out a promising new item—say, a pencil that would last twice as long as present kinds. What sorts of developments might discourage you from making this investment? How much would your final decision hinge on what you anticipated for the future, compared with what you knew to be the situation today?

4. How can the money you put into a savings bank get back into someone's hands as his income? The money you put into a newly-formed business? The money you put into insurance?

5. If your income (or your parents') was suddenly reduced to half, by how much would your expenditures fall? What sorts of businesses would be hit by your reduced spending? Would they in turn curtail their expenditures?

6. Why is investment so critical in determining the level of prosperity?

"This nation asks for action, and action now.... We must act and act quickly."

The words are from the inaugural address of the incoming President Franklin Delano Roosevelt. It is hard today to reconstruct the urgency, the sense of desperation, against which the words were addressed on March 4, 1933. A few hours before the actual inauguration ceremony, every bank in America had locked its doors. The monetary system was at the point of collapse. Nearly thirteen million Americans were without work. A veterans' march on Washington, 15,000 strong, in the previous year had been dispersed with tear gas, tanks, and bayonets. On the farms, mortgage-lifting parties, at which a noose was tactfully displayed, served as powerful deterrents to any representatives of insurance companies or banks who might be thinking of bidding in foreclosed land. Meanwhile, a parade of business leaders before the Senate Finance Committee had produced a depressing sense of impotence. Said the president of a great railroad: "The only way to beat the depression is to hit the bottom and then slowly build up." "I have no solution," said the president of one of New York's biggest banks. "I have no remedy in mind," testified the president of U.S. Steel. "Above all we must balance the budget," urged a long string of experts.[1] The crisis was a deep and genuine one; it is doubtful if the United States has ever stood closer to economic collapse and social violence.

THE NEW DEAL

The new President's response was immediate and vigorous: in the three months after Roosevelt's inauguration, writes Arthur Schlesinger, "Congress and the country were subjected to a presidential barrage of ideas and programs unlike anything known to American history." This was the famous Hundred Days of the New Deal—the days in which, half by design, half by accident, the foundation was laid for a new pattern of government

[1] Arthur Schlesinger, Jr., *The Crisis of the Old Order* (Boston: Houghton Mifflin, 1957), pp. 457–58.

relationship to the private economy, a pattern that was to spell a major change in the organization of American capitalism.

We begin to trace its general outline in the main measures of the Hundred Days. In all, some fifteen major bills were passed: the Emergency Banking Act, which reopened the banks under what amounted to government supervision; the establishment of the Civilian Conservation Corps to absorb at least some of the young unemployed; the Federal Emergency Relief Act to supplement the exhausted relief facilities of states and cities; the Emergency Farm Mortgage Act, which loaned four times as much to farmers in seven months as all federal loans in the previous four years; the Tennessee Valley Authority Act, setting up TVA, a wholly new venture into government enterprise; the Glass-Steagall Banking Act, divorcing commercial banks from their stock-and-bond floating activities and guaranteeing bank deposits; the first of the Securities Acts aimed at curbing stock speculation and reckless corporate pyramiding.

The Hundred Days only inaugurated the New Deal; it did not by any means complete it. Social Security, housing legislation, the National Recovery Act, the dissolution of public utility holding companies, the establishment of a Federal Housing Authority were yet to be passed. So was the Wagner Act. Indeed, it would not be until 1938 that the New Deal would be "completed" with the passage of the Fair Labor Standard Acts, establishing minimum wages and maximum hours and banning child employment for interstate commerce.

It would take us beyond the boundaries of our survey of general economic history to investigate the content of each of these important pieces of legislation, but we can gain an over-all view of the New Deal by summarizing its achievements against the backdrop of the problems and issues of economic history that we have already encountered. Then we can see that the New Deal is important as marking a genuine change in the development of the market economy itself. With its advent we begin to trace the evolution of a new kind of capitalism, different in significant ways from that which we have heretofore studied. We must understand the nature of this evolution if we are to bring our survey of general economic history to its contemporary terminus in our own society.

One general problem that confronted the New Deal, we have noted earlier in this chapter. It was the severe misfunction of the market mechanism in agriculture.

The problem, we will remember, arose in large part from two causes: the nature of the inelastic demand for farm products, and the highly competitive, "atomistic" structure of the agricultural market itself. The New Deal could not alter the first cause, the inelasticity of demand, for this arose from the nature of the consumers' desire for food. But it could change the condition of supply which hurled itself, self-destructively, against an unyielding demand. Hence, one of the earliest pieces of New Deal legislation—the Agricultural Adjustment Act—sought to establish machinery by which farmers, as a group, could accomplish what they could not as competitive individuals: curtailment of output.

The curtailment was sought by offering payments to farmers who agreed to cut back their acreage or in other ways hold down their output. In the first year of the act, there was no time to cut back acreage, so that every fourth row of growing cotton had to be plowed under, and six million pigs were slaughtered. In a nation still hungry and ill-clad, such a spectacle of waste aroused sardonic and bitter comment. And yet, if the program reflected an appalling inability of a society to handle its distribution problem, its attack on over-production was not without results. In both 1934 and 1935 more than thirty million acres were taken out of production in return for government payments of $1.1 billion. Farm prices rose as a result. Wheat, which had slumped to 38¢ a bushel in 1932, rose to $1.02 in 1936. Cotton doubled in price, hog prices tripled, and the net income of the American farmer climbed from the fearful low of $2.5 billion in 1932 to $5 billion in 1936.

We need not here retrace the many later developments in the agricultural programs of the New Deal and its successors. Suffice it rather to make the point that the *central idea* of the AAA has remained. Farmers' incomes no longer reflect the extreme fluctuations characteristic of an inelastic demand, but are cushioned by government payments earned by adhering to some form of crop limitation. The uncontrolled competitive struggle to market crops has given way to a continuing effort to achieve a balance between supply and demand by limiting supply itself.

Has the idea worked well? It might have, but for one thing. Belatedly, technology caught up with American agriculture. Starting in the years before World War II and continuing thereafter with accelerating effect, productivity on the farm began to soar—in fact, it rose faster than productivity in industry. Hence, despite the limitation of *acreage*, the actual output of *crops* increased steadily: between 1940 and the late 1960s, for instance, the amount of harvested acreage declined by 15 percent, but the yield per acre increased by *more than 70 percent.* The result was a flood of output, huge quantities of which had to be purchased and stored by the government under its support programs. Only the gradual distribution of these surpluses to the underdeveloped lands during the 1960s prevented the surplus problem from becoming a permanent national embarrassment.*

At best, the attempt to solve the farm problem has been but a partial success. It has not, for instance, succeeded in much improving the economic status of the million-and-a-half least productive small farmers, for these farmers are not able to raise enough crops to benefit substantially from crop supports. Nor has it succeeded in bringing about a sufficient reduction in farm output, so that the normal interplay of supply and demand would lift crop prices above their support levels and relieve the government of its purchase obligations.

Yet the attempt to improve the farm picture must not be brushed aside as ineffective. Without doubt, agriculture, as an income-producing activity, has benefited substantially—especially for the million-odd successful farmers who produce 90 percent of our marketed farm products. Between 1940 and 1964 the farm operator families enjoying the use of electricity increased from 33 percent to more than 95 percent; telephones increased from 25 percent to 76 percent; refrigerators from 15 percent to more than 90 percent. In the West, Midwest, and Northeast, the independent farm operator is today, as he was never before, at a close parity to the urban middle class in terms of living standards.

Our primary interest, however, is not to assess the relative success or failure of the farm programs from early New Deal days to the present. It is, rather, to note that all of the programs spelled a fundamental change in the role of the government in a market society. *The essence of that change was that the government sought to alter the structure of certain markets to allow the competitive process to produce socially acceptable results.*

For it was not only in the agricultural sector that the government tried to ameliorate the functioning of the competitive process. In the industrial sector, as well, a new policy of active intervention tried to bring about a better working of the economic mechanism.

In industry as in agriculture, during the first years of acute economic distress, intervention mainly took the form of an attempt to limit supply. Under the provisions of the National Industrial Recovery Act (NIRA) passed in 1933, business was permitted to make sweeping price-and-production agreements (in return for wage agreements designed to better the

---

* Actually, technology had been catching up with—and creating problems for—the farmer for a long time. One of the reasons for the overproduction of the 1920s was that we were steadily cutting back on the acreage needed to sustain horses and mules, as tractors came into general use. Before World War I, we used to devote over a quarter of our cropland to sustaining draft animals. After 1940, this fell to just over 10 percent. Much of the land not needed for animals went into production for the market, thereby adding its load of straw to the camel's back. I am indebted to Professor Eldon Weeks for this point.

incomes of the poorest paid). In other words, recovery was aimed at by legalizing the partial oligopolization of business.

The NIRA was greeted with great enthusiasm, and nearly 800 industrial "codes" were elaborated under it. But as the demoralized markets of the early 1930s regained some degree of orderliness, a new source of complaint arose. Smaller producers within many industries claimed that the codes favored the large producer. By the time the experiment was declared unconstitutional by the Supreme Court in 1935, it had already become apparent that the problem was not too much competition, but too little.

There arose a radical shift in policy signaled by the vigorous prosecution of the antitrust laws, a development we traced in Chapter 7. Yet, although the angle of attack had changed completely, the objective was much the same: *to make the market work.*

To what extent can the government make markets work? The answer, as we have seen, is far from clear-cut. Against the powerful forces of oligopoly on the one hand, and the self-defeating competition of "atomistic" industries on the other, the market-shaping powers of government may well prove to be inadequate. But in the formulation of the aim itself is evidence of a profoundly important change in the philosophy of the market society. No longer does laissez faire constitute the ideal relationship between government and economy. *Slowly there has arisen the conception of active public intervention to insure the orderly operation of the system.*

COUNTERING THE DEPRESSION

But the market system had broken down in a much more important way than was revealed in the farm glut or even in the troubles of the manufacturing sector. Its real collapse in the 1930s was its inability to solve the basic production problem itself—its inability to put together human beings, capital, and land, in order to produce a satisfactory level of output for the nation.

It is curious that the Roosevelt administration had little clear idea of how to remedy this situation when it first took office. Neither, as we have seen, did the business community. Indeed, for nearly everyone, economists included, the only "remedy" for the Depression was thought to be a balanced budget for the government.

Yet there were emergencies to be faced that could not be deferred, even if they unbalanced the budget. Many of the unemployed were literally at the brink of starvation, and the resources of private, state, and local charities were in most instances exhausted. President Roosevelt, unlike his predecessor, did not believe that the receipt of federal relief would "demoralize" the unemployed any more than the receipt of federal loans from the Reconstruction Finance Corporation had "demoralized" business. By May of the inaugural year, a relief organization had been established; and a year later, nearly one out of every seven Americans was receiving relief. In nine states, one out of five families—in one state one out of three families—was dependent on public support. Not that relief did much more than keep these unfortunate families from starvation—the average grant per family was less than $25 per month—but it did provide an economic floor, no matter how rickety.

The immediate aims of relief were humanitarian. Shortly, however, they were followed by thoughts of the *useful* possibilities of relief expenditures. Soon the great bulk of relief spending was being paid for public works of various sorts: schools, roads, parks, hospitals, slum clearance—and even federal art, theater, and writing projects.

As the public-works program grew, however, the finances of the federal government took a turn for the worse, until, by the mid-1930s, it was clear that something like a chronic deficit of $2 to $3 billion a year had been achieved. Each year the government spent more than it took in through taxes—not only for relief, but for conservation, farm subsidies, veterans' bonuses, public housing, aid to the states. To meet its bills it borrowed the necessary money from the public through the sale of government bonds to private individuals, to corporations, and to the commercial banks. Obviously, as the total amount of bonds outstanding grew each year, so did the total debt of the nation. In 1929, the national debt totaled $16.9 billion. By 1935 it had risen to $28.7 billion, and each year it steadily rose: to $36 billion in 1937, to $40 billion in 1939, to $42 billion in 1940.

At first the heavy spending of the federal government was greeted with wary acceptance by the business and banking communities as a necessary temporary expedient. Before long, however, even within the administration itself, the mounting deficit was regarded with considerable misgivings. The recurrent excess of government expenditure over tax receipts was thereupon apologized for as "pump priming"—as an injection of government fuel which would, so to speak, start up the stalled motor of private expenditures, making further injections unnecessary. Thus, a few billions of government spending, it was hoped, would set into motion an upward spiral of spending and job expansion by the business sector.

But the upward spiral did not materialize. After 1933, helped by government spending, *consumption* expenditures began to rise, but private capital expenditures lagged behind. Although they, too, improved after 1933, by 1938 they were still 40 percent below 1929.

Why did private investment fail to rise? The answer lies partly in the fact that the very government deficits that were supposed to cure the Depression only frightened business into a condition of economic paralysis that prolonged it. Coupled with the reform legislation of the New Deal, the new presence of government's large-scale economic activity caused business to lose its former "confidence." The businessman felt uncomfortable and ill-at-ease in a changing economic and political climate and was in no mood to plan ahead boldly for the future. The general outlook stressed caution rather than promise; cycles rather than growth; safety rather than gain. And then behind the psychological factors, real forces were also at work. A much slower rate of population growth in the 1930s depressed the important housing market. Even more serious, no major industry-creating technological breakthrough, comparable to the railway or the automobile, held sufficient promise of profitable growth to tempt private capital into a major capital-building boom of its own.

Thus, for many reasons, the new federal expenditures did not prime the pump. Private investment did not spontaneously rise to take over its traditional propulsive function, now "temporarily" carried out by the government. This did not mean, however, that the economic influence of government was therefore relegated to a minor role. On the contrary, the failure of pump priming—conceived as an emergency measure—caused a widening in the conception of the government's role. Government now began to be envisioned as a *permanent stabilizing and growth-promoting agency for the market economy as a whole.*

COMPENSATORY
GOVERNMENT
SPENDING

The idea was slow in taking form and did not, in fact, receive its full-dress exposition until the middle 1930s.* As is often the case with new ideas, it seemed at first complicated and difficult, and even among professional economists its basic concepts were the subject of murky discussion for a number of years. Yet in retrospect, it appears as a very simple argument.

The key to prosperity or depression, it had become increasingly evident, lay in the *total volume of expenditure* that a market society laid out for its goods and services. When that volume was high, employment and incomes were high; when it declined, output and employment declined as well. And what determined the volume of expenditure? As we have seen, the stream of consumption spending tended to be a passive factor, rising when individuals' incomes rose and diminishing when they fell. The volatile item, as both history and theory made clear, was the stream of capital expenditure.

From this starting point it is not difficult to take the next step. If lagging private capital expenditures were responsible for lagging employment and output, why could not the government step in to make up whatever deficiencies arose from private expenditure? There had always been, after all, a fairly regular flow of public expenditure, much of it for capital-creating purposes, such as roads or schools. Why could not this flow of public spending be deliberately enlarged when the occasion demanded, to maintain the needed total volume of expenditure? True, this required the government to borrow and spend and thereby increase its debt. But did not much private capital spending also result in corporate debts? And why

---

* The most influential book setting forth the concept—albeit, in highly technical terms—was John Maynard Keynes' *General Theory of Employment, Interest and Money* published in 1936. Few books have roused such controversy or left so permanent a mark.

could not the debt, itself, be handled as corporate debts which were never "paid off" in the aggregate but refunded, with new bond issues being sold to take the place of those coming due?

To the economists of the Roosevelt administration, the answers to these questions seemed plain enough. The government not only could, but should, use its spending powers as an economic instrumentality for securing full employment. By this, they did not have in mind a "radical" revision of capitalism. Rather, they envisaged the evolution of a new form of *guided* capitalism—a market society in which the all-important levels of employment and output would no longer be left to the vagaries of the market but would be protected against decline and stimulated toward growth by public action.

This was not how matters appeared to many members of the nation, however, and especially to the business community. They saw government spending as inherently "wasteful," and the mounting debt as evidence that we would spend ourselves into "bankruptcy." Beneath these arguments there lurked a deeper suspicion, a suspicion that government spending, whatever the protestations to the contrary, was the entering wedge for socialism or worse.

The controversy raged through 1940. But in a sense, it was an empty debate. At its peak, the annual deficit never touched $4 billion, and federal government purchases never contributed more than 6 percent to gross national product. Judged by the importance of government in the economy, probably no industrial nation in the world was *less* socialist than the United States. Yet, if the fears of the conservatives were hardly realistic, neither were the hopes of the liberals. For in the prevailing atmosphere of distrust, the remedy of government spending could never be more than half-heartedly applied. Deficit spending in the 1930s was a holding operation and not an operation of growth. By 1939, although conditions had improved considerably over the levels of 1932, there were still 9.5 million people—17 percent of the labor force—without work.

In the end, it was not theory that settled the history of compensatory government spending, but history that settled the theory. With the outbreak of World War II came a tremendous forced expansion in government outlays. Year by year, spending for war purposes rose, until in 1944 federal expenditures totaled just over $100 billion, and with this unprecedented rise in expenditure came an equally swift rise in GNP. By 1945, our gross national product had risen by 70 percent in real terms over 1939, and unemployment had dwindled to the vanishing point. The demonstration that public spending could indeed impel the economy forward—indeed, could lift it beyond all previously imagined bounds—was unmistakable. So was the fact that a government could easily carry an enormously much larger debt, a debt that now towered over $250 billion, provided that its gross national product was also much larger.

And then, with the war had come a marked change in attitude both toward the government and to the economy in general. After four years of unprecedented effort, the American people looked to massive government action with a more accustomed eye; so, too, after four years of record output, they looked back upon the days of mass unemployment with a new feeling of shame. Perhaps most important of all, they looked ahead to the postwar period with considerable trepidation. Virtually every economist, contemplating the huge cutback in spending consequent upon a termination of hostilities, feared the rise of a vast new army of the unemployed. Even the most conservative opinion was uneasy at the political possibilities of such a return to the 1930s.

The upshot of the change in attitude was the passage of the Employment Act of 1946, one of the truly historic pieces of American economic legislation. The act recognized (although in carefully circumspect terms) that it was "the continuing policy and responsibility of the Federal Government ... to promote maximum employment, production, and purchasing power." It was, as we shall see, one thing to write such an act and another thing to implement it; but without question, the Employment Act marked the end of an era. The idea that the best thing the government could do to promote recovery was to do nothing, the belief that a balanced budget was in all cases the goal for government fiscal policy, and beyond that the trust in the blind forces of the market as inherently conducive to prosperity—all these once firmly held ideas of the past had been abandoned. The debate within capitalism was no longer whether or not government should undertake the responsibility for the overall functioning of the market system; only the specific means were questioned: how best to achieve that end.

AFTERMATH OF THE WAR: INFLATION

The war ended in 1945; within a year, federal spending dropped by $40 billion, and the nation waited tensely for the expected fall in employment, incomes, and prices.

Instead, it found itself confronting the least anticipated of all eventualities: a rousing inflationary boom. It is true that unemployment doubled, rising to two million, but this was still less than 4 percent of the labor force. Meanwhile, the number of people at work showed a steady rise: 54 million jobs in 1945; 57 million in 1946; 60 million in 1947; 63 million in 1950. Industrial production, after a brief postwar dip, was buoyant: by 1953 it would surpass its wartime peak with no sign of more than momentary turndown. Most striking of all was what happened to prices. Year by year, the cost of living rose: up a third between 1945 and 1948, up another 10 percent between 1948 and 1952, up still another 7 percent from then to 1957. In all, the purchasing power of the dollar declined by more than a third in the first twelve postwar years.

What was the cause of this totally unforeseen turn of events?

There was no one single cause, but several. To begin with, the end of the war found America in a situation of "classic" inflationary potential: too much money and too little goods. The too little goods was, of course, the result of four years of wartime shortage; the too much money was the result of having added $150 billion to liquid savings during those same years of high incomes and consumer scarcity. With the end of the war, Americans lost no time in entering upon a mammoth spending spree. In fact, it was this unexpected surge of consumption that was the main reason why the gloomy postwar economic forecasts were not fulfilled. Meanwhile, the nation's supply of money itself, in the form of bank deposits, was also high, owing to wartime financing. Banks and other credit institutions were all too happy to supply loans to consumers or corporations. Thus an enormous pressure of pent-up demand, financed out of past savings and current incomes, exerted its pressure on the price level.

A second reason for the inflationary boom was that spending was high in the nonconsumer areas. Government expenditures ceased falling in 1947 and sparked by rising state and local needs, began to increase again, augmented in 1950, when the Korean War added its fillip to federal expenditures. High exports and Marshall aid to Europe provided another stimulus. Perhaps more significant was that private capital expenditures proved themselves unexpectedly strong. Encouraged by the avalanche of consumer buying, by a host of new inventions and industries stemming from the war, by a new impetus toward research and development, the longest and steadiest period of capital accumulation in American history added its expenditures to the flow of purchasing power.

And then there was a third cause of the inflationary trend. In "pattern-setting" areas of industry, such as automobiles or steel, powerful unions succeeded in winning sharp wage increases. That, in itself, was not so unusual; but in these years of "easy money," there was nothing to prevent corporations from passing along the increases in terms of higher prices. What made matters still worse was that the wage increases (particularly in the mid-1950s) were often in excess of productivity increases, while the corporation price boosts (especially in the critical case of steel) were in excess of the wage boosts. Easy money, strong labor unions, and oligopolistic industry all combined to create inflationary pressure points at strategic locations of the economy.

This is by no means a full explanation of the inflationary problem from which America suffers. For that analysis, a student must study the formal subject of economics itself.

It is clear, however, that the nation faced a postwar situation very different from the one anticipated during the late 1930s by the fervent advocates of government spending. All through the 1950s it was the problem of inflation that occupied the authorities—and without much more success than had attended their efforts to curb mass unemployment twenty years earlier. Yet the confrontation with the problem of inflation was not without results; for out of the debate which it created, there emerged for the first time a general consensus on the nature of the mechanisms the government was entitled to use in seeking to affect the over-all operation of the system.

Once again, a full understanding of the mechanisms requires a study of technical economics. But it is not difficult to grasp the basic devices of control. They were three.

The first were *monetary controls*, mainly centered in the Federal Reserve banking system. By easing or tightening the reserve requirements which all banks had to maintain behind their deposits, the Federal Reserve was able to encourage or discourage lending, the source of much economic activity. In addition, by buying or selling government bonds, the Federal Reserve was able to make the whole banking system relatively flushed with funds, when these were needed, or relatively short of funds when money seemed in excess supply.

The second were *tax adjustments*. The pressure of consumer buying during the postwar boom served as a reminder of the fact that the largest fraction of the volume of total expenditure was always consumption spending. By raising or lowering taxes, particularly income taxes, the government could quickly increase or diminish this broad flow of purchasing power.

The third was *the federal budget*. By the 1950s, the great debate over the virtues of a balanced government budget had virtually come to an end. Among academic groups and in a widening circle of business leaders, the budget was recognized as a tool for regulating total national expenditure. In inflationary times, a budget surplus would serve to "mop up" part of the inflationary purchasing flow. In depressed times, a budget deficit (covered by borrowing) was a mechanism for generating a desired increase in that flow.

The idea of monetary controls was not new, but the general consensus on the use of taxes and budgets as deliberate instruments of economic policy to counter boom and recession *was* new. Once again, as in the case with government spending, it was not the force of theoretical argument which had won this historic agreement. Rather, it was the fact of historic change which had placed theory in a new light. For essentially what commended the new means of influence over the market system were profound changes in the structure of that system. Let us see what those changes were.

REDISTRIBUTION OF INCOME

In our concentration on the functional problems of the economy in its years of depression, war, and inflation, we have omitted one very significant development. This was a marked movement away from the extreme inequalities of reward which so vividly marked the capitalism of the past.

In part, this was brought about by a decline in unemployment, in part by aiding lower income groups through the support of trade unions, through the enactment of minimum wage floors, and through the passage of welfare legislation. The change was not entirely due to public policy, however. The occupational shifts which we noted at the commencement of our previous chapter also played a powerful role, as workers shifted out of low-paid agricultural and unskilled labor into the semiskilled and skilled categories of the factory.

However varied the causes, the results were striking.

TABLE 9 • 1

INCREASED
INCOME

PERCENT INCREASE IN PRE-TAX AVERAGE INCOME (1950 DOLLARS)	
	1935–36 to 1962
Lowest fifth	120%
Second fifth	136
Third fifth	131
Fourth fifth	115
Highest fifth	74
Top 5 percent	47
All groups	98

Source: *Statistical Abstract*, 1965, p. 340.

Note in Table 9-1 that the lowest and second fifths benefited almost twice as much as the highest fifth and almost three times as much as the top 5 percent. While the bottom was moving up, owing to a variety of causes, the top was coming down—in large part owing to the pressure of higher tax rates. For beginning with the New Deal, then receiving an even stronger impetus from the war, stiffer tax schedules and stricter enforcement had borne down upon the relative affluence of upper income groups. Table 9-2 gives us some idea of the change.

TABLE 9 • 2

RELATIVE
AFFLUENCE

PERCENT SHARES OF TOTAL INCOME RECEIVED BY TOP 1 PERCENT AND TOP 5 PERCENT OF TOTAL POPULATION				
	1929	1941	1946	1968
Top 1% (after tax)	19.1%	9.9%	7.7%	n.a.
Top 5% (before tax)	30.0	24.0	21.3	17.0

Source: *Historical Statistics*, G135, 105 (1929–1946). Figures for 1968 estimated from data, *Statistical Abstract*, 1970, p. 323.

What had happened was quite extraordinary. The share of income going to the top 1 percent had been cut by over 60 percent. That going to the top 5 percent had been cut by more than one third.

To be sure, we must exercise a good deal of caution in interpreting these figures. Without question they give evidence of a substantial improvement in the relative distribution of income in the United States since the lopsided days of the late 1920s. However we must not therefore leap to the conclusion that the existing distribution is "fair." Table 9-3 shows us the share of money income received by family units in 1960 and 1968. Note that the scales have begun to tilt slightly the other way and that the share of the top income group is beginning once again to rise faster than the bottom groups. Note as well that there has been virtually no change in the past eight to ten years; and that the top 10 percent of families get *thirty times* as much income as the bottom 10 percent.

TABLE 9•3

SHARE OF TOTAL INCOME BY FAMILY UNITS

Income rank	Percent of total income	
	1960	1968
Lowest tenth	1%	1%
Second tenth	3	3
Third tenth	5	4
Fourth tenth	7	6
Fifth tenth	8	8
Sixth tenth	9	9
Seventh tenth	11	11
Eighth tenth	13	13
Ninth tenth	16	15
Highest tenth	27	30

Source: *Statistical Abstract,* 1970, p. 323.

INCOME AND WEALTH

Finally, two last and very important cautions. The official statistics of income distribution do not take into account very large flows of personal receipts that are legally exempted from classification as "income," such as stock options and expense accounts. We do not know the extent to which such legal (not to mention many illegal) ways of "smuggling" income reduce the reliability of the figures, but it may be by a very substantial amount.

Second, the data on incomes do not tell us about the distribution of *wealth*—bank accounts, home ownership, and above all, stocks and bonds. There is little evidence that wealth ownership has become less concentrated in the United States in recent years. For instance, it is estimated that the top 1 percent of all "spending units" own at least 65 percent of all corporate stock and that the wealthiest one-tenth of 1 percent own 35 percent of it—and here too concentration may be increasing.[2]

These figures make it plain that we must exercise caution when we talk of the degree of change that history has brought. Yet, despite the remaining unfairness of income distribution, there is no doubt that a basic change has overtaken the economic profile of American society since the Great Depression. With all the misery that remains at the bottom of the nation and all the luxury at the top, what has emerged more and more clearly is a society in which "middle incomes" describes the facts and the psychology of the American people. In 1969 about 40 percent of all households received incomes of $10,000 or more before taxes, and 18 percent received over $15,000. If GNP grows at the rate of 4.3 percent for the next decade—a rate slightly higher than the historic trend, but by no means impossible of attainment—*40 percent of all families will be over the $15,000 mark (in terms of 1970 dollars) by 1980.*[3]

These present and projected realities go a long way in explaining the predominantly "middle-class" viewpoint of American society (and may help explain as well our indifference to the social neglect that penalizes those who are least fortunate in the competitive struggle for incomes). But in this chapter, where our main theme is the evolution of a new "guided" capitalism, it is important to stress that the *upward escalation of incomes has also provided the government with a new and powerful means of economic influence.* As Table 9-4 shows, the upward shift in the economic center of gravity of the nation has brought about a situation in which, for the first time, a change in income taxes can directly affect *mass* purchasing power.

TABLE 9•4

IMPACT OF
INDIVIDUAL
INCOME
TAXES

Year	Number of individual returns (millions)	Total income tax paid ($ billions)	Total income tax as % of total con- sumption	Income tax liability of median family ($)
1929	2.5	$ 1.0	1%	$ 17
1940	7.4	1.4	2	101(1941)
1968	73.4	76.6	14	1,044

Source: *Statistical Abstract*, 1970, p. 387, *Historical Statistics*, Series Y 292, 299, 303, 307.

[2] See F. Lundberg, *The Rich and the Super Rich* (New York: Lyle Stuart, 1968), pp. 15ff., and supporting citations.
[3] *Fortune* Magazine (February 1971), p. 80.

The redistribution of income thus provides us with an understanding of why tax policy has become such a potent new instrument of economic manipulation. An insight into the second of our new instruments—fiscal policy, or the use of the government's budget—is provided if we examine another structural alteration in the economy: the change in the relative size of the government contribution to gross national product. Table 9-5 gives us the magnitude of the change.

TABLE 9•5

GROWTH OF THE PUBLIC SECTOR (current dollars)

Year	GNP (billions)	Gov't. purchases of goods and services (billions)		All gov't. purchases as percent of GNP
		Federal	State & local	
1929	$104.4	$ 1.3	$ 7.2	8.1%
1940	100.6	6.2	7.9	14.0
1970	976.5	99.7	120.9	22.5

Source: *Historical Statistics,* Series F, 67, 81, 86; *Economic Indicators.*

It is clear from the table that a major shift has taken place. Whereas in 1929 less than one dollar in ten of national production owed its origin to government purchasing, today about one dollar in five of all goods and services produced is sold to some branch of the government.

What has accounted for this striking shift? Three-quarters of the rise in *federal* expenditures is due solely to the growth of the military subeconomy, whose economic significance remains very great. But a second look at the table reveals that the growth of the public sector is by no means entirely a matter of federal spending. State and local expenditures have also grown enormously. In fact, federal nonwar expenditures plus state and local expenditures amount to about double the fraction of GNP represented by these public expenditures in 1929.

What lies behind this rise in the public sector? The cause of the growth of the armaments economy is the Cold War—a problem we will examine in our final chapter. As for the growth of the nonwar public sector, this is a phenomenon we find in all industrialized countries. It stems in part from the increase in population that has steadily spurred the growth of huge urban complexes; in part from a widening government concern with education and welfare; in part from the omnipresent automobile with its necessary road systems and supervisory personnel. Perhaps ultimately the cause is the growing dependence of man on man, of which we spoke in Chapter 6—a dependence in turn traceable to the relentless entrance of a technology that both heightens the collective productivity of man and intensifies his helplessness as an individual.

But at this juncture we are not as interested in tracing the reasons for the rise of the public sector, as we are in bringing home its consequences. For in the evolution of a guided, rather than laissez-faire capitalism, the growth of public economic activity, whether for war or peace, brought a signal change to the economy. It has meant that today the government is in a position of such commanding economic strength that it cannot *avoid* influencing the trend of total expenditure, even by relatively modest changes in its budgetary balance. For example, a 10 percent fall in government receipts and a 10 percent rise in expenditures will add to total GNP expenditures an amount equal to one-and-a-half times all manufacturing investment; in 1929, a similar change in the budget position would have contributed new purchasing power equal to much less than one-half of all manufacturing investment.

Does the existence of these government "stabilizers" and the general consensus on the mechanisms of influence mean that economic fluctuations such as the Great Depression cannot recur?

It is certainly unlikely in the extreme that the terrible experience of the early 1930s will be repeated. Many of its causes, as we noted, were rooted in particular excesses of the times, and these, to a very large extent, have been corrected. The flimsiness of the credit structure, the vulnerability of the banks—and perhaps most important of all, the barrier of inadequate economic understanding—have all been removed or much improved. Although history teaches us the virtues of caution in announcements of this kind, it seems fair to state that we now understand, as we never did before, the economic policies required to avoid or cure severe economic depressions.

In this regard the Kennedy tax cut proposed in 1962 is an interesting example of the New Economics in action. There had been a mild recession in 1960 from which the nation had not fully recovered by mid-1962, and President Kennedy's advisers were much concerned about the mounting level of unemployment in the country at large. To cure this unemployment, all agreed, the economy's rate of growth would have to increase, and this in turn required a major economic stimulus. But where was the stimulus to come from? Relying on the New Economics, the President's advisers recommended that taxes be cut across the board, despite mounting federal expenditures, so that a "deficit" in the nation's budget would be *deliberately* incurred.

As was to be expected, voices of disaster were raised. "At the heart of our national finances," declared Representative Cannon, then Chairman of the House Appropriations Committee, "is a simple inescapable fact, easily grasped by anyone. It is that our government—any government—like individuals and families—cannot spend and continue to spend more than they take in without inviting disaster."

What Representative Cannon did not seem to grasp, however, was that the government was not proposing to spend more than it took in. It was proposing to spend more than it took in *in taxes, borrowing the rest from the nation's savings.* This was an operation that was, economically speaking, in no way different from the nation's business sector which in a normal year of growth took in, in sales, less than it spent for its running expenses plus its capital investments, and which regularly borrowed the difference.

Thus at its core the so-called New Economics proposed that the government be considered not as an individual "household," but as a full economic *sector,* no different from the business sector in its operation, except that it was subject to deliberate public control and could thus be used to help move the economy in a desired direction. This is a central aspect of modern economic policy.

After much debate, the controversial tax cut was finally passed in early 1964. Was it a success? As is often the case in economics, we cannot produce laboratory proof. Certainly the economy responded vigorously and unemployment fell after the tax cut. But by then other factors were also at work, including higher spending for the Vietnam war. Indeed, by the end of 1965, spending on Vietnam had already strained the economy to the point that the President's advisers recommended a tax *increase* to dampen inflationary pressures.

Hence we can only say that economists *think* the New Economics works. Perhaps more important, it is increasingly clear that business thinks so too and bases its plans on the assumption that government will no longer "let" depressions go unchecked. It is perhaps too early to be absolutely certain that the suspicions and misunderstandings of the 1930s have been overcome. Yet it seems likely that the graduates of the colleges and business schools who now play an important part in the direction of corporate affairs are not so likely to be panicked by government action to cure a slump as were their fathers thirty years ago. There is a hypothesis that should cheer the despairing instructor of economics!

REMAINING
PROBLEMS

This general reassurance should not lead us to the easy assumption that economic fluctuations of considerable severity and unemployment of uncomfortable magnitude are not still possibilities. The basic cause of instability in the market system remains; and so long as anticipated profit is the critical link between savings and investment, it will continue to remain. Irregular bursts of capital formation and recurrent downward revisions of profit anticipations are virtually inseparable from an economic system in which the process of technical change and its conversion into real capital are left to the unguided impulses of individual business firms.

Yet, we now possess powerful instruments of economic compensation against the *cumulative effects* of these shocks—protections we have never enjoyed (or understood) before. To be sure, the mere existence of these instruments does not guarantee that they will, in fact, be used. Lingering fears of an unbalanced budget may delay or even prevent the use of compensatory government expenditure. Then, too, nearly half our present total government expenditure (and 85 percent of our *federal* expenditure) goes for defense purposes. The effective use of a compensatory mechanism in a truly *peacetime* economy might be much more difficult than in an economy where a large defense sector offers a politically acceptable area for public spending. Finally, we must remember that the New Economics is designed to be an instrument of restraint as well as one of stimulus—that it is meant to be used against inflation as well as recession. Recently we have been discovering that to translate restraint into effective political action may be much more difficult than we had thought. The New Economics is no panacea against the old politics, if it calls for unpopular measures like raising taxes.

Nevertheless, there can be no doubting the change since the early days of the New Deal with which we began this chapter. However difficult to control or disconcerting to predict, something like a "guided" system has emerged. The great central problem of capitalism, which threatened the very existence of the system in the dark days of the 1930s, can be considered essentially solved.

Does that mean that capitalism is therefore secure—that its place in history will remain unchanged and unchallenged for many years? The panorama with which we began in Chapter 1 should be enough to make it clear that no such conclusion can be drawn. If the problem of deep depression has been more or less effectively diagnosed and strong remedies concocted, new problems of no less severity have risen to take its place. Social neglect, the stubborn continuance of poverty amid a growing general affluence, the growth of an arms subeconomy, the problem of pollution, the ghetto—to mention only some of the issues that agitate our times—are far from solved and pose dangers perhaps as grave as depression itself.

Are these problems inherent to capitalism? That central question is still unanswered. And for a few chapters it must remain hanging in midair, for we have yet to fill out our understanding of the market system with the experience of Europe and the communist nations and the underdeveloped world. Only after we have looked into the problems and prospects of the market system in those areas will we be able to tackle the question that forms the ultimate focus of our inquiry.

New Deal

1. *The New Deal* was a major effort to reverse the downward spiral of the Great Depression. A many-pronged attack, it sought both to correct the failures of the economy, and to strengthen its workings.

2. The New Deal *interfered with the structure of markets* to a greater extent than had been tried by an American government before. Not only agricultural, but many industrial markets were regulated in an effort to bring about an orderly economic recovery. Although many of these efforts failed or were declared unconstitutional, the heritage of the New Deal has been a new concept of *government intervention* and an effective end to the philosophy of laissez faire.

Pump-priming

3. The most important of the New Deal policies was the deliberate initiation of *government spending,* first for relief, then for public works, as a means of stimulating private investment—so-called priming the pump. Owing to the small scale of the public spending and the prevailing business attitude of fear and suspicion to government intervention, the pump priming did not work.

Compensatory government spending

4. Out of the New Deal experience evolved a new conception of how the economy operated, and of how government might counteract depression. The key was now recognized to be the *total volume of expenditure.* And the new conception urged that whenever private expenditure was insufficient to maintain full employment, the government should add *compensatory spending* of its own.

Employment Act of 1946

5. The war provided convincing evidence that public expenditure could indeed bring about a high level of employment and output. After the war, the *Employment Act of 1946* recognized the role of the government in promoting "maximum employment."

Fiscal policy

6. Postwar experience brought inflation, rather than the generally expected recession. But the period also saw the formulation of a general consensus on the tools of the *New Economics:*
   - *Monetary controls* to encourage or discourage private spending.
   - *Tax adjustments* to induce or to dampen consumer and business spending.

Monetary controls

Federal budget

   - The use of the *federal budget* as a balance wheel in the economy.

7. These new tools were made more workable by a considerable *redistribution of income* that had taken place and by *the enlargement of the public sector.*

Public sector

8. The New Economics is by no means a cure for all economic ills, but it does hold the promise of *greater economic stability* than in the past.

QUESTIONS

1. What do you think is the prevailing attitude of big businessmen to government today? Of little businessmen? Farmers? Students?

2. "Even if the Hoover administration had wanted to take a more active role in combatting the Depression, it would have been difficult in those times for it to do so." Why?

3. Do you consider inflation to be as dangerous a condition as depression?

4. The farm problem will always be difficult to solve as long as agriculture is a highly competitive industry, faced with an inelastic demand and with a technology that continuously increases productivity. Explain why.

5. Do you think that all government spending is wasteful? Some? All private spending? Some? How does one measure "waste"?

6. In what ways has history provided the testing ground for the theory of government spending? Was the war such a test? Was it conclusive? What would invalidate the theory that government spending can properly supplement private investment to cure a depression?

The challenge

to the

market system

In the last several chapters, we focused our narrative of economic history on the rise of modern capitalism in America. But our initial narrative is not yet complete. For the central subject of our early pages was not just the rise of American capitalism, but the emergence of the market system itself, and in describing its development in America we have by no means described it everywhere. That will be our task in this final section of our book. We must follow the fortunes of the market first in Europe and Russia, and then in the underdeveloped world. Then we will hazard a concluding generalization about the market system in the long evolution of economic society.

TRIALS OF
CAPITALISM
ABROAD

One thing is immediately apparent when we direct our eyes away from America to the continents of the East, West, and South. It is that the trajectory of economic evolution there has been utterly different from that in the United States. No doubt we recall that when we left the European scene in the early 1800s capitalism was fast becoming the dominant form of economic society. England was the very cradle of industrial capitalism itself; elsewhere on the Continent, if capitalism was not already established, it was clearly waiting in the wings for the last remnants of feudalism to disappear. Moreover, had we looked abroad from America at any time in the nineteenth century, our expectations would have been fully justified. By then, all of Europe was unquestionably capitalist in orientation. And not only Europe. By the end of the nineteenth century, capitalism had reached out to touch most of the other continents of the world. In Asia and Africa, the main European nations had established colonies or spheres of influence that projected the imprint of capitalism into these societies, many of which had barely awakened from an age-long slumber of ancient ways. In South America, as well, capitalism was clearly the main fertilizing influence. Even in reactionary Russia—the last of the great European powers to abolish the legal fetters of feudalism—by the early 1900s, capitalism had succeeded in creating a small but active nucleus from which further growth seemed assured.

Yet what do we find today? To our astonishment, the seemingly unopposed evolution of the world into a capitalist market system has not taken place. In Europe, its original birthplace, capitalism continues to be the dominant economic system; and yet we find that socialist parties either hold power or constitute the main opposition in England, France, Belgium, Netherlands, Italy, Sweden, Norway, Denmark, Germany, and Austria. In Russia, the nucleus of capitalism has been entirely swept away by a communist society. In the huge continents of East and South—in Asia and Africa and South America—we find that the original organizing impetus of capitalism has given way, in many of the most important nations, to a noncapitalist framework of economic organization. China is more communist than communist Russia. India proclaims herself a socialist state. So do Burma, Ceylon, Egypt, Guinea, Syria. Only in South America do we find socialism largely absent from the official ideologies of political economy; and even there, the examples of Cuba and the rumblings elsewhere hardly make it possible to anticipate the kind of capitalist development that we would have expected fifty years ago.

What happened outside America to abort the seemingly assured development of capitalism? A full answer to such a question would require much more than a book in itself, but we can begin to grasp the main picture of evolutionary trends if we follow, first, the factors that caused capitalism in Europe to take on a form different from that in America. From Europe it is not so long a jump, geographically or historically, to Russia; and from Russia we can turn with increased understanding to the so-called underdeveloped world.

What are the reasons behind the turn of events in Europe? They must be sought, to begin with, not in the economic tendencies of European capitalism but in the social and political background whence those tendencies emerged.

Certainly the social background was significantly different from that of America. In the New World, capitalism developed with a population that had, to a large degree, spiritually and physically shed the feudal encumbrances of the Old World; but in that Old World, many of the social

EUROPEAN CAPITALISM: FEUDAL HERITAGE AND NATIONAL RIVALRY

outlooks and habitudes of the past lingered on. An awareness of class position—and more than that, an explicit recognition of class hostility—was as conspicuous by its presence in Europe as by its absence in America. In Vienna, in 1847, writes one social historian:

At the top were the nobles who considered themselves the only group worth noticing. The human race starts with barons, said one of them. Then there were the big businessmen who wanted to buy their way into the human race; the little businessmen; the proud but poor intellectuals; the students who were still poorer and still prouder; and the workers who were poor and had always been very, very humble.[1]

The result was a totally different climate for the development of an economic society. Capitalism in America, building on a new and vigorous foundation, was, from the beginning, a system of social consensus. Capitalism in Europe, building on a feudal base, was deeply tinged with class conflict. It was without effort that American capitalism secured the loyal support of its "lower orders"; but in Europe, by the time of the revolutions of 1848, those lower orders had already turned their backs on capitalism as a vehicle for their hopes and beliefs.

Second and no less important in explaining the divergence of American and European economic evolution was the profound difference between the political complexion of the two continents. In America, save only for the terrible crisis of the Civil War, a single national purpose fused the continent; in Europe, a historic division of languages, customs, and mutually suspicious nationalities again and again prevented just such a fusion.

Accordingly, American capitalism came of age in an environment in which political unity permitted the unhindered growth of an enormous unobstructed market, while in Europe a jigsaw puzzle of national boundaries forced industrial growth to take place in cramped quarters and in an atmosphere of continued national rivalry. It is curious to note that whereas Europe was considered "wealthier" than America all through the nineteenth century, American productivity in many fields began to outstrip that of Europe from at least the 1850s, and perhaps much earlier. For instance, at the Paris Exposition of 1854, an American threshing machine was twice as productive as its nearest (English) rival and eleven times as productive as its least (Belgian) competitive model.[2]

These advantages of geographic space, richness of resources, and political unity were widened by subsequent developments in European industry. Not surprisingly, European producers, like those in America, sought to limit the destructive impact of industrial competition, and for this purpose they turned to *cartels*—contractual (rather than merely voluntary) agreements to share markets or fix prices. Unlike the case in America, however, this self-

[1] Priscilla Robertson, *Revolutions of 1848* (New York: Harper, Torchbooks, 1960), p. 194.
[2] Thomas Cochran and William Miller, *The Age of Enterprise*, rev. ed. (New York: Harper, Torchbooks, 1961), p. 58.

protective movement received the blessing, overt or tacit, of European governments. Although "anticartel" laws existed in many European countries, these laws were almost never enforced: by 1914 there were more than 100 international cartels, representing the most varied industries, in which most European nations participated.*

Cartelization was undoubtedly good for the profit statements of the cartelized firms, but it was hardly conducive to growth—either for those firms or new ones. By establishing carefully delineated and protected "preserves," the cartel system rewarded unaggressive behavior rather than economic daring; and together with the ever-present problem of cramping national frontiers, it drove European producers into a typical high-cost, high profit-margin, low-volume pattern rather than into the American pattern of very large plants with very high efficiencies. The difference in economic scale is dramatically illustrated by steel. In 1885, Great Britain led the world in the production of steel; fourteen years later her entire output was less than that of the Carnegie Steel Company alone.

As a result, by the early twentieth century, European productivity lagged very seriously behind American. A study by Professor Taussig in 1918 showed that the daily output of coal per underground worker was 4.68 tons in the United States, as contrasted with 1.9 tons in Great Britain, 1.4 tons in Prussia, and 0.91 tons in France. In 1905, the output of bricks per person employed was 141,000 in the United States and 40,000 in Germany; U.S. pig iron production was 84.5 tons per worker in 1909, compared with only 39 tons in Great Britain in 1907.[3] Parts of these differences were attributable to geological differentials, but these, too, were made worse by restrictive business practices. The result was a steady falling-behind in Europe as the twentieth century went on.

The divergence was strikingly noticeable in per capita incomes. In 1911, for example, when per capita income in the United States was $368, the corresponding figure for Great Britain was $250, for Germany $178, for France $161, for Italy $108. By 1928, American per capita income was $541 (in unchanged dollar values), while that of the United Kingdom was only $293; of Germany, $199; of France, $188; and of Italy, $96.[4] While American per capita incomes had grown by nearly 46 percent, English and French per capita incomes had increased only one-third as rapidly. German incomes rose only about one-quarter as fast, and Italian per capita incomes had actually declined.†

* In 1939 an estimated 109 cartels also had American participation, since American companies were not prohibited by antitrust laws from joining international restrictive agreements.

[3] Heinrich E. Friedlaender and Jacob Oser, *Economic History of Modern Europe* (Englewood Cliffs, N.J.: Prentice-Hall, 1953), p. 224.

[4] *Ibid.,* p. 522.

† We must be wary of placing too much faith in the translation of one income—say £500—into its "equivalent"—$1,200. Until we know the price levels, the living standards and customs of the nations we are comparing, we make such translations strictly at our own risk. But changes *within* a country, from year to year, are, of course, as meaningful in one currency as in another.

Still another consequence followed from the division of European industry and agriculture into national compartments. To a far greater extent than in America, it made the development of European capitalism subject to the expansion of international trade.

For the division of the European Continent into many national units made international trade a continuous and critical preoccupation of economic life abroad. For instance, a study has shown that in 1913, when manufactured imports provided but 3.6 percent of United States' consumption of manufactured goods, they provided 9 percent of Germany's, 14 percent of England's, 21 percent of Sweden's.[5] Perhaps even more striking is the degree to which some nations in Europe depended on international trade for the foodstuffs on which they lived: in the five years preceding World War I, for instance, England produced less than 20 percent of the wheat she consumed and barely over 55 percent of the meat.[6] We find the same dependence on foreign trade in the export side of the picture. Whereas the United States in 1913 exported a mere fifteenth of its national product, France and Germany exported a fifth, and Britain exported nearly a quarter of theirs.

Thus, to a far greater degree than America, Europe lived by foreign trade. Here we clearly see the advantage to America of its enormous unbroken market over the fragmented national markets of Europe. All the gains from trade that were realized in the swift rise of American productivity were denied to Europe. To put it differently, in America, the division of labor was permitted to attain whatever degree of efficiency technology made possible, for in the end virtually all products entered into a single vast market where they could be exchanged against one another. In Europe, where the need for, and the potential benefits of, a far-reaching division of labor were no less pressing, a tangle of national barriers prevented the optimal specialization of effort from taking place.

Instead, what was visible in Europe was a struggle between the need for international trade as a primary means for advancing productivity, and the retarding hand of national suspicions, rivalries, and distrust. A striking example was provided as recently as the early 1950s by the great cluster of European steel and coal industry near the German-Belgian-Luxembourg borders. Here, in a triangle, 250 miles on a side, was gathered 90 percent of European steelmaking capacity in a kind of European Pittsburgh. But this natural geographic division of labor had to contend with political barriers which largely vitiated its physical productivity. Typically, German coal mines in the Ruhr sold their output to French steelmakers at prices 30 percent higher than to German plants; while, in turn, French iron-ore producers charged far higher prices in Germany than at home. As a result,

[5] *Der Deutsche Aussenhandel* (Berlin: 1932), II, 23.
[6] Friedlaender and Oser, *Economic History of Modern Europe*, p. 206.

while American steel production soared 300 percent between 1913 and 1950, the output of Europe's steel triangle rose but 3 percent during the same period.

Our example, itself, poses a question, however. Prior to 1913, as we have seen, something like a great international division of labor did, in fact, characterize the European market, albeit to nothing like the extent seen in America. By 1913, we will remember, a very considerable flow of international trade was enhancing European productivity, despite the hindrances of cartels and national divisiveness. It was only the beginning of a truly free and unhampered international market, but at least it *was* a beginning.

What brought this promising achievement to an end? Initially, it was the shock of World War I, with its violent sundering of European trade channels and its no less destructive aftermath of punitive reparations, war debts, and monetary troubles. In a sense, Europe never recovered from its World War I experience. The slow drift toward national economic separatism, at the expense of international economic cooperation, now accelerated fatefully. Tariffs and quotas multiplied to place new handicaps before the growth of international trade.

Then came the Depression of 1929 as the final blow. As the Depression spread contagiously, nation after nation sought to quarantine itself by erecting still further barriers against economic contacts with other countries. Starting in 1929, an ever-tightening contraction of trade began to strangle economic life around the world. For 53 grim months following January 1929, the volume of world trade was lower each month than in the preceding month. Between the late 1920s and the mid-1930s, manufactured imports (in constant prices) fell by a third in Germany, by nearly 40 percent in Italy, by almost 50 percent in France. As international trade collapsed, so did Europe's chance for economic growth. For two long decades there followed a period of stagnation which earned for Europe the name of the "tired continent."

Against this background of economic malfunction it is easier to understand the growing insecurity that afflicted European capitalism. During the 1930s serious rumblings were already heard. In England the Socialist Labour Party had clearly displaced the middle-class Liberals as the Opposition. In France, a mildly socialist "Popular Front" government came to the fore, albeit insecurely. Even in Italy and Germany, the fascist dictators repeatedly declared their sympathy with "socialist" objectives—and whereas their declarations may have been no more than a sop to the masses, it was certainly indicative of the sentiments the masses wanted to hear.

Note that the socialist movements were not communist—that is, they were pledged strongly to democratic political principles and envisaged a "takeover" through education and persuasion rather than by revolution and coercion. In addition, the socialists sought to convert only the strategic centers of production into public enterprises, rather than to "socialize" all of industry and agriculture. Thus socialism was always a much more evolutionary program than communism. Nevertheless, to the European conservatives of the 1930s, the Socialist leaders appeared every bit as dangerous as did the Socialists' bitterest enemies, the Communists.

By the end of World War II, socialist ideas were clearly ascendant throughout most of Europe. Even before the war was concluded, the Labour Party swept into office in England and rapidly nationalized the Bank of England, the coal and electricity industries, much of the transportation and communications industry, and finally steel. As the first postwar governments were formed, it was evident that a socialist spectrum extended across Europe from Scandinavia through the Lowlands and France to Italy (where the communists came within an ace of gaining power). To many observers, it seemed as if capitalism in Europe had come to the end of its rope.

RECOVERY OF EUROPEAN CAPITALISM

Yet, European capitalism did not come to an end. Instead, beginning in the late 1940s and early 1950s, it embarked on what is unquestionably its period of strongest economic growth. Indeed, a comparison not only with the past but with United States performance during the same period shows the remarkable change that had come over the Continent.

TABLE 10 • 1

COMPARATIVE GROWTH RATES

	AVERAGE ANNUAL RATES OF PER CAPITA INCREASE				
	France	Germany	Italy	U.K.	U.S.
Pre-World War I (1870–1913)	1.4	1.8	0.7	1.3	2.2
Post-World War II (1948–1962)	3.4	6.8	5.6	2.4	1.8 (1950–64)

Source: M. M. Postan, *An Economic History of Western Europe* (London: Methuen, 1967), p. 17.

Note that the nations of Europe not only doubled and tripled their pre-World War I rates of per capita growth, but actually outstripped the contemporary performance of the United States economy by a margin almost as large.

To bring about such results, important changes obviously must have taken place in these economic societies. One of them, it is hardly surprising to learn, was political. The postwar socialist governments quickly showed that they were not revolutionary but reform-minded administrations. Once in power they quickly instituted a number of welfare and social planning measures, such as public health facilities, family benefits and allowances, improved social security, and the like; but they did not engage in sweeping changes. Hence, when many of the socialist governments, facing the exigencies of the postwar period, were voted out again, they bequeathed to the conservatives the framework of a welfare state *which the conservatives accepted*. Harking back to one of the traditional weaknesses of European capitalism, we can say that this represented a conservative attempt to create a social service state which would mend the historic antagonism of the lower classes. As a result, we find today that in most European states, welfare expenditures form a considerably higher proportion of government expenditures than they do in the United States.

The second reason was even more important. This was the rise of a movement within the conservative ranks to overcome a still more dangerous heritage of the past—the national division of markets. This great step toward creating a full-scale Continental market for European producers is called the European Community—or more usually, the Common Market.

To some extent, the Common Market was born out of the vital impetus given to postwar European production by the so-called Marshall plan, under which Europe received some $12 billion in direct grants and loans from the United States to rebuild its war-shattered industry. Despite Marshall aid, it soon became apparent that Europe's upward climb would necessarily be limited if production were once again restrained by cartels and national protectionism. To forestall a return to the stagnation of the prewar period, a few farsighted and courageous statesmen, primary among them Jean Monnet and Robert Schuman, proposed a truly daring plan for the abolition of Europe's traditional economic barriers.

The plan as it took shape called for the creation of a *supranational* (not merely an international) organization to integrate the steel and coal production of France, Germany, Italy, Belgium, Luxembourg, and the Netherlands. The new Coal and Steel Community was to have a High Authority with power to eliminate all customs duties on coal and steel products among members of the Community, to outlaw all discriminatory pricing and trade practices, to approve or disapprove all mergers, to order the dissolution of cartels, and to provide social and welfare services for all Community miners and steelworkers. The Authority was to be given direct power to inspect books, levy fines, and enforce its decrees—and still more remarkable, it was to be responsible not to any single member government but to a multinational Parliament and a multinational Court, both to be created as part of the Community. A Council of Ministers was to act as a *national* advisory and permissory body, but even here action could be taken by majority vote, so that no single nation (or even two nations) could block a decision desired by the Community as a whole.

By the fall of 1952, the Coal and Steel Community was a reality, and it lost no time going about its business. At mid-1954, customs duties and discriminatory pricing within the coal and steel "triangle" had been virtually eliminated, and roughly 40 percent more coal and steel was being shipped across national boundaries than had been shipped prior to the establishment of the Community. Cartels and secret agreements still remain, but the restrictive influence on production was much less than it was formerly.

The success of the Coal and Steel Community led, in 1957, to the next two organizations: Euratom, a supranational atomic power agency, and the Common Market itself, an organization that was to do for commodities in general what the Coal and Steel Community had done for its products. Under the Common Market treaty, a definite schedule of tariff cuts was laid down, envisaging within slightly more than a decade an entirely unimpeded Continental market for Common Market members, with a single "external" tariff vis-à-vis the world. In addition, there were to be a single agricultural policy and, perhaps most imaginative, full freedom for the intermember mobility of both capital and labor.

The Common Market is still in the process of achieving some of these goals, although it is well ahead of its timetable.* Already, however, it has led to a remarkable increase in European trade and production. Trade among member countries has grown from $6.8 billion in 1958 to $28.4 billion in 1968. As a result, the Community's rate of growth has surged ahead, as Table 10-2 shows.

TABLE 10•2

PERCENT AVERAGE ANNUAL GROWTH IN REAL GNP

	1950–1960	1958–1968
Common Market	5.9%	5.3%
Rest of Europe	3.1	3.8
United States	3.2	4.7

Source OECD; *Basic Statistics of the Community*, p. 24.

Notice that during the decade of the 1950s, the Common Market's growth was almost twice that of the United States; and although the pace of expansion has slowed somewhat abroad and quickened at home in recent years, it is clear that the doldrums of the European past are well behind us.

The figures, of course, only point to the real changes that have occurred. For the first time the style of life and level of consumption of the European working and middle classes have begun to resemble that of America. The number of autos in use has been growing at the rate of 12

---

* The first agreements have now been signed for the introduction of a single currency throughout the Community, although this will take many years to work out fully.

percent a year; the number of TV sets, at 30 percent. Not less important, the boom in European trade has led to an even greater boom in world trade.

There is much in these prosperous statistics that reminds us of the general course of affairs in the United States. After its time of trial, European capitalism, like American capitalism, seems to have achieved a high degree of economic success. It is true that socialist parties continue to constitute a strong political movement in Europe, but the thrust of these programs is no longer directed mainly toward nationalization or other fundamental economic changes, but aims instead at correcting social privileges or at buttressing still further the welfare arrangements that we find in every European country. Equality—social as well as economic—is the present main objective of European socialism, and although equality requires adjustments in the existing distribution of rewards, the socialists do not see it as requiring the destruction of the system by which those rewards are determined.

Yet if socialism has made its peace with modern capitalism in Europe, there is a deeper reason than a mere change of mind on the part of Europe's socialists. The reason is that capitalism in Europe has borrowed a central idea of socialism and adapted it to conservative uses—the idea of *national economic planning.*

SOCIALISM AND MODERN EUROPEAN CAPITALISM

For all through Europe we see a reliance on planning that is both greater and more outspoken than anything we have encountered in the United States. In our country, we recall from Chapter 9, we have arrived at a consensus as to fiscal and monetary policy as the proper implements for achieving a stable and satisfactory rate of growth. But in most European nations, there is visible a further commitment to planning as a means of achieving publicly determined patterns of resource allocation as well as adequate rates of growth.

In France, for example, a central planning agency, working in consultation with Parliament and with representatives of industry, agriculture, labor, and other groups, sets a general plan for French growth—a plan that not only establishes a desired rate of expansion, but determines whether or not, for example, the provincial cities should expand faster or slower than the nation as a whole, or where the bulk of new housing is to be located, or to what degree social services are to be increased. Once decided, the plan is then divided into the various production targets needed for its fulfillment, and their practicality is discussed with management and labor groups in each industry concerned.

From these discussions arise two results. First, the plan is often amended to conform with the wishes or advice of those who must carry it

CONSERVATIVE PLANNING

out. Second, the general targets of the plan become part of the business expectations of the industries that have helped to formulate them. To be sure, the government has substantial investment powers that can nudge the economy along whatever path has been finally determined. But in the main, French "indicative" planning works as a *self-fulfilling prophecy*—the very act of establishing its objectives setting into motion the behavior needed to realize them.

In England, Germany, the Netherlands, Italy, and Scandinavia, we see other forms of government planning, none so elaborately worked out as the French system, but all also injecting a powerful element of public guidance into the growth and disposition of the resources of their economies.

The plans have not been wholly successful. Inflation has been the curse of Europe to an even greater degree than it has been here; and nothing like a successful "incomes policy" has been worked out in any nation. But considerable success has been attained in the allocation of resources for public purposes through planning, and in the shaping of the general contours of national development.

What is beyond dispute is that a basic commitment to planning seems to have become an integral part of modern European capitalism. *Note, however, that all these planning systems utilize the mechanism of the market as a means for achieving their ends.* The act of planning itself is not, of course, a market activity; but the realization of the various desired production tasks for industry is entrusted largely to the pull of demand acting on independent enterprises. Thus the market has been utilized as an instrument of social policy.*

EUROPE
AND AMERICA
How do we account for the fact that in Europe the evolution into a guided capitalism has evidently progressed much further than in America? In part, the reason is no doubt ascribable to the problems that have racked Europe and have forced upon it a much greater degree of necessary government intervention for survival. The Common Market, for example, would never have been brought into being had Europe not suffered from the effects of economic fragmentation, and the Common Market in turn stimulated and supported the development of purely national planning efforts.

To some extent the difference may be due, as well, to the survival in Europe of those "feudal" (or at least monarchical) attitudes that contrast so sharply with the democratic climate in America. Europeans are used to, and accept, a larger role for public authority in the economic direction of affairs; whereas Americans have traditionally tended to resist and reject such a role. Hence the movement toward planning in Europe has not encountered the fierce ideological opposition it has met in America, where the very word still

---

* Anyone who wishes to learn more about the important subject of European planning should read Andrew Shonfield, *Modern Capitalism* (New York: Oxford University Press, 1965).

conjures up fearsome "socialistic" visions to some people. This is a matter we will discuss again in our last chapter. But we cannot put these questions into focus until we have looked into another significant drift—in the opposite direction. But to see that striking development we must now examine the rise of a totally different economic structure: the socialist economy of the Soviet Union.

We cannot here recount in detail the history of Soviet socialism. Let us, rather, begin by noting the extraordinarily difficult problem that faced the revolutionary leaders who had secured the victory of "socialism" in Russia in 1917. In the first place, Russia was a semifeudal society in which capitalism was restricted to a small industrial and commercial sector. Second, both production and distribution were highly disorganized in the chaotic situation following the civil war.

Finally, there was little guidance in the official literature of the Communist movement as to how a socialist society should be run. Marx's *Das Kapital*, the seminal work of communism, was entirely devoted to a study of capitalism; and in those few essays in which Marx looked to the future, his gaze rarely traveled beyond the watershed of the revolutionary act itself. With the achievement of the revolution, Marx thought, a temporary regime known as "the dictatorship of the proletariat" would take over the transition from capitalism to socialism, and thereafter a "planned socialist economy" would emerge as the first step towards a still less specified "communism."* In the latter state—the final terminus of economic evolution according to Marx—there were hints that the necessary but humdrum tasks of production and distribution would take place by the voluntary cooperation of all citizens and that society would turn its serious attention to matters of cultural and humanistic importance.

In reality, the Revolution presented Lenin, Trotsky, and the other leaders of the new Soviet Union with problems far more complex than this utopian long-term design. Shortly after the initial success of the Revolution, Lenin nationalized the banks, the major factories, the railways, and canals. In the meantime, the peasants themselves had taken over the large landed estates on which they had been tenants, and they had carved them up into individual holdings. The central authorities then attempted for several years to run the economy by requisitioning food from the farms and allocating it

---

* What is the difference between *socialism* and *communism?* We have already noted one difference in the West, where socialism implies an adherence to democratic political mechanisms, whereas communism does not. But within the socialist bloc there is another interesting difference of definition. Socialism there represents a stage of development in which it is still necessary to use "bourgeois" incentives in order to make the economy function; that is, people must be paid in proportion to the "value" of their work. Under communism, a new form of human society will presumably have been achieved in which these selfish incentives will no longer be needed. Then will come the time when society will be able to put into effect Karl Marx's famous description of communism: "From each according to his ability; to each according to his need."

to factory workers, while controlling the flow of output from the factories themselves by a system of direct controls from above.

This initial attempt to run the economy was a disastrous failure. Under inept management (and often cavalier disregard of "bourgeois" concerns with factory management), industrial output declined precipitously: by 1920 it had fallen to *14 percent* of prewar levels. As goods available to the peasants became scarcer, the peasants, themselves, were less and less willing to acquiesce in giving up food to the cities. The result was a wild inflation followed by a degeneration into an economy of semibarter. For a while, toward the end of 1920, the system threatened to break down completely.

To forestall the impending collapse, in 1921 Lenin instituted a New Economic Policy, the so-called NEP. This was a return toward a market system and a partial reconstitution of actual capitalism. Retail trade, for instance, was opened again to private ownership and operation. Small-scale industry also reverted to private direction. Most important, the farms were no longer requisitioned but operated as profit-making units. Only the "commanding heights" of industry and finance were retained in government hands.

There ensued for several years a bitter debate about the course of action to follow next. While the basic aim of the Soviet government was still to industrialize and to socialize (i.e., to replace the private ownership of the means of production by state ownership), the question was how fast to move ahead—and, indeed, *how* to move ahead. The pace of industrialization hinged critically on one highly uncertain factor: the willingness of the large, private peasant sector to deliver food with which the city workers could be sustained in their tasks. To what extent, therefore, should the need for additional capital goods be sacrificed in order to turn out the consumption goods that could be used as an inducement for peasant cooperation?

THE DRIVE
TO TOTAL
PLANNING

The student of Russian history—or, for that matter, of economic history—will find the record of that debate an engrossing subject.[7] But the argument was never truly resolved. In 1927, Stalin moved into command, and the difficult question of how much to appease the unwilling peasant disappeared. Stalin simply made the ruthless decision to appease him not at all, but to *coerce* him by collectivizing his holdings.

The collectivization process solved in one swoop the problem of securing the essential transfer of food from the farm to the city, but it did so at a frightful social (and economic) cost. Many peasants slaughtered their livestock rather than hand it over to the new collective farms; others waged outright war or practiced sabotage. In reprisal, the authorities acted with brutal force. An estimated five million "kulaks" (rich peasants) were executed or put in labor camps, while in the cities an equally relentless policy

[7] See Alexander Erlich, *The Soviet Industrialization Debate: 1924–1928* (Cambridge: Harvard University Press, 1960).

showed itself vis-à-vis labor. Workers were summarily ordered to the tasks required by the central authorities. The right to strike was forbidden, and the trade unions were reduced to impotence. Speed-ups were widely applied, and living conditions were allowed to deteriorate to very low levels.

The history of this period of forced industrialization is ugly and repellent, and it has left abiding scars on Russian society. It is well for us, nonetheless, to attempt to view it with some objectivity. If the extremes to which the Stalinist authorities went were extraordinary, often unpardonable, and perhaps self-defeating, we must bear in mind that industrialization on the grand scale has always been wrenching, always accompanied by economic sacrifice, and always carried out by the more or less authoritarian use of power. We have already seen what happened in the West at the time of the industrial revolution with its heavy-handed exploitation of labor; and without "excusing" these acts, we have seen their function in paving the way for capital accumulation.

In much the same fashion, when the Soviet leaders deliberately held down consumption, regimented and transferred their labor forces into the new raw industrial centers, and ruthlessly collected the foodstuffs to feed their capital-building workers, they were, in fact, only enforcing the basic process of industrialization. What was new about the Soviet program was that totalitarian control over the citizenry enabled the planners to carry out this transformation at a much faster tempo than would have been possible had protests been permitted. Under Stalin's iron will, the planners did not scruple to exercise their industrializing power to the hilt.

Without seeking to justify the Russian effort, it is worth pondering one last question. Can rapid industrialization, with its inescapable price of low consumption, ever be a "popular" policy? Will poor people willingly vote for an economic transformation which will not "pay out" for twenty or forty years?* Does rapid and large-scale industrialization *necessitate* a large degree of authoritarian political control? We will return to these problems when we turn to underdevelopment, but we might well begin to think about them now.

THE PLANNING
MECHANISM

A massive industrialization drive requires a determined effort to hold consumption to a minimum and to transfer resources to capital-building, an effort greatly facilitated, as we have seen, by the totalitarian political apparatus. But there is still another question to be considered. How are the freed resources to find their proper destination in an integrated and workable industrial sector?

---

* We might note in passing that universal male suffrage was not gained in England until the late 1860s and 1870s. Aneurin Bevan has written: "It is highly doubtful whether the achievements of the Industrial Revolution would have been permitted if the franchise had been universal. It is very doubtful because a great deal of the capital aggregations that we are at present enjoying are the results of the wages that our fathers went without." (From Gunnar Myrdal, *Rich Lands and Poor.* New York: Harper, 1957, p. 46.)

Let us remind ourselves again of how this is done under a market economy. There, the signal of profitability serves as the lure for the allocation of resources and labor. Entrepreneurs, anticipating or following demand, risk private funds in the construction of the facilities which they hope the future will require. Meanwhile, as these industrial salients grow, smaller satellite industries grow along with them to cater to their needs.

The flow of materials is thus regulated in every sector by the forces of private demand, making themselves known by the signal of rising or falling prices. At every moment there emanates from the growing industries a magnetic pull of demand on secondary industries, while, in turn, the growth salients themselves are guided, spurred, or slowed down by the pressure of demand from the ultimate buying public. And all the while, counterposed to these pulls of demand, are the obduracies of supply—the cost schedules of the producers themselves. In the cross fire of demand and supply exists a marvelously sensitive social instrument for the integration of the overall economic effort of expansion.

And in the absence of a market? Clearly, the mechanism must be supplied by the direct orders of a central controlling and planning agency. *In a growing industrial economy, a planning agency must act as a substitute for the market.* Let us reflect for a moment what this entails.

To begin with, it means that the planning agency must provide a substitute for the forward-looking operations of the great entrepreneurs in a market economy. In place of a Carnegie or a Ford, building their plants in anticipation of, or response to, an insistent demand for their products, the planning body must itself set overall goals and objectives for economic growth. Not the consumer but the planners' own judgment and desires determine the force of "demand."*

Establishing the overall objectives is, however, only the first and perhaps the easiest part of the planning mechanism. It is not enough to set broad goals and then assume that they will be fulfilled by themselves. We must remember that planning in a totalitarian economy is not superimposed on a market structure in which individuals take care of the "details" of production according to the incentives of price and profit. In a totally planned economy, each and every item which goes into the final plan must also be planned. Schedules of production are needed for steel, coal, coke,

---

* In the case of the Soviet Union, the planning authority has typically set its demand goals in terms of Five-Year Plans. The first of these, from 1928 to 1932, had as its basic objective the intensification of industrialization in heavy industry, with special emphasis on electrification; the second took as its main goal the development of transportation and the beginning of agricultural planning; the third plan (1938-1942) was essentially occupied with producing the needs for a war economy; the fourth, from 1946 to 1950, was mainly a plan of reconstruction from wartime damage, with continuing emphasis on heavy industry; a fifth plan, 1951-1955, emphasized a steep increase in output with some stress being given (for the first time) to consumer goods. A sixth plan was scrapped in midcourse; a seventh (1959-1965) aimed to increase industrial output by 80 percent, agricultural output by 70 percent, and to bring significant increases in housing (a sector long neglected in the interests of industrialization) and in consumer goods, generally. We know that many of these objectives were not met, but there is no doubt of growing emphasis on consumer goods and housing.

lumber, on down to nails and paper clips, for there is no "automatic" device by which these items will be forthcoming without a planning directive. Supplies of labor must also be planned; or if labor is free to move where it wishes, wage rates must be planned in order to draw labor where it is wanted.

Thus supplementing and completing the master objective of the overall plan must be a whole hierarchy of subplans, the aggregate of which must bring about the necessary final result. And here is a genuine difficulty. For an error in planning, small in itself, if it affects a strategic link in the chain of production, can seriously distort—or even render impossible—the fulfillment of the total plan.

How is this infinitely complicated planning system carried out in the Soviet Union? It is begun by breaking down the overall, long-term plan into shorter one-year plans. These one-year plans, specifying the output of major sectors of industry, are then transmitted to various government ministries concerned with, for example, steel production, transportation, lumbering, and so forth. In turn, the Ministries refer the one-year plans further down the line to the heads of large industrial plants, to experts and advisers, and so on. At each stage, the overall plan is thus unraveled into its subsidiary components, until finally the threads have been traced as far back as feasible along the productive process—typically, to the officials in charge of actual factory operations. The factory manager of, for instance, a coking operation is given a planned objective for the next year, specifying the output needed from his plant. He confers with his production engineers, considers the condition of his machinery, the availability of his labor force, and then transmits his requirements for meeting the objective back upward along the hierarchy. In this way, just as "demand" is transmitted downward along the chain of command, the exigencies of "supply" flow back upward, culminating ultimately in the top command of the planning authority (the Gosplan) itself.[8]

From this description of the tasks of planning, it is obvious that planning is an enormously complex task. Indeed, the very complexity of the task is such that more than one economist in the first days of chaos following the Russian Revolution declared socialism—meaning by this, centralized decision-making—to be "impossible."

Central planning is not impossible for certain kinds of economic tasks: for "forcing" growth, in particular, it may be more effective than any other means of bringing about the needed allocation of resources. The most recent investigation into Soviet economic performance, for example, indicates that over the period 1929 to 1961, Soviet output rose between 5.2 and 7.2

[8] For an excellent description of Soviet planning, see Robert W. Campbell, *Soviet Economic Power,* 2nd ed. (Boston: Houghton Mifflin, 1966).

percent per annum—roughly twice as fast as the United States' growth over these years.[9] Part of this extraordinary record, to which must be credited Russia's passage from a peasant society to an industrial one, is certainly due to the ability of central planning to bring about tremendously high levels of investment: measured in 1937 prices, investment was pushed from 8.4 percent of GNP in 1928 to 30.6 percent in 1961.

The trouble comes when we look to the planning system for its *efficiency* in allocating resources, rather than to its success in forcing total volumes of output. An economy may be very successful in producing larger and larger quantities of steel and electric power, but it may be very unsuccessful in producing the right kinds of steel or in locating its electric power plants effectively or in producing its goods at the lowest possible cost. Sooner or later, such inefficiency will interfere with the rate of growth, and that is exactly what we see in the case of the U.S.S.R. From many indications it appears that the Soviet rate of expansion has been declining in recent years and that the economy is increasingly plagued with difficulties arising from a failure to produce the right goods at the best possible prices. The result is a system that has operated more and more unevenly and awkwardly, as first one and then another of the gears in the great machine jammed.

In 1962, for example, an observer reports:

The Byelorussian Tractor Factory, which has 227 suppliers, had its production line stopped 19 times ... because of the lack of rubber parts, 18 times because of ball bearings, and 8 times because of transmission components. The pattern of breakdowns continued in 1963. During the first quarter of 1963 only about one-half of the plant's ball bearing and rubber needs were satisfied, and only half of the required batteries were available. One supplier shipped 19,000 less wheels than called for in the contract. In total, they were short of 27 items.[10]

Stories such as these abound in any book describing the Soviet economic system. They should not be taken to mean that Russian planning is a "failure" or that it is on the point of collapse. Taken as a whole, the system continues to produce at good rates. But the bottlenecks do point to deepseated troubles in running the economy smoothly, even now when industrial needs are still relatively simple and consumers are not yet highly critical. These troubles are apt to exact a higher price as the Soviet economy turns its attention to the more complex and demanding problems of a highly integrated industrial process and a much more demanding citizenry.

What is at the root of the inefficiency of central planning? *Essentially the problem is to find a means of guiding the production of individual firms.* Do not forget that a Russian factory manager has very little leeway in what he

[9] Richard Moorsteen and Raymond P. Powell, *The Soviet Capital Stock, 1928-1962* (Homewood, Ill.: Irwin, 1966).

[10] Barry Richman, *Soviet Management* (Englewood Cliffs, N.J.: Prentice-Hall, 1965), p. 123.

produces or the combination of factors that he uses for production. Both his inputs and his outputs are carefully specified for him in his plan. What the manager *is* supposed to do is to beat the plan, by "overproducing" the items that have been assigned to his plant. Indeed, from 30 to 50 percent of a manager's pay will depend on bonuses tied directly to his "overfulfillment" of the plan, so that he has a very great personal incentive to exceed the output "norms" set for him.

All this seems sensible enough. Trouble comes, however, because the manager's drive to exceed his factory's quota tends to distort the productive effort from the receivers' point of view. For example, if the target for a textile factory is set in terms of yards of cloth, there is every temptation to weave the cloth as narrowly as possible, to get the maximum yardage out of a given amount of thread. Or if the plan merely calls for tonnages of output, there is every incentive to skimp on design or finish or quality, in order to concentrate on sheer weight. A cartoon in the Russian satirical magazine *Krokodil* shows a nail factory proudly displaying its record output: one gigantic nail suspended from an immense gantry crane. (On the other hand, if a nail factory has its output specified in terms of the *numbers* of nails it produces, its incentive to overfulfill this "success indicator" is apt to result in the production of very small or thin nails.)

What is the way out of this kind of dilemma? A few years ago, a widely held opinion among the Russian planners was that more detailed and better integrated planning performed on a battery of computers would solve the problem. Few still cling to this belief. The demands of planning have grown far faster than the ability to meet them: indeed, one Soviet mathematician has predicted that at the current rate of growth of the planning bureaucracy, planning alone would require the services of the entire Russian population by 1980. Even with the most complete computerization, it seems a hopeless task to attempt to beat the problem of efficiency by increasing the "fineness" of the planning mechanism.[11]

Rather, the wind for reform in the Soviet Union is now blowing from quite another quarter. Led by economist E. G. Liberman, there is a growing demand that the misleading plan directives of weight, length, etc., be subordinated to a new "success indicator" that will, all by itself, guide the manager to results that will make sense from the overall point of view. And what is that overriding indicator? It is the *profit* that a factory manager can make for his enterprise!

Note several things about this profit. To begin with, it is not envisaged that it can arise from price manipulations. Factory managers will continue to operate with the prices established by the planners; but they will now

---

[11] For an interesting glimpse into the Russian change of mind, see *Planning, Profit and Incentives in the U.S.S.R.*, Myron E. Sharpe, ed. (White Plains, N.Y.: International Arts and Sciences Press, 1966).

have to *sell* their output and *buy* their inputs, rather than merely deliver or accept them. This means that each factory will have to be responsive to the particular needs of its customers if it wishes to dispose of its output. In the same way, of course, its own suppliers will now have to be responsive to the factory's needs if the suppliers are to get the factory's business.

Second, the profit will belong not to the factory or its managers, but to the State. A portion of the profit will indeed be allocated for bonuses and other rewards, so that there is a direct incentive to run the plant efficiently, but the bulk of the earnings will be transferred to the State.

Thus, profits are to be used as an *efficiency-maximizing indicator*. Indeed, to view the change even more broadly, we can see that the reintroduction of the use of profits implies a deliberate return to the use of the *market mechanism* as a means of achieving economic efficiency. Not only profits but also interest charges—a capitalist term that would have been heresy to mention in the days of Stalin—are being introduced into the planning mechanism to allow factory managers to determine for themselves what is the most efficient thing to do, both for their enterprises and for the economy as a whole.

The drift toward the market mechanism is still new in the Soviet Union, and we do not know how far it will ultimately progress. The objectives of the 1971-1975 Plan call for a much greater emphasis on consumer goods, but speak of "an extensive use of economic-mathematical methods," which implies something of a return to the computer rather than a rapid movement in the direction of freer trade. Nonetheless, there seems to be no doubt from which quarter the winds blow most steadily. As Soviet economist A. Birman has put it: "Only three years ago, no one would have thought that there would be anything but the direct physical allocation of goods. Now economists talk of *torgovat* (trading) instead of *snabzhat* (allocating)."[12] Furthermore, the government has warmly endorsed the idea of "production associations,"—groups of geographically separate plants that coordinate their marketing, purchasing, research, and management, just like corporations. The market idea of economies of large-scale production has triumphed over the political idea of production organized by locality.

Meanwhile, the trend toward the market has proceeded much further in a large part of Eastern Europe, and above all in Yugoslavia. There, the market rules very nearly as supreme as it does in Western capitalist countries. Yet the Yugoslavs certainly consider themselves a socialist economy. As in the U.S.S.R., enterprise profits do not go to the "owners" of the business but are distributed as incentive bonuses or used for investment or other purposes under the overall guidance of the State. And again as in

[12] From Marshall I. Goldman, *The Soviet Economy: Myth and Reality* (Englewood Cliffs, N.J.: Prentice-Hall, 1968), p. 129.

the U.S.S.R., the market is used as a deliberate instrument of social control, rather than as an institution that is above question. Thus, the main determination of investment, the direction of development of consumers' goods, the basic distribution of income—all continue to be matters established at the center as part of a planned economy. More and more, however, this central plan is allowed to realize itself through the profit-seeking operations of highly autonomous firms, rather than through being imposed in full detail upon the economy.*

How far will this drift toward the market proceed? That is a question to which we will return in our penultimate chapter. What is important to recognize at this juncture is that there has been a visible movement toward the market mechanism in every *European* communist nation (we will see shortly why it is only in these nations). One ironic consequence is that we find the same ideological alarm being expressed in these nations as in the United States, as each sees itself in danger of being subverted by the introduction of some elements of the other system: indeed, one of the reasons behind the Soviet invasion of Czechoslovakia was its concern that Czech economic (as well as political) liberalization had gone too far.

Before we look further into this "convergence" of systems, however, there is a last development of the market economy into which we must inquire.

---

* One of the most interesting aspects of Yugoslav socialism is its effort to introduce worker-run enterprises. At least in theory, the top authority in most enterprises is a Worker's Council, which has the right to *fire* the boss of the plant, and which also determines wage and bonus payments, plant investments, and so on. We do not yet know whether this economic democracy exists in fact as well as on paper. If it does, it may prove to be one of the important social developments of our time. See Paul Blumberg, *Industrial Democracy* (New York: Schocken Books, 1969).

1. The development of European capitalism was considerably hampered by a number of factors absent from the American scene. Among these were a *feudal heritage* that brought serious political problems and *severe national rivalry* that prevented economic unification. As a result, productivity in Europe lagged behind that of the United States. Compounding the problem of slow growth was the *breakdown of international trade* following World War I.

National planning

European Community

Common Market

2. Capitalism in Europe was seriously threatened by the rise of a *socialist opposition*. However following World War II, conservative parties generally accepted the reformist ideas of socialism and backed large programs of *social welfare and a commitment to national economic planning.*

3. Equally, or more, important was the creation of the *European Community* with its *Common Market,* a successful attempt to revive inter-European trade.

Indicative planning

4. Among the many European planning mechanisms, the most elaborate is the French system of *"indicative planning."* A centrally formulated plan is discussed among representatives of industry, labor, and other groups, and in the process of discussion and amendment becomes part of the general expectations of these groups. This leads to the requisite investment needed to bring the plan about. Thus the system works as a *self-fulfilling prophecy.*

5. All the European planning systems *rely on the market mechanism.* While the commitment of the European nations to a guided economy is in most cases greater than our own, a similar drift toward planning is visible in American capitalism as well.

Central planning

6. The U.S.S.R. has followed a totally different course. Following the Revolution of 1917, a system of *central planning* was initiated, but it early collapsed. Thereafter a semimarket system was introduced as a rescue measure.

Collectivization

7. Following long debates about how to secure agricultural production to feed workers engaged in industrial projects, Russia under Stalin began a *total collectivization* that used naked force to solve the food transfer problem and the industrialization program.

Success indicators

8. The planning mechanism by which Russia carries out its industrial growth requires the formulation of *highly detailed and accurately interlocked subplans,* any one of which, if wrongly designed or unmet, can wreck the larger one. *Inefficiency* has been the plague of the central planning system, although the system did succeed in achieving its larger objectives. The problem has been that "success indicators" have led to misallocation of resources.

9. As a result, we see the *introduction of the market mechanism,* using profit as *the* success indicator, into the European communist economics. *The market is being introduced into socialism just as planning is being introduced into capitalism.*

QUESTIONS

1. Discuss how the fragmentation of a continent can affect the gains from trade. Does the experience of Europe illustrate that the bias of nationalism constitutes the main source of international economic difficulties?

2. In what ways is communism different from socialism? Are these differences merely economic?

3. What is the difference between indicative planning, as we find it in France, and the kind of planning we find in the U.S.S.R.?

4. What is a "self-fulfilling prophecy"? If you were a bank president and said in a speech that you thought your bank would fail, might that provoke behavior that would make your prediction true? Can you think of another example?

5. Imagine that you were in charge of automobile production in Russia. How would you decide how many cars to make? How expensive to make them? What materials to order? What prices to pay for various grades of labor? How to mix land, labor, and capital?

6. How is the transfer of food from country to city accomplished under capitalism? Why was the problem so acute under early Soviet rule? Do you think a program of rapid industrialization can be managed without recourse to coercion of some sort?

7. Do you think that profit-seeking enterprise is compatible with a planned economy? What kind of planning could utilize such enterprises? What kinds could not?

We have looked fairly carefully into the advantages and disadvantages of the market as a means of organizing the economic activity of nations, and we shall have something more to say about it when we study the problems of the underdeveloped world. But in this chapter we must add a new dimension, that of international economics. Everything we have heretofore learned has had to do with the internal production and distribution of goods and services. What we must now consider is a revolutionary development in international economics, having to do with the *international production* of goods and services. To understand what this means we must learn about a new institution that has sprung up as the most important agency for international production: the multinational corporation.

THE
MULTINATIONAL
CORPORATION·

What is a multinational corporation? Essentially, we mean a corporation that has producing branches or subsidiaries located in more than one nation. Take PepsiCo, for example. PepsiCo does not ship its famous product around the world from bottling plants in the United States. It *produces* Pepsi Cola in 512 plants located in 114 countries. When you buy a Pepsi in Mexico or the Philippines or Israel or Denmark, you are buying an American product that was manufactured in that country.

PepsiCo is a far-flung, but not a particularly large multinational corporation: in 1969 it was only the 119th largest industry. More impressive by far is the Ford Motor Company, a multinational that consists of a network of 60 subsidiary corporations, 40 of them foreign-based. Of the corporation's total assets of $8 billion, 36 percent are invested in 27 foreign nations; and of its 388,000 employees (as of 1966) 150,000 were employed outside the U.S. And, if we studied the corporate structures of GM or IBM or the great oil companies, we would find that they, too, are *international* companies—not only because they export their goods (or import their materials), but also because they all have substantial portions of their total wealth invested in productive facilities outside the United States.

Indeed, if we broaden our view to include the top 100 American firms, we find that 62 have such production facilities in at least 6 nations. Moreover, the value of output that is produced overseas by the largest corporations by far exceeds the value of the goods they still export from the United States. In 1968, sales of manufacturing foreign affiliates of U.S. firms (which means their wholly or partially owned overseas branches) came to over $59 billion.[1] In the same year, our total exports of manufactures amounted to $24 billion, only 40 percent as much as American firms produced abroad. Indeed, *all* U.S. exports, including agricultural and other nonmanufactures, amounted to $9 billion less than our manufacturing output abroad.[2]

But that is still only a part of the picture. The $59 billion refers only to *manufacturing* abroad. If we add the sale of all goods and services produced abroad (which brings oil into the picture, as well as U.S. trade and retail activities abroad) our total foreign-produced flow of output probably amounted to over $110 billion in 1968.[3] One estimate for 1970 places the value of all U.S. overseas output at a staggering $200 billion.[4]

Another way of establishing the spectacular rise of international production is to trace the increase in the value of U.S. foreign direct investment; that is, the value of foreign-located, U.S.-owned plant and equipment (*not* U.S.-owned foreign bonds and stocks). In 1950 the value of U.S. foreign direct investment was $11 billion. In 1970 it was over $70 billion. Moreover, this figure, too, needs an upward adjustment, because it includes only the value of American dollars invested abroad and not the additional value of foreign capital that may be controlled by those dollars. For example, if a U.S. company has invested $10 million in a foreign enterprise whose total

INTERNATIONAL
DIRECT
INVESTMENT

[1] *Survey of Current Business,* October 1970, p. 20; *Statistical Abstract,* p. 696.

[2] *Ibid.*

[3] Estimate by Emile Benoit in *World Business,* Courtney Brown, ed. (New York: Macmillan, 1970), p. 19.

[4] Estimate by Judd Polk before the Subcommittee for Economic Policy of the Joint Economic Committee, July 27, 1970.

net worth is $20 million, the U.S. official figures for our foreign investment take note only of the $10 million of American equity (ownership) and not of the $20 million of wealth that our equity actually controls. If we include the capital controlled by our foreign direct investment as a whole, the value of American overseas productive assets almost certainly exceeds $120 billion and may be as large as $200 billion.[5] In general, something between a quarter and a half of the real assets of our biggest corporations are located abroad.

THE
"AMERICAN
CHALLENGE"

The stunning expansion of American corporate production overseas, especially in Europe, has given rise to what has been called *The American Challenge*. In a book with that title, Jean-Jacques Servan-Schreiber describes the "take over" of French markets by dynamic American firms that have seized 50 percent of Europe's semiconductor market, 80 percent of its computer market, and 95 percent of its integrated circuit production. Servan-Schreiber fears that the American Challenge portends the Americanization of Europe's fastest growing industries. "Fifteen years from now," he writes, "it is quite possible that the world's third greatest industrial power, just after the United States and Russia, will not be Europe, but American industry in Europe."[6]

Servan-Schreiber argues that Europe must fend off this American threat by the formation of equally efficient, large pan-European corporations. But he fails to see that the movement toward the internationalization of production is not a strictly American but a truly multinational phenomenon. If the American multinationals are the most imposing (of the world's biggest 500 corporations, 306 are American), they are closely challenged by non-American multinationals. Philips Lamp Works, for example, is a huge Dutch multinational company with operations in 68 countries. Of its 225,000 employees, 167,000 work in nations other than the Netherlands "home" nation. Royal Dutch/Shell is another vast multinational, whose "home" is somewhere between the Netherlands and the United Kingdom (it is jointly owned by nationals of both countries): Shell *in the United States* ranks among our top 20 biggest companies. Another is Nestlé Chocolate, a Swiss firm, 97 percent of whose $2 billion revenues originate outside Switzerland.

Thus if we look at the world picture of production, we find that European (and Japanese) firms have been expanding their production overseas just as rapidly as, or even more rapidly than, American firms; and although American companies have been growing very rapidly in Europe, thereby scaring the daylights out of their European competition, non-American firms have been growing even faster in other parts of the world market,

[5] Estimate by Kenneth Waltz in Brown, *World Business,* p. 219; also Louis Turner, *Invisible Empires* (New York: Harcourt, 1971), p. 71; and Polk testimony, *op. cit.*
[6] J.-J. Servan-Schreiber, *The American Challenge* (New York: Atheneum, 1968), pp. 3, 13.

including America itself.[7] (Think, for example, of the invasion of the American automobile market within the last 15 years by Volkswagen, Toyota, and a host of British and French makes.)

The point is that the change in international economic relations is truly worldwide. If we take the ten leading capital-exporting nations together (including the United States), we find that in 1967 their combined exports came to over $130 billion, but their combined overseas production amounted to well over $240 billion. For 1970, Judd Polk, economist for the International Chamber of Commerce, estimates that total international production—U.S. production abroad, foreign production here, and foreign production in other foreign countries—may account for as much as *one-sixth* of the total value of all world output, and a much higher fraction of the world output of industrial commodities.[8]

Because we do not have complete statistics on many aspects of international production, the full extent of this new form of economic relationship is still uncertain. But a number of economists have made projections based on the continuance of the rapid growth of international production. Professor Harold Perlmutter, for example, predicts that by 1988 most noncommunist trade will be dominated by 300 large corporations, of which 200 will be American, and that these corporations will account for roughly half of total world industrial output.[9] Professor Adolf Berle has remarked that some corporations "can be thought of only in somewhat the way we have heretofore thought of nations." No more than a glance at the table below, Table 11-1, comparing the GNPs of various countries with the sales of selected

TABLE 11 • 1

GNP OF VARIOUS COUNTRIES COMPARED WITH SALES OF SELECTED
MULTINATIONAL CORPORATIONS (billions of current dollars, 1967)

Netherlands	$26.6	Norway	$8.3
General Motors	**20.0**	**General Electric**	**7.7**
Belgium	19.7	Greece	7.1
Switzerland	15.9	**Chrysler**	**6.2**
Standard Oil (N.J.)	**13.3**	**Mobil**	**5.7**
Denmark	12.2	**Unilever**	**5.6**
Austria	10.6	**IBM**	**5.3**
Ford	**10.5**	Portugal	4.6
Royal Dutch/Shell	**8.4**		

Source: Louis Turner, *Invisible Empires* (New York: Harcourt, (1970), pp. 135–36.

[7] See Robert Rowthorn and Stephen Hymer, *International Big Business* (New York: Cambridge University Press, 1971), pp. 84-85.
[8] Polk testimony, *op. cit.*
[9] Turner, *Invisible Empires,* p. 191.

multinational corporations, shows that Berle's statement was not just rhetoric.

Cautionary note: Corporate sales are not the equivalent of GNPs. The table vastly overstates the relative importance of corporations with respect to manpower: Portugal, for instance, has a population of 9 million, whereas GM employs less than 1 million. On the other hand, the table understates the economic strength of corporations: GM can borrow a great deal more easily than Portugal; and it controls *all* of its receipts, whereas Portugal gets only the taxes from its GNP. Nonetheless, the table makes it clear that Berle's comparison was not a wholly fanciful one.

EMERGENCE OF MULTINATIONAL PRODUCTION

Why has the multinational phenomenon arisen? The question is not altogether simple to answer. After all, it is cheaper to export goods or to license production abroad than to establish a branch in a faraway nation and encounter troubles and risks, which we will look into. Why, then, has production itself leaped overseas?

The initial reason arises from a characteristic of the firm, to which we have heretofore paid only passing attention. This is the drive for expansion that we find in nearly all capitalist enterprises. In our overview of the rise of American big business, we saw the emergence of giant enterprise as a consequence of the pull of markets and the push of a mass production.* Much the same logic has driven firms, from early times, to expand their market overseas. Samuel Colt, the inventor of the first "assembly line" revolver, opened a foreign branch in London in the mid-1850s (and promptly failed). But in those same years American entrepreneurs were already successfully pushing a railway line to completion across the Panama isthmus, and by the 1870s the Singer Sewing Machine was gaining half its revenues from overseas production and exports.

But what drives a firm to *produce* overseas, rather than just to sell overseas? The answers are many. One of them may be that transport costs become too large, once a certain volume of exports is reached, and simple economics dictates overseas production instead. Another may be a desire to locate a factory behind the tariff walls that a country may have erected in the hope of keeping out imports of the very goods the factory will produce. Another is simply the growth of the "horizon" of the giant companies, so that it becomes a matter of as great importance for IBM to win a commanding share of production overseas as it is to gain dominance at home. At some point in their expansion many companies make the transition from the

* Alfred Chandler has shown in a brilliant book, *Strategy and Structure* (Cambridge, Mass.: M.I.T. Press, 1962), that the typical domestic firm went through a series of "logical" changes in organization, growing from the single-product, single-plant firm (in which every operation was supervised personally by the founder-owner) to the multidivisional, multiproduct enterprise in which a tiered organizational structure became necessary to superintend the strategic requirements of national geographic scope and increasing technical complexity.

viewpoint of a "national" enterprise to that of a genuinely international one, whose markets are now worldwide in extent and whose production facilities must be located wherever these global markets are served most efficiently.* This is a matter we will return to when we consider the problem of imperialism.

What economic changes have followed from the startling rise of international production? One clear answer is that the growth of the multinational enterprise has dramatically changed the *geographic location* and the *technological character* of international economic activity.

The shift away from exports and imports to international production has introduced two changes into the international economic scene. One change is a movement of foreign investment away from its original concentration in the underdeveloped areas of the world toward the richer markets of the developed areas. Fifty years ago, in the era of high imperialism, most of the capital leaving one country for another flowed from rich to poor lands. Thus foreign investment in the late nineteenth and early twentieth centuries was largely associated with the creation of vast plantations, the building of railways through jungles, and the development of mineral resources.

But the growth of the multinational enterprise has coincided with a decisive shift away from investment in the underdeveloped world to investment in the industrial world. In 1897, 59 percent of American foreign direct investment was in agriculture, mining, or railways, mainly in the underdeveloped world. By the end of the 1960s, our investment in agriculture, mining, and railways, as a proportion of our total overseas assets, had fallen to about 20 percent; and its geographical location in the backward world came to only 36 percent of all our overseas direct investments. More striking, almost three-quarters of our huge rise in direct investment during the decade of the 1960s had been in the developed world; and the vast bulk of it has been in manufacturing (and oil) rather than in plantations, railroads, or ores.[10] *Thus the multinational companies are investing in each others' territories rather than invading the territories of the underdeveloped world.* This is not to say that they do not wield great power in the backward regions, as we shall see, but their thrust of expansion has been in other industrial lands, not in the unindustrialized ones.

The second economic change is really implicit in the first. It is a shift away from "heavy technology" to "high technology" industries—away from

---

* The internal dynamics that send some firms overseas, but not others, are by no means wholly understood. The internationalization of production is much more widely spread in some industries, such as glass, than in others, such as steel. Drugs are widely produced on an international basis; machine tools are not.

[10] See Mira Wilkins, *The Emergence of Multinational Enterprise* (Cambridge: Harvard University Press, 1970), p. 110; also *Survey of Current Business,* October 1970, pp. 28-29.

enterprises in which often vast sums of capital were associated with large, unskilled labor forces, as in the building of railways or plantations—toward industries in which capital is perhaps less strategic than research and development, skilled technical manpower, and sophisticated management techniques typical of computer, petrochemical, and other new industries.

Table 11-2 sums up the overall shift.

TABLE 11•2

SIZE AND DISTRIBUTION OF U.S. FOREIGN DIRECT INVESTMENT			
	1929	1950	1969
Total (millions)	**$7,528**	**$11,788**	**$70,763**
Percent distribution, by market			
Canada	27	30	30
Europe	18	14	30
Latin America	47	41	20
Asia, Africa, other	8	15	18
Percentage distribution, by industrial sector			
Manufacturing	24	31	42
Petroleum	15	29	29
Transport and utilities	21	12	4
Mining	15	9	8
Trade	5	7	8
Agriculture	12	5 }	9
Other	8	6 }	

Sources: *Historical Statistics of the U.S.*, p. 566; *Survey of Current Business*, October 1970, pp. 29, 31.

Note the dramatic shift away from Latin America and away from transport, mining, and agriculture into Europe and manufacturing, a shift that would be even more accentuated if we were not still dependent on oil as a major source of the world's energy. If nuclear power or the fuel cell displace oil within the next two decades, we can expect a still more rapid decline in investment in the backward areas (especially in the Near East), and a proportionately still larger concentration of foreign direct investment in manufacturing.

POLITICAL ECONOMICS OF MULTINATIONAL ENTERPRISE

Thus the international corporations have served as vehicles for the redirection of the world's international allocation of capital investment. But the economic effects of the multinationals are perhaps less important than their political effects, for international production has a political factor that makes international economic relationships sharply different from those of pre-multinational days.

In the main, the "classical" conception of international trade was based on the familiar model of a competitive world in which factors of production were free to move about to find their points of highest return *within* their own national territories. The result was a final equilibrium in which each nation discovered the best allocation of resources both with regard to its own resources and to the advantageous exchanges it could make with other nations. In this final equilibrium, political considerations might enter in the form of tariffs or other trade barriers, but these were always considered by economists as the product of national nearsightedness, so that in theory— and to some extent in practice—it was possible to use the notion of *an equilibrium determined entirely by economic considerations.*

Not so, under the peculiar conditions of international production. For now the unit of economic activity is no longer the tiny "factor of production" subject to market forces, but a giant corporation capable of the maneuvers, tactics, and strategies characteristic of oligopolistic, rather than competitive, economic units. *Within* a given country, as we have seen, oligopolies tend to "settle down" to a more or less steady division-of-the-market, usually by tacit agreement not to engage in price warfare. But this division-of-the-market becomes rudely disturbed when a newcomer from the "outside" establishes his production unit within the home market of another nation. Moreover, the new division-of-the-market between the invader and the established giants will not be determined solely by the economic growth potentials of the various contestants. *There is an inescapable political element that will also play an important, perhaps determinative, role.*

This political element has two aspects. On the one hand, it depends on the ability of smaller nations, such as those we find in Europe, to relinquish their feelings of national pride sufficiently to allow the creation of big enough pan-European enterprises to challenge the (American) invader successfully. (Here is Servan-Schreiber's problem in a nutshell.) The cost of IBM's research and development, for example, is more than the entire sales earnings of its largest British competitor. To stand up against IBM, therefore, it may be necessary for British companies to merge with French or German ones, to form a competitor with the economies of scale, the ability to generate finance, the command over technical talent that will put it in a league with IBM. But that will require a *political* decision on the part of England or France or Germany to give up exclusive national control over "their" biggest computer companies.

A few such genuinely international companies have come into existence. Royal Dutch/Shell and Unilever are truly bi-national enterprises run by boards of directors that represent both Dutch and English directors and an effort is being made to create more such genuinely "European" enterprises. Whether or not this effort will be successful, it is too early to tell. But

CREATING
PAN-NATIONAL
ENTERPRISES

surely the critical element in the final division of the market among the multinationals will depend fully as much on the politics of international merger as on the economics of market tactics.

There is, moreover, a second political element that enters into the new multinational thrust. This is the question of the extent to which foreign governments will *permit* "foreign" corporations to operate within their borders.

This problem has its counterpart in the political decision on how much to tax (by tariffs) the goods that foreign companies sell to a given nation. But the problem of permitting the entry of a foreign-owned production unit is much more important—and much more difficult to resolve—because this may be the only way that a nation can "import" the *technology* and the *productivity* that the multinational invader will bring with it.

For example, the French government has been extremely uneasy over the virtual preemption of its high technology computer industries by American firms. Thus when General Electric sought to buy a 20 percent interest in Machines Bull, a leading French manufacturer of computer and desk machinery, the French government balked at the "Americanization" of the firm and forbade the transaction. That was in 1962. Within a very few years it became apparent that without an infusion of American technology, Machines Bull could not stand up to the competition of IBM, and the French government unhappily acquiesced in the American "takeover." But then it *was* a takeover, for G.E. demanded (and got) 50 percent control of Machines Bull.*

Thus, the pan-national thrust of economic activity unavoidably hinges on political decisions concerning the national independence of the economies into which the multinationals seek to move. Canadians, for example, have recently awakened to the fact that they own only *15* percent of their "own" industry. All the rest is foreign owned. Americans alone control 46 percent of Canadian manufacturing, 58 percent of its oil and gas, and almost 100 percent of its auto industry. The next biggest slice is owned by various European, mainly British, interests. Canada is thus a minority stockholder in its own economy, a situation that has led to strong sentiments to block further foreign ownership. But there would, of course, be a real economic price—a diminished rate of growth—for such a blockage.

This conflict between the jealous claims of nation-states who seek to retain national control over productive activity within their own borders and the powerful thrust of pan-national corporations for new markets in foreign territories introduces profound tensions into the political economics of multinational production. On the one hand, the multinational is in a position to

* An investment that did not work out very successfully, by the way, for G.E.

win hard bargains from the "host" country into which it seeks to enter (as in the case of France and G.E.), because the corporation *is* the main bearer of new technologies and management techniques that every nation seeks. Therefore, if one country—say France—refuses to give a would-be entrant the right to come in (and possibly to cause financial losses to its established firms), the multinational may well place its plants, with their precious economic cargo of productivity, in another country, leaving the recalcitrant nation the loser in the race for international growth.

On the other hand, the power is by no means entirely one-sided; for once a multinational *has* entered a foreign nation, it becomes a *hostage* of the host country. It is now bound by the laws of that country and may find itself forced to undertake activities that are "foreign." For example, in Japan it is an unwritten law that workers engaged by giant corporations are *never* fired, but become permanent employees. Japan has been extremely reluctant to allow foreign capital to establish manufacturing operations on Japanese soil, to the great annoyance of foreign companies. But if, as now seems likely, Japan is opened to American and European capital, we can be sure that American or European corporations will be expected to behave in the Japanese way with their employees. This will not be an easy course to follow, since these corporations are not likely to receive the special support that the Japanese government gives to its own big firms.

Or take the problem of a multinational that is forced by a fall in demand to cut back the volume of its output. A decision made along strictly economic lines would lead it to close its least profitable plant. But this may bring very serious economic repercussions in the particular nation in which that plant is located—so serious that the government will threaten to take "action" if the plant is closed. What dictates shall the multinational then follow: those of standard business accounting or those of political accounting?

Or consider the multinational seeking to expand or to alter its operations in an underdeveloped country. This, too, may lead to friction, for as former Undersecretary George Ball has candidly asked: "How can a national government make an economic plan with any confidence if a board of directors meeting 5,000 miles away can, by altering its pattern of purchasing and production, affect in a major way the country's economic life?"[11]

As we have seen in Peru, Bolivia, and Chile (*before* the victory of the socialist party there in 1970), this incompatibility of aims may become so great that the underdeveloped country eventually seizes and nationalizes the assets of the multinational.

Is there an "answer" to this conflict between the business rationality of the multinational corporation and the political priorities of the nation-state? At this stage in the development of both institutions, none is in sight. The

[11] Brown, *World Business,* p. 334.

very idea of pan-national production is itself so new that we lack even a conceptual model of how to deal with its problems, much less a set of practical rules and regulations to follow. Take something so simple—but so important—as the location of the "head office" of the corporation to which a nation would make representations if the action of an international corporation were contrary to national interest. From one nation to another the legal definition of the *head office* differs: in the U.S. and the U.K., it is the place where the company is formally incorporated; in Morocco it is the location of the "registered" home office; in France, Germany, and Belgium, it is the main center of management; in Italy and Egypt it is the place of principal business activity. Which of these will respond when a country in search of legal redress calls out: "Will the real head office please stand up?"

Or take the question of the patriotic accountability of the multinational enterprise. Suppose a company wishes to move its profits from country A to country B, but that country A has balance-of-payments difficulties. Is the company bound to obey the wishes of A? Suppose the government in B also has balance-of-payments difficulties and desires the company to import capital? What should the corporation do? In 1966, for example, the United States government asked corporations not to export capital, lest our precarious balance of payments be worsened. But the Ford Motor Company decided that its long-term interests required the purchase of British Ford, so that despite objections of the U.S. government, Ford exported $600 million of capital to make the purchase. Was Ford "unpatriotic," if its actions were in the long-term interests of the company? Was it similarly "unpatriotic" (from a British point of view) for a group of English investors to export British capital to finance the building of the Pan Am skyscraper in New York?

Or suppose a multinational company, in one of its foreign plants, undertakes work that is integral to the defense of that nation; and that the foreign policy of the nation in question brings its military strength to bear against another country in which the multinational is also located? Is the company supposed to "take sides"?

UNRESOLVED QUESTIONS

There are no answers to such questions, only speculations.[12] Here are some of them.

Speculation 1. Will the conglomerate serve as a means of mediating between the demands of business production efficiency and political "national" control? For example, why didn't Ford build the Pan Am building, and why didn't the British investors put their pounds into autos? Both sides would have told you (in 1966) that they weren't "in the business" of real estate or cars, as the case may be. But the rise of the conglomerates (see pp. 123-24)

---

[12] For a searching commentary see Detlev F. Vagts, "The Multinational Enterprise: A New Challenge for Transnational Law," *Harvard Law Review,* February 1970.

opens new possibilities in this direction. If, in the future, the controlling center of Ford becomes (as I.T.&T. has already become) a capital-allocation office rather than the headquarters of an auto firm, it is possible that Ford *will* build buildings and that British realtors *will* build automobiles. In that case, the big corporation may surrender some of its multinationality in exchange for multi-industrial coverage.

Speculation 2. Will the multinationals, if they continue their growth, constitute the skeleton of a new form of world order? Some economists and businessmen see the rise of a pan-national system of oligopolies controlled by boards of directors that represent many nations (rather than mainly one, as is now the case), whose operations will pave the way for a much more pragmatic, down-to-earth, effective system of world production and distribution than the present competition of hostile, suspicious, and dangerous nation-states. Such an international rationalization of production, they believe, could bring a "businessman's peace," in which the big companies serve to accelerate world growth, to introduce efficiency into the backward areas, and to assert the logic of economic performance over the outmoded rivalries of jealous nation-states.

Speculation 3. Will the multinationals, on the contrary, serve to heighten the tension of a world which, for better or worse, must continue to use the powerful appeal of nationhood? How can giant corporations, necessarily dedicated to profit-making, adjust their operations to the often unprofitable needs of national development? How can corporations, jockeying for market position, provide the basis for a stable world economic system? The opponents of the multinationals see in them not a force for progress but only a means of imposing a calculus of profits on a world whose needs at the moment often demand an entirely different set of fundamental values.

It is much too early to determine which of these arguments will eventually be proven correct. Perhaps the safest guess is that all will be, at least in our lifetimes. The big corporations are likely to continue to go in both multinational and conglomerate directions. To some extent they will be the international carriers of efficiency and development, especially in the high technology areas for which they seem to be the most effective form of organization. But if the power of the nation-state will be challenged by these international production units, it is not likely to be humbled by them. There are many things a nation can do that a corporation cannot, including, above all, the creation of the spirit of sacrifice necessary both for good purposes such as development and for evil ones such as war.

Perhaps all we can say at this stage of human development is that both nation-states and huge corporations are necessary, in that they seem to be the only ways in which we can organize mankind to perform the arduous and sustained labor without which humanity itself would rapidly perish. Perhaps after the long age of capital accumulation has finally come to an end and sufficient capital is available to all peoples, we may be able to think seriously about dismantling the giant enterprise and the nation-state, both of which overpower the individual with their massive organized strength. However desirable that ultimate goal may be, in our time both state and corporation promise to be with us, and the tension between them will be part of the evolutionary drama of our period of history.

KEY CONCEPTS AND KEY WORDS

Multinational
corporations

1. The basic conception of international trade has entered a new stage marked by *international production carried on by the multinational corporation.*

2. The natural impetus of the drive for growth has pushed most large U.S. corporations into multinational operations. As a result, our exports of manufactures are today only 40 percent of our overseas production of manufactured commodities. In fact, *overseas production is now considerably larger than the exports of all U.S. goods.*

Foreign direct
investment

3. As a result of the thrust of the multinationals, U.S. foreign direct investment has risen to approximately $70 billion of foreign direct American investment and may be much larger than that if the value of foreign capital controlled by American equity is included.

4. The rise of the American multinational in Europe has been very rapid and has led to a European fear of an "American challenge." However justified in Europe, this fear masks the fact that *European (and Japanese) foreign investment is rising as rapidly as American—and much of it in America.*

Internationalization
of production

5. *The prospect is for a genuine internationalization of production within the next few decades.* A few hundred large firms, of which the majority will probably be American, are apt to control a very large fraction of the production of industrial commodities on a worldwide basis.

6. *The rise of multinational production has resulted in striking shifts in the geographic location and technological character of international investment.* The trend has been away from investment in underdeveloped nations to investment in the markets of high-consumption countries; and away from low-skilled labor-intensive or capital-intensive industries to high skill-intensive industries.

High technology

7. The *incursion of the multinationals across national boundaries has raised sharp new problems of political economics.* An equilibrium in international production will depend on political decisions as well as economic forces. These are:
   - The ability of smaller nations to abandon national prerogatives in order to form effective international corporations to challenge American or other companies.
   - The willingness of countries to allow foreign companies to dominate industries that they may consider vital to their national interests.
   - The ability of most nations to import new high technology if they deny entry to the multinationals.

8. Equally perplexing problems are posed for the multinationals themselves. *If they are often in a position to drive hard bargains before entrance, once they have committed themselves, they are "hostages."* To which of the many countries where they may be located do they owe allegiance if the interests of those countries clash? To what extent should the dictates of profit determine their international allocations of manpower and capital? To what extent can a multinational "defy," and to what extent must it "bow before," the demands of a host country?

9. There are no answers to the questions above. *We still have no established rules or procedures or laws to cover this new mode of organizing the world's production.* Nor do we know if the growth of multinational enterprise will serve as a force for order and rationality or for friction and tension.

QUESTIONS

1. How many products produced in America can you identify as "foreign"? (You might start with the detergents and soaps produced by Lever Brothers, the office machinery produced by Olivetti-Underwood, the gas and oil refined by Shell.)

2. Can you suggest a hypothesis that might be testable as to why certain industries seem to go "overseas" more rapidly than others? Why autos and tractors but not washing machines? Why plate glass but not sheet steel? (Little is known about this, so you might become famous if you come up with an idea that tests out.)

3. Do you think a nation is right to exclude a foreign company from producing in certain areas? Would you wish to exclude from the U.S. Japanese production of, say, high-speed computers if *this were the only way we could get high-speed computers?*

4. What do you think is the duty of a company that is active in nations A, B, and C, when all have balance-of-payments problems and request domestic corporations not to make unnecessary international payments? Suppose the headquarters of the company is in A and the stockholders want the profits from B and C repatriated?

5. Can you draw up a plan for a company that would be privately owned and managed but not officially "headquartered" in any one nation? From whom would it receive its charter? Under what laws will it operate so far as the top management is concerned?

6. Do you think that the rise of multinational production opens the way for a more rational world or a more divided one?

We must begin this very important chapter with a sobering realization. It is that our account of the long sweep of Western economic advance has largely ignored the economic existence of four out of five human beings on earth. Mere parochialism was not, however, the reason for this concentration on Western progress. Rather, it was the shocking fact that, taken in the large, *there was no economic progress in the rest of the world.*

This is not to say that tides of fortune and misfortune did not mark these areas, that great cultural heights were not achieved, and that the political or social histories of these regions do not warrant interest and study. Yet the fact remains that the mounting tide of *economic* advance that has engaged our attention was a phenomenon limited to the West. It is no doubt something of an oversimplification, but it is basically true to claim that in Asia, Africa, South America, or the Near East, economic existence was not materially improved for the average inhabitant from the twelfth— and, in some cases, the second—to the beginning of the twentieth century. Indeed, for many of them it was worsened. A long graph of non-Western material well-being would depict irregular rises and falls but an almost total absence of cumulative betterment.

The near end of such a graph would show the standard of living of three-quarters of the human race who inhabit the so-called underdeveloped areas today. Most of this mass of humanity exists in conditions of poverty that are difficult for a Westerner to comprehend. When we sum up the plight of the underdeveloped nations by saying that a billion human beings have a standard of living of "less than $100 a year," and that another, more fortunate, billion people enjoy in a year one-quarter to one-half the income a typical American family spends in a single *month*, we give only a pale statistical meaning to a reality that we can scarcely grasp.*

* In Iran, for instance, in years of famine, the children of the poor examine the droppings of horses to extract morsels of undigested oats. In Calcutta, 250,000 people have no home whatsoever and live in the streets. In Hong Kong, large numbers of families of four or more live in one bed-space in a squalid dormitory. In Cali, Colombia, when the river rises, the city's sewers run through the homes of the poor. In Hyderabad, Pakistan, child labor employed in sealing the ends of bangles over a kerosene flame is paid eight cents—per *gross* of bangles.

Why are the underdeveloped nations so pitiably poor? Only a half-century ago it was common to attribute their backwardness to geographic or climatic causes. The underdeveloped nations were poor, it was thought, either because the climate was too debilitating or because natural resources were lacking. Sometimes it was just said that the natives were too childlike or racially too inferior to improve their lot.

Bad climates may have had adverse effects. Yet, many hot areas have shown a capacity for sustained economic growth (for example, the Queensland areas of Australia), and we have come to recognize that a number of underdeveloped areas, such as Argentina and Korea, have completely temperate climates. So, too, we now regard the lack of resources in many areas more as a *symptom* of underdevelopment than a cause—which is to say that in many underdeveloped areas, resources have not yet been *looked for.* Libya, for instance, which used to be written off as a totally barren nation, has been discovered to be a huge reservoir of oil. Finally, little is heard today about native childishness or inherent inferiority. (Perhaps we remember how the wealthy classes similarly characterized the poor in Europe not too many centuries ago.) Climate and geography and cultural unpreparedness unquestionably constitute obstacles to rapid economic growth—and in some areas of the globe, very serious obstacles—but there are few economists who would look to these disadvantages as the main causes of economic backwardness.

Why then are these societies so poor?

The answer takes us back to an early chapter of our book. These are poor societies because they are *traditional* societies—that is, societies which have developed neither the mechanisms of command nor of the market by which they might launch into a sustained process of economic growth. Indeed, as we examine them further we will have the feeling that we are encountering in the present the anachronistic counterparts of the static societies of antiquity.

Why did they remain traditional societies? Why, for instance, did Byzantium, which was economically so advanced in contrast with the Crusaders' Europe, fall into decline? Why did China, with so many natural advantages, not develop into a dynamic economic society? There are no simple, or even fully satisfactory, answers. Perhaps the absence of economic progress elsewhere on the globe forces us to look upon our Western experience not as the paradigm and standard for historic development, but as a very special case in which various activating factors met in an environment peculiarly favorable for the emergence of a new economic style in history. The problem is one into which we cannot go more deeply in this book. At any rate, it is today an academic question. The dominant reality of our times is that the backward areas are now striving desperately to enter the mainstream of economic progress of the West. Let us examine further their chances for doing so.

CONDITIONS OF BACKWARDNESS

Every people, to exist, must first feed itself; there is a rough sequence to the order of demands in human society. But to go beyond existence, it must achieve a certain level of efficiency in agriculture, so that its efforts can be turned in other directions. What is tragically characteristic of the underdeveloped areas is that this first corner of economic progress has not yet been turned.

Consider the situation only a few years ago in that all-important crop of the East, rice. Table 12-1 shows the difference between the productivity of rice fields in the main Asiatic countries and those of the United States and Australia as of the later 1950s.

What is true of rice can be duplicated in most other crops.* It is a disconcerting fact that the backward peasant nations which depend desperate-

TABLE 12 • 1

RICE PRODUCTION

(100 kilograms per hectare)	
U.S.	34.3
Australia	45.9
Burma	14.8
China (1954)	24.7
India	12.6
Indonesia	16.5
Thailand	14.3
Philippines	11.9

Source: Benjamin Higgins, *Economic Development* (New York: Norton, 1959), p. 16.

* Table 12-1 shows only the productive differentials of equal *areas* of land. When we consider that a single American farmer tends up to a hundred times as large an acreage as a peasant in an underdeveloped area, the difference in output *per man* would be much more striking. The "Green Revolution" (see p. 222) has improved the situation, but we do not yet have the data we need to determine outputs for the new rice strains. Despite the improvement, a vast gulf still separates U.S. agricultural productivity from that of the underdeveloped nations.

ly on their capacity to grow food cannot even compete in these main products with the advanced countries: U.S. Louisiana rice undersells Philippine rice, California oranges are not only better but cheaper than Indonesian oranges.

Why is agriculture so unproductive? One apparent reason is that the typical unit of agricultural production in the underdeveloped lands is far too small to permit efficient farming. What has been called "postage stamp cultivation" marks the pattern of farming throughout most of Asia and a good deal of Africa and South America. John Gunther, reporting the situation in India thirty years ago, described it vividly. It has not changed since that time.

There is no primogeniture in India as a rule, and when the peasant dies his land is subdivided among all his sons with the result that most holdings are infinitesimally small. In one district in the Punjab, following fragmentation through generations, 584 owners cultivate no less than 16,000 fields; in another, 12,800 acres are split into actually 63,000 holdings. Three-quarters of the holdings in India as a whole are under ten acres. In many parts of India the average holding is less than an acre.[1]

In part, this terrible situation is the result of divisive inheritance practices which Gunther mentions. In part, it is due to landlord systems in which peasants cannot legally own or accumulate their own land; in part, to the pressure of too many people on too little soil. There are many causes, with one result: agriculture suffers from a devastatingly low productivity brought about by grotesque man/land ratios.

These are, however, only the first links in a chain of causes for low agricultural productivity. Another consequence of these tiny plots is an inability to apply sufficient capital to the land. Mechanical binders and reapers, tractors and trucks are not only impossible to use efficiently in such tiny spaces, but they are costly beyond the reach of the subsistence farmer. Even fertilizer is too expensive: in much of Asia, animal dung is used to provide "free" fuel rather than returned to the soil to enrich it.

This paralyzing lack of capital is by no means confined to agriculture. It pervades the entire range of an underdeveloped economy. The whole industrial landscape of a Western economy is missing: no factories, no power lines, no machines, no paved roads meet the eye for mile upon mile as one travels through an underdeveloped continent. Indeed, to a pitiable extent, an underdeveloped land is one in which human and animal muscle power provide the energy with which production is carried on. In India in 1953, for instance, 65 percent of the total amount of productive energy in the nation was the product of straining man and beast.[2] The amount of usable electrical power generated in all of India would not have sufficed to light up New York City.

[1] *Inside Asia* (New York: Harper, 1939), p. 385.
[2] Daniel Wit and Alfred B. Clubok, "Atomic Power Development in India," *Social Research,* Autumn 1958, p. 290.

A lack of agricultural and industrial capital is not the only reason for low productivity. As we would expect in traditional societies, an endemic cause of low per capita output lies in prevailing social attitudes. Typically, the people of an underdeveloped economy have not *learned* the "economic" attitudes that foster rapid industrialization. Instead of technology-conscious farmers, they are tradition-bound peasants. Instead of disciplined workers, they are reluctant and untrained laborers. Instead of production-minded businessmen, they are trading-oriented merchants.

For example, Alvin Hansen reports from his observations in India:

Agricultural practices are controlled by custom and tradition. A villager is fearful of science. For many villagers, insecticide is taboo because all life is sacred. A new and improved seed is suspect. To try it is a gamble. Fertilizers, for example, are indeed a risk. ... To adopt these untried methods might be to risk failure. And failure could mean starvation.[3]

In similar vein, a UNESCO report tells us:

In the least developed areas, the worker's attitude toward labour may entirely lack time perspective, let alone the concept of productive investment. For example, the day labourer in a rural area on his way to work, who finds a fish in the net he placed in the river the night before, is observed to return home, his needs being met....[4]

An equally crippling attitude is evinced by the upper classes, who look with scorn or disdain upon business or production-oriented careers. UNESCO also reports that of the many students from the underdeveloped lands studying in the United States—the majority of whom come from the more privileged classes—only 4 percent were studying a problem fundamental to all their nations: agriculture.[5]

All these attitudes give rise to a *social inertia* that poses a tremendous hurdle to economic development. A suspicious peasantry, fearful of change that might jeopardize the slim margin yielding them life, a work force unresponsive to monetary incentive, a privileged class not interested in production—all these are part of the obdurate handicaps to be overcome by an underdeveloped nation.

Many of these problems, as we anticipated, remind us of the premarket economies of antiquity. But in addition, the underdeveloped lands face an obstacle with which the economies of antiquity did *not* have to cope: a crushing rate of population increase threatens to nullify their efforts to emerge from backward conditions.

[3] *Economic Issues of the 1960s* (New York: McGraw-Hill, 1960), pp. 157-58.
[4] *Report on the World Social Situation,* UNESCO, March 9, 1961, p. 79.
[5] *Ibid.,* p. 81.

Only a few figures are needed to make the point. Let us begin with our southern neighbor, Mexico. Today, Mexico has a population equal to that of New York State, Pennsylvania, New Jersey, and Connecticut. Thirty years from now, if Mexico's present rate of population increase continues, it will have as many people as the present population of these four states *plus* the rest of New England, *plus* the entire South Atlantic seaboard, *plus* the entire West Coast, *plus* Ohio, Indiana, Illinois, Michigan, and Wisconsin. Or take the Caribbean and Central American area. That small part of the globe has a population of around 70 million. In some thirty years, at present growth rates, its population will outnumber by 30 million the entire population of the United States today. South America, now 20 percent less populous than we, will be 200 percent larger than our present population. India will then very likely number a billion souls. China will probably number 1.6 billion.

We have already seen one result of the relentless proliferation of people in the fragmentation of landholdings. But the problem goes beyond mere fragmentation. Eugene Black, formerly president of the International Bank for Reconstruction and Development (the World Bank) tells us that in India a population equivalent to that of all Great Britain has been squeezed out of any landholding whatsoever—even though it still dwells in rural areas.[6] Consequently, population pressure generates massive and widespread rural poverty, pushing inhabitants from the countryside into the already overcrowded cities. Five hundred families a day move into Jakarta from the surrounding Javanese countryside where population has reached the fantastic figure of 1,100 per square mile.

Even these tragic repercussions of population growth are but side effects. The main problem is that population growth adds more mouths almost as fast as the underdeveloped nations manage to add more food. They cancel out much economic progress by literally eating up the small surpluses which might serve as a springboard for faster future growth.

Ironically, this population "explosion" in the underdeveloped countries is a fairly recent phenomenon, attributable largely to the incursion of Western medicine and public health into the low income areas. Prior to World War II, the poorer countries held their population growth in check because death rates were nearly as high as birth rates. With DDT and penicillin, death rates have plunged dramatically. In Ceylon, for example, death rates dropped 40 percent in one year following the adoption of malaria control and other health measures. As death rates dropped in the underdeveloped areas, birth rates, for many reasons, continued high, despite efforts to introduce birth control. In the backward lands, children are not only a source of prestige and of household labor for the peasant family, but also the only possible source of "social security" for old age. The childless older

[6] Eugene R. Black, *The Diplomacy of Economic Development* (Cambridge: Harvard University Press, 1960), p. 9.

couple could very well starve; as parents or grandparents they are at least assured of a roof over their heads.

Is there a solution for this grim question? Until very recent years, any candid expert could have answered only with a discouraged shake of the head. In the long run there was always the hope that industrialization would eventually bring the lower birth rates characteristic of all urban societies. But the problem was how to reach the long run against the overwhelming tides of population increase.

Today there is some hope. New techniques of birth control—especially the IUD (for *intra-uterine device*)—have shown promising results in those areas—mainly Taiwan and South Korea—where they have been introduced. There seems now to be a chance, if the underdeveloped countries apply their full efforts with the assistance of Western *expertise,* that the floodtide can be stemmed, perhaps within another generation or two. That still leaves the prospect of a Niagara of births to come. But there is new hope that the human torrent can be dammed before it has washed away all possibility of progress.

NINETEENTH-CENTURY IMPERIALISM

This gives us a brief introduction to underdevelopment as it exists today. Before we turn to the problem of how this condition can be remedied, we must inquire into one more question. Why did not the market society, with all its economic dynamism, spread into the backward areas?

The answer is that the active economies of the European and American worlds *did* make contact with the underdeveloped regions, beginning with the great exploratory and commercial voyages of the fifteenth and sixteenth centuries. Until the nineteenth century, unfortunately, that contact was little more than mere adventure and plunder. And then, starting in the first half of that century and gaining momentum until World War I, came that scramble for territory we call the Age of Imperialism.

What was this imperialism? It was, in retrospect, a compound of many things: militarism, jingoism, a search for markets and for sources of cheap raw materials to feed growing industrial enterprises. Insofar as the colonial areas were concerned, however, the first impact of imperialism was not solely that of exploitation. On the contrary, the incursion of Western empires into the backward areas brought some advantages. It injected the first heavy dose of industrial capital: rail lines, mines, plantation equipment. It brought law and order, often into areas in which the most despotic personal rule had previously been the order of the day. It introduced the ideas of the West, including, most importantly, the idea of freedom, which was eventually to rouse the backward nations against the invading West itself.

Yet if imperialism brought these positive and stimulating influences, it also exerted a peculiarly deforming impulse to the underdeveloped—indeed, then, totally undeveloped—economies of the East and South. In the eyes of the imperialist nations, the colonies were viewed not as areas to be brought along in balanced development, but essentially as immense supply dumps to be attached to the mother countries' industrial economies. Malaya became a vast tin mine; Indonesia, a huge tea and rubber plantation; Arabia, an oil field. In other words, the direction of economic development was steadily pushed in the direction that most benefited the imperial owner, not the colonial peoples themselves.

The result today is that the typical underdeveloped nation has a badly lopsided economy, unable to supply itself with a wide variety of goods. It is thereby thrust into the international market with its one basic commodity. For instance, in South America we find that Venezuela is dependent on oil for some 90 percent of its exports; Colombia, on coffee for three-quarters of its exports; Chile, on copper for two-thirds of its foreign earnings; Honduras, on bananas for half of its foreign earnings. On the surface, this looks like a healthy specialization of trade. We shall shortly see why it is not.

Economic lopsidedness was one unhappy consequence of imperialism. No less important for the future course of development in the colonial areas was a second decisive influence of the West: its failure to achieve political and psychological relationships of mutual respect with its colonial peoples. In part, this was no doubt traceable to an often frankly exploitative economic attitude, in which the colonials were relegated to second-class jobs with third-class pay, while a handful of Western whites formed an insulated and highly paid managerial clique. But it ran deeper than that. A terrible color line, a callous indifference to colonial aspirations, a patronizing and sometimes contemptuous view of "the natives" runs all through the history of imperialism. It has left as a bitter heritage not only an identification of capitalism with its worst practices, but a political and social wariness toward the West which deeply affects the general orientation of the developing areas.

What about imperialism today? Certainly it has changed. The naked power grabs are in the past, when imperialism often meant only the acquisition of territory that would look good on a map. In the past, also, are the seizures of raw materials on the unfair terms characteristic of mineral empires built in the late nineteenth century. Gone as well are attitudes of racial "superiority" so infuriating to peoples whose culture was often of far greater delicacy and discrimination than that of the West.

Yet that is not the whole story. For there is also no doubt that some Western capitalist nations continue to exercise a mixed political and economic hegemony over "independent" governments: Portugal over Angola, England over portions of Africa, and above all, the United States over South and Central America and Southeast Asia.

The nature of this imperialism is now changing, partly under the pressures exerted by a restive Third World, partly as a result of developments within the advanced nations themselves. The rise of the so-called multinational corporation, for example, puts the problem of the economic relationship of advanced and backward countries in a new light. The backward nations are extremely wary of the power inherent in a giant U.S. or European corporation. Yet they also need the big companies. Big multinationals pay higher wages, keep more honest books, provide better working conditions and fancier career opportunities, and bring in more technological expertise than do the domestic enterprises of the "host" nation.

The result is that the problem of imperialism in our day, at least so far as the United States is concerned, has taken an unexpected turn. On the economic side of the question, the *danger now is as much that the big companies will bypass the backward nations as that they will dominate them.*

Meanwhile, the political element of imperialism seems to be diminishing. The erstwhile capitalist empires of Germany, Belgium, Netherlands, England (with a few exceptions), have disappeared. Portugal, for all its ruthless domination of Angola, is an archaic remnant of the past, not an entering wedge of the future. What is left is a strong effort on the part of the United States to preserve its ideological and political influence, particularly in Latin America and Southeast Asia, but the election of a Marxist president in Chile and the debacle of the American Vietnam policy indicate that the prospects for a "successful" imperialism of this kind are limited, at best.

The Engineering of Development

Up to this point we have concentrated our attention mainly on the background of underdevelopment. Now we must ask a more forward-looking, more technically "economic" question: How can an underdeveloped nation emerge from its poverty?

From what we have learned, we know the basic answer to this question. The prerequisite for economic progress for the underdeveloped countries today is not essentially different from what it was in Great Britain at the time of the industrial revolution, or what it was in Russia in 1917. To grow, an underdeveloped economy must build capital.

How is a starving country able to build capital? When 80 percent of a country is scrabbling on the land for a bare subsistence, how can it divert its energies to building dams and roads, ditches and houses, railroad embankments and factories which, however indispensable for progress tomorrow, cannot be eaten today? If our postage-stamp farmers were to halt work on their tiny unproductive plots and go to work on a great project like, say, the Aswan Dam, who would feed them? Whence would come the necessary food to sustain these capital workers?

At first sight, the problem looks insuperable. If an underdeveloped country is to amass capital, it will have to swing labor from agricultural tasks to capital-building tasks. But when a country can barely feed itself, how can it make this switch?

At second look, however, the prospect is not quite so bleak. These economies *do* have unemployed factors, and a large number of peasants who till the fields are not feeding themselves. They are, also, in a sense, taking food from one another's mouths.

As we have seen, the crowding of peasants on the land in these areas has resulted in a diminution of agricultural productivity far below that of the advanced countries. Hence the abundance of peasants working in the fields obscures the fact that *a smaller number of peasants, with little more equipment—perhaps even with no more equipment—could raise a total output just as large.* One observer has written: "An experiment carried out near Cairo by the American College seems to suggest that the present output, or something closely approaching it, could be produced by about half the present rural population of Egypt."[7] Here is an extreme case, but it can be found to apply, to some degree, to nearly every underdeveloped land.

Now we begin to see an answer to the predicament of the underdeveloped societies. In nearly all of these societies, there exists a disguised and hidden surplus of labor which, if it were taken off the land, could be used to build capital. Most emphatically, this does not mean that the rural population should be literally moved, en masse, to the cities where there is already a hideous lump of indigestible unemployment. It means, rather, that the inefficient scale of agriculture conceals a reservoir of both labor and the food to feed that labor if it were elsewhere employed. By raising the productivity of the tillers of the soil, a work force can be made available for the building of roads and dams, while this "transfer" to capital building need not result in a diminution of agricultural output.

This rationalization of agriculture is not the only requirement for growth. When agricultural productivity is enhanced by the creation of larger farms (or by improved techniques on existing farms), *part of the ensuing larger output per man must be saved.* In other words, the peasant who remains on the soil cannot enjoy his enhanced productivity by raising his standard of living and eating up all his larger crop. Instead, the gain in output per cultivator must be siphoned off the farm. It must be "saved" by the peasant cultivator and shared with his formerly unproductive cousins, nephews, sons, and daughters who are now at work on capital-building projects. We do not expect a hungry peasant to do this voluntarily. Rather, by taxation or exaction, the government of an underdeveloped land must arrange for this indispensable transfer. Thus in the early stages of a *successful* development program there is apt to be no visible rise in the individual peasant's food *consumption,* although there must be a rise in his food *production.* What is apt to be visible is a more or less efficient—and sometimes harsh—mechanism for assuring that some portion of this newly added productivity is not consumed on the farm but is made available to support the capital-building worker. We see here the problem that caused the Russian planners such trouble in the early days of Soviet industrialization.

[7] Ragnar Nurkse, *Problems of Capital Formation in the Underdeveloped Countries* (New York: Oxford University Press, 1958), p. 35, fn. 2.

What we have just outlined is not, let us repeat, a formula for immediate action. In many underdeveloped lands, as we have seen, the countryside already crawls with unemployment, and to create, overnight, a large and efficient farming operation would create an intolerable social situation. We should think of the process we have just outlined as a long-term blueprint which covers the course of development over many years. It shows us—as did our earlier model—that the process of development takes the form of a huge internal migration from agricultural pursuits, where labor is wasted, to industrial and other pursuits, where it can yield a net contribution to the nation's progress.

PROBLEM
OF
EQUIPMENT

Our model also showed us that capital-building is not just a matter of freeing hands and food. Peasant labor may construct roads, but it cannot, with its bare hands, build the trucks to run over them. It may throw up dams, but it cannot fashion the generators and power lines through which a dam can produce energy. In other words, what is needed to engineer the great ascent is not just a pool of labor. It is also a vast array of industrial equipment.*

How is this equipment obtained? In our model, by expanding the machine-tool—that is, the capital-equipment-building—subsector. But an underdeveloped economy does not have a capital-equipment-building sector. Consequently, *in the first stages of industrialization, before the nucleus of a self-contained industrial sector has been laid down, a backward nation must obtain its equipment from abroad.*

This it can do in one of three ways. (1) It can buy the equipment from an industrialized nation by the normal process of *foreign trade.* Libya, for example, can sell its oil and use the foreign currency it receives to purchase abroad the tractors, lathes, and industrial equipment it needs. (2) It can receive the equipment by *foreign investment* when a corporation in an advanced nation chooses to build in a backward area. This is the route by which the United States got much of its capital from Britain during the nineteenth century, and it is the means by which the underdeveloped nations themselves received capital during their colonial days. (3) It may receive the foreign exchange needed to buy industrial equipment as a result

---

* An allied problem of no less importance arises from the lack of technical training on which industrialization critically depends. At the lowest level, this is evidenced by appalling rates of illiteracy (up to 80 or 90 percent) which make it impossible, for instance, to print instructions on a machine or a product and expect them to be followed. And at a more advanced level, the lack of expert training becomes an even more pinching bottleneck. Before its catastrophic civil war, United Nations economists figured that Nigeria alone would need some 20,000 top-level administrators, executives, technicians, etc., over the next ten years and twice as many subordinates. On a worldwide scale, this implies a need for at least 700,000 top-level personnel and 1,400,000 second-level assistants. Not 1 percent of these skilled personnel exists today, and to "produce" them will be a task of staggering difficulty. Yet, without them it is often impossible to translate development plans into actuality.

of a grant or a loan from another nation or from a United Nations agency such as the World Bank. That is, it can buy industrial equipment with *foreign aid.*

Of these three avenues of industrialization, the most important is foreign trade. In all, the underdeveloped nations earn from $30 to $40 billion a year from foreign trade. Not all of this, by any manner of means, however, is available for *new* industrial capital. A lion's share of export earnings, unfortunately, must go to pay for indispensable imports—replacements of old equipment, or even food—or to pay interest on loans contracted with the industrialized world.

In addition, another problem plagues the underdeveloped nations in foreign trade. We have seen how international trade is the means by which a great international division of labor can be achieved—that is, by which productivity can be enhanced in all trading countries, by enabling each to concentrate on those products in which it is most efficient.

With the underdeveloped nations, however, this international division of labor has worked badly. First, as we have seen, their structural backwardness has prevented them from developing their productivities even in their main occupational tasks. Second, most of them suffer from another problem. As sellers of raw commodities—usually only one raw commodity—typically, they face a highly inelastic demand for their goods. Like the American farmer, when they produce a bumper crop, prices tend to fall precipitously, and demand does not rise proportionately. At the same time, the industrial materials they buy in exchange tend to be firm or to rise in price over the years. Thus the "terms of trade"—the actual *quid pro quo* of goods received against goods offered—are likely to move against the poorer nations, who must give more and more coffee for the same amount of machinery.* In 1957 and 1958, when commodity prices took a particularly bad tumble, the poor nations actually lost more in purchasing power than the total amount of all foreign aid they received. In effect they subsidized the advanced nations! As another example, it has been estimated that falling prices have cost the African nations more, in the two decades since World War II, than all foreign funds given, loaned, or invested there.[8]

That is why all the underdeveloped nations are seeking commodity stabilization agreements (not altogether dissimilar from the support programs that stabilize American farm incomes). Recently, the advanced nations of the West have come to recognize the need for some such device if the underdeveloped nations are to be able to plan ahead with any assurance of

---

* It should be noted that not everyone agrees with this argument which has been advanced mainly by Dr. Raul Prebisch, a famous Chilean economist. The argument on the other side claims that the quality of machinery and industrial products is constantly improving, whereas the quality of raw commodities is not, so that the higher prices of industrial goods are offset by their greater productivity when put to use.

[8] Reginald H. Green and Ann Seidman, *Unity or Poverty* (Baltimore: Penguin, 1968), p. 400.

stability, and agreements have been signed for the international stabilization of coffee prices.

Another possibility lies in the prospect of encouraging diversified exports from the underdeveloped nations—handicrafts, light manufactures, and others. The difficulty here is that these exports may compete with the domestic industry of the advanced nations: witness the problems of the American textile industry in the face of textile shipments from Hong Kong. No doubt, a large source of potential earnings lies along this path, but it is unlikely to rise rapidly as long as the advanced nations refuse to allow the backward ones equal access to their own markets.

LIMITATIONS ON PRIVATE FOREIGN INVESTMENT

A second main avenue of capital accumulation for the backward nations is foreign investment. Indeed, before World War II, this was *the* source of their industrial wealth. Today, however, it is a much diminished avenue of assistance for reasons we have learned in our exploration of the multinational corporation. On the one hand, the former capital-exporting nations are no longer eager to invest private funds in areas over which they have lost control and in which they fear to lose any new investments they might make. On the other hand, many of the poorer nations, for reasons that we have discussed, view Western capitalism with ambivalence. On the one hand, they need capital, technology, expertise. On the other, they see in the arrival of a branch of a powerful corporation run by faraway "headquarters" another form of the domination they have just escaped. As a result, foreign investment is often hampered by restrictive legislation in the underdeveloped nations, even though it is badly needed. Consequently, not much more than $3 billion to $4 billion a year from all the advanced nations goes overseas as foreign investment into the underdeveloped world.

Another difficulty is that Western corporations partially offset the growth-producing effects of their investments by draining profits out of the country. In the period 1950–1965, for example, the flow of income remitted from Latin America to the United States was $11.3 billion, three times larger than the flow of new capital into Latin America. From 1968 to 1969, income of $3.2 billion was transmitted to the United States, and only $0.7 billion was sent back to Latin America. This pattern of economic flows should not be misinterpreted as implying that foreign investment is a "negative" influence: the plant and equipment that the West has sent abroad remains in the underdeveloped world, where it continues to enhance the productivity of labor. But the *earnings* on this capital are not typically plowed back into still more capital goods, so that their potential growth-producing effect is far from realized.

THE CRUCIAL AVENUE OF AID

These considerations enable us to understand the special importance that attaches to the third channel of capital accumulation: foreign aid. Surprisingly, perhaps, in the light of the attention it attracts, foreign aid is not a very large figure. International assistance, from *all* individual nations and from the UN and its agencies, has run at a rate of about $6 billion to $7 billion per year through the 1960s and is now *diminishing*. This is an insignificant contribution to the gross output of the noncommunist underdeveloped world.

It is, however, a substantial fraction—perhaps as much as 15 percent—of the *gross investment* of that world. Thus, foreign aid makes possible the accumulation of industrial capital much faster than could be accomplished solely as a result of the backward lands' export efforts or their ability to attract foreign private capital.* To be sure, an increase in foreign earnings or in private capital imports would have equally powerful effects on growth. But we have seen the difficulties in the way of rapidly increasing the receipts from these sources. For the near future, foreign aid represents the most effective channel for *quickly* raising the amount of industrial capital which the underdeveloped nations must obtain.

Foreign aid, particularly from UN sources, is also an extremely important source of *technical assistance* which enables the backward regions to overcome the handicaps imposed by their lack of skilled and trained personnel. For the near term, this may be even more important than the acquisition of the industrial capital itself in promoting growth. Largely because of this bottleneck of skills, it is estimated that the underdeveloped countries could absorb at best $8 billion to $10 billion a year in foreign aid during this decade.

Against these handicaps, can the underdeveloped nations grow? Can the terrible conditions of poverty be relegated to the past? Economic analysis allows us to ask these questions systematically. For growth depends on the interplay of three variables.

ECONOMIC POSSIBILITIES FOR GROWTH

1. *The rate of investment that an underdeveloped nation can generate.*

As we know, this depends on the proportion of its current effort that it can devote to capital-creating activity. In turn, the rate of saving, the success in attracting foreign capital, the volume of foreign aid—all add to this critical fraction of effort on which growth hinges.

2. *The productivity of the new capital.*

The saving that goes into new capital eventually results in higher output. But not all capital boosts output by an equal amount. A million-dollar steel mill, for example, will have an impact on GNP very different from that of a

---

* Note "makes possible." There is some disturbing evidence that foreign aid may displace domestic saving, that an underdeveloped country receiving aid may relax its own efforts to generate capital. Much depends on the political will of the recipient country. (See K. B. Griffin and J. L. Enos, "Foreign Assistance: Objectives and Consequences," *Economic Development and Cultural Change,* April, 1970.)

million-dollar investment in schools. In the short run, the mill may yield a higher return of output per unit of capital investment; in the long run, the school may. But in any event, the effect on output will depend not merely on the amount of investment, but on the marginal capital-output ratio of the particular form of investment chosen.

3. *Population growth.*

Here, as we know, is the negative factor. If growth is to be achieved, output must rise faster than population. Otherwise, per capita output will be falling or static, despite seemingly large rates of overall growth.

THE CRITICAL BALANCE

  With these basic variables, is growth a possibility for the backward lands? We can see that if investment were 10 percent of GNP and if each dollar of new investment gave rise to a third of a dollar of additional output,* then a 10 percent rate of capital formation would yield a 3.3 percent rate of growth (10 percent × one-third). This is about equal to population growth rates in the nations with the highest rates of population income.

  The trouble is that most of the backward nations have investment rates that are closer to 5 percent than 10 percent of GNP. In that case, even with a marginal capital-output ratio of one-half, growth rates would not be enough to begin a sustained climb against a population growth of 2.5 percent (5 percent × $\frac{1}{2}$ = 2.5 percent). And this gloomy calculation is made gloomier still when we confront the fact that the labor force is rising faster than the population as a whole, as vast numbers of children become vast numbers of workers. In 1960 in Latin America it was estimated that at least *25 percent* of the working-age population was unemployed. In the decade since then, unemployment as a percent of the labor force seems to have increased in virtually every country.[9]

ECONOMIC PROSPECTS: THE "GREEN REVOLUTION"

  Nobody can confront these economic realities and make optimistic forecasts for the developing countries. Yet the situation is not hopeless. For many nations, an increase in their capital formation rates of 50 or 100 percent—a difficult but by no means impossible task—should bring them to the point of cumulative growth. What is then needed is a program of encouragement to small industry, to absorb the flood of unemployed while the essential industrial core is being built, and an all-out effort to bring

---

* This seems to be *roughly* what the marginal capital-output ratio of new investment in the underdeveloped areas may be.

[9] See William Thiesenhausen, "Latin America's Employment Problem," *Science,* March 1971; also H. Oshima in *Economic Development and Cultural Change,* January 1971.

about manageable rates of population growth through the IUD and other means. These are also difficult, but again not impossible, undertakings.

Meanwhile a vitally important breakthrough has been scored on the agricultural front with the development of new crops that can literally double and triple yields. This so-called Green Revolution, in effect in parts of India, has almost certainly removed the spectre of mass famine, which haunted the food officials of the world during the 1960s when they looked ahead to the 1970s. The Green Revolution will require vast amounts of fertilizer, huge irrigation projects, and much administration; so it is far from a simple "solution" to the development problem, but it offers vital time for a critical effort to stop the juggernaut of population growth and to institute an all-out developmental effort.

Thus it is possible, not only in theory but in actuality, to foresee a long, slow developmental climb. But this is not the end of our analysis, for it is impossible to think of development only in terms of economics. As we have seen in the case of Western growth, *economic development is nothing less than the modernization of an entire society.* When we talk of building capital or redirecting agriculture, we must not imagine that this entails only the addition of machines and farm equipment to a peasant society. In entails the conversion of a peasant society into an industrial one. It means a change in the whole tenor of life, in the expectations and motivations, the environment of daily existence itself.

SOCIAL AND POLITICAL PROBLEMS

We have already noted some of the changes that economic development imposes on a society. Illiterate peasants must be made into literate farmers. Dispirited urban slum-dwellers must be made into disciplined factory workers. Old and powerful social classes, who have for generations derived their wealth from feudal land tenure, must be deprived of their vested rights and oriented toward often despised business pursuits. Above all, the profligate generation of life, conceived in dark huts as the only solace available to a crushed humanity, must give way to a responsible and deliberate creation of children as the chosen heirs to a better future.

These changes will *in time* be facilitated by the realization of development itself. A growing industrial environment breeds industrial ways. The gradual realization of economic improvement brings about attitudes that will themselves accelerate economic growth. A slowly rising standard of living is likely to quicken the spread of birth control, as it did in the West.

All these changes, as we have said, may take place in time. But it is time itself that is so critically lacking. The changes must begin to take place now—today—so that the process of development can gain an initial momentum. The transition from a backward, tradition-bound way of life to a modern and dynamic one cannot be allowed to mature at its own slow pace. Only an enormous effort can inaugurate, much less shorten, the transition from the past into the future.

These sobering considerations converge in one main direction. They alert us to the fact that *in the great transformation of the underdeveloped areas, the market mechanism is apt to play a much smaller role than in the comparable transformation of the West during the industrial revolution.*

We will recall how lengthy and arduous was the period of apprenticeship through which the West had to pass in order for the ideas and attitudes, the social institutions and legal prerequisites of the market system to be hammered out. When the industrial revolution came into being, it exploded within a historic situation in which market institutions, actions, customs had already become the dominant form of economic organization.

None of this is true in the underdeveloped nations today. Rather than having their transition to a market society behind them, many of those nations must leap overnight from essentially tradition-bound and archaic relationships to commercialized and industrialized ones. Many of them are not even fully monetized economies. None of them have the network of institutions—and behind that, the network of "economic" motivations—on which a market society is built.

Hence it is not difficult to foresee that the guiding force of development is apt to be tilted in the direction of central planning. Regardless of the importance of private enterprise in carrying out the individual projects of development, the driving and organizing force of economic growth will have to be principally lodged with the government.

POLITICAL
IMPLICATIONS

But the outlook indicates more than a growth of economic command. Implicit also in the harsh demands of industrialization is the need for strong political leadership, not only to initiate and guide the course of development, but to *make it stick.* For it is not only wrong, but dangerously wrong, to picture economic development as a long, invigorating climb from achievement to achievement. On the contrary, it is better imagined as a gigantic social and political earthquake. Eugene Black, ex-president of the World Bank, soberly pointed out that we delude ourselves with buoyant phrases such as "the revolution of rising expectations" when we describe the process—rather than the prospect—of development.[10] To many of the people involved in the bewildering transformations of development, the revolution is apt to be marked by a loss of traditional expectations, by a new awareness of deprivation, a new experience of frustration. For decades, perhaps generations, a developing nation must plow back its surplus into the ugly and unenjoyable shapes of lathes and drills, conveyor belts and factory smokestacks. Some change toward betterment is not ruled out, particularly in health, basic diet, and education; but beyond this first great step, material improvement in everyday living will not—cannot—materialize quickly.

[10] *The Diplomacy of Economic Development,* p. 9.

As a consequence, many of the policies and programs required for development, rather than being eagerly accepted by all levels of society, are apt to be resisted. Tax reform, land reform, the curtailment of luxury consumption are virtually certain to be opposed by the old order. In addition, as the long march begins, latent resentments of the poorer classes are likely to become mobilized; the underdog wakens to his lowly position. Even if his lot improves, he may well feel a new fury if his *relative* well-being is impaired. The late anthropologist Oscar Lewis warned:

The political stability of Mexico is grim testimony to the great capacity for misery and suffering of the ordinary Mexican. But even the Mexican capacity for suffering has its limits, and unless ways are found to achieve a more equitable distribution of the growing national wealth and a greater equality of sacrifice during the difficult period of industrialization, we may expect social upheavals, sooner or later.[11]

These considerations enable us to understand how, along with a rise in economic standards can come a *rise* in social tensions, and this prospect, in turn, enables us to appreciate the fearful demands placed upon political leadership, which must provide the impetus, the inspiration—and, if necessary, the discipline—to keep the great ascent in motion. The strains of the early industrial revolution in England, with its widening chasm between the proletariat and capitalist, are not to be forgotten when we project the likely course of affairs in the developing nations.

In the politically immature and labile areas of the underdeveloped world, this exercise of leadership typically assumes the form of "strong man" government. In large part, this is only the perpetuation of age-old tendencies in these areas, but in the special environment of development, a new source of encouragement for dictatorial government arises from the exigencies of the economic process itself. Powerful, even ruthless, government may be needed, not only to begin the development process, but to cope with the strains of a *successful* development program.

It is not surprising, then, that the political map reveals the presence of authoritarian governments in many developing nations today. The communist areas aside, we find more or less authoritarian rule in Egypt, Pakistan, Burma, South Korea, Indonesia, and the succession of South American junta governments. From country to country, the severity and ideological coloring of these governments varies. Yet in all of them we find that the problems of economic development provide a large rationale for the tightening of political control. At least in the arduous early stages of growth, some form of political command seems as integral to economic development as the accumulation of capital itself.

[11] *The Children of Sanchez* (New York: Random House, 1961), pp. xxx-xxxi.

To this endless list of problems one last one must now be added. It is
the fact that the sheer resources of the earth may be insufficient, at least
with modern technology, to make possible a "Western" standard of living
for all the peoples of the world. Paul and Anne Ehrlich, of Stanford
University, write:

To raise all the 3.6 billion people of the world of 1970 to the American standard of
living would require the extraction of almost 30 billion tons of iron, more than 500
million tons of copper and lead, more than 300 million tons of zinc, about 50
million tons of tin, as well as enormous quantities of other minerals. That means the
extraction of some 75 times as much iron as is now extracted annually, 100 times as
much copper, 200 times as much lead, 75 times as much zinc and 250 times as much
tin. The needed iron is theoretically available, and might be extracted by tremendous efforts over long periods of time, but ... needed quantities of the other
materials far exceed *all* known or inferred reserves. Of course, to raise the standard
of living of the projected world population of the year 2000 would require doubling
all of the above figures.[12]

    The solution to this problem reinforces the political argument above.
For it is clear that the free play of market forces, *insofar as these are
permitted to develop along the lines of traditional capitalism,* would lead
rapidly to an ecological impasse. Instead, the development of the backward
nations, once an initial momentum has been attained, will have to be
planned to economize on materials and production to a degree unknown in
the West. The absurd waste of resources involved in providing transportation through the proliferation of private automobiles instead of public con-
veyances; the encouragement of individual ownership of washing machines
and television sets and domestic conveniences—the very center of the Western ideal of a "high standard of living"—will be impossible to duplicate on
a global scale.
    What will be required in their place is a new pattern of *public consump-
tion,* new ideals of stable rather than ever-rising standards of material
achievement, perhaps even a wholly new conception of what is meant by an
advanced society. All this will be required not as a matter of ideological
preference, but as one of long-run necessity. The ecological barriers of
resource availability and the absorption capacity of the earth thus pose truly
staggering problems for the underdeveloped nations, once they manage to
escape from the stagnation that still characterizes most of them. No one
knows how these obdurate limitations of nature will be translated into the
realities of social life, but it is certain that the relatively laissez-faire attitudes of Western capitalism will be hopelessly inadequate to the task.

[12] *Population, Resources, Environment* (San Francisco: Freeman, 1970), pp. 61-62.

Does this imply that the underdeveloped nations are apt to follow the route of communism?

It is a possibility. For its political and social ugliness notwithstanding, communism—or perhaps we should say, *revolutionary socialism*—offers a means of achieving the Great Ascent. There is no secret about this means. A communist nation, like a capitalist one, must transfer its workers from traditional pursuits to modern ones, must rationalize its agriculture, must build an industrial center, and must relentlessly plow back its increments of output, at least in the initial stages of the Ascent, into more capital, more capital, ever more capital. The difference is that communism or revolutionary socialism does the job without the handicaps of a free society. Where land is needed, it is simply taken; where workers are required, they are moved; where opposition is encountered, it is suppressed.

As was the case with Russia, all this is likely to be accomplished at a fearful social cost and with huge waste. In communist China, large numbers of people have been put to death for opposing the regime, and life is regimented to a chilling degree. Even in Cuba, where an initial great burst of enthusiasm carried the revolution forward with a minimum of repressiveness, a creeping militarization now seems to be entering the economy, as enthusiasm wanes and the economy staggers under the burdens of forced and inefficiently planned growth. One of the bitterest facts of the present era is that even with all the will of a revolutionary party, growth has been painful and excruciatingly slow, so that the chances for a tolerant and mild socialist regime in the backward areas are not good. All the more will this be true if environmental restrictions make it plain that the dazzling (if wasteful) achievements of the West are doomed to remain forever beyond duplication on a mass scale.

Yet it would be wrong to concentrate wholly on the negative side of revolutionary socialism. Oppression weighs less heavily on a people if it believes that a regime imposes it not for personal gain, but on behalf of children who would otherwise be born to lives of misery and want. This last point is crucial. It must not be forgotten that for all its cruel errors, Russia is still the only peasant nation that has escaped from poverty in the twentieth century; and that for all their turmoil and disappointments, China and Cuba are making an unparalleled effort to escape from poverty. Communism or iron collectivism *is* a way out of underdevelopment, at least in the beginning, and to see it in any less serious—and in this regard, respectful— light is to underestimate its challenge.

It would be fatuous to pretend that somewhere, concealed in this picture, is an answer which will solve all problems happily. Rather, the likelihood is very great that the West, quite as much as the underdeveloped areas themselves, will have to make bitter choices and to follow unwelcome paths for many years. Yet, the fact that many alternatives are closed does not mean that none remain. There are degrees of command, political as well as economic, which result in a very different tenor of existence for those who must bear the burden of development and which offer very different possibilities for the future. Nothing could be more disastrous for the West than to overlook these differences and to brand all nonmarket economies or all nondemocratic governments as constituting a single undesirable species. In the mold of economic development is being cast the shape of much of world civilization for the long-term future. On the capacity of the West to overcome its stereotyped conception of other societies, on its capacity to discriminate between mere oppression and purposeful social direction, on its capacity to persevere in the encouragement of development despite inevitable disappointments and failures will depend much of the outcome of this central process of historic change in our time.

KEY CONCEPTS AND KEY WORDS

Underdevelopment

1. *Underdevelopment* constitutes the economic environment for the vast majority of mankind. It is ascribable in part, perhaps, to bad climates or inadequate resources, but in the main it springs from the inability of traditional societies to mount sustained programs of investment and change.

Population explosion

2. The main attributes of underdevelopment are *very low levels of productivity,* especially in agriculture where man/land ratios often impose highly inefficient scales of production. No less important, and more difficult to correct, are deep-seated *attitudes of inertia* on the part of the population. And constituting a main obstacle to a development effort are very high rates of *population growth.* (Here the new birth control techniques now offer some hope for the future.)

Industrialization

3. The development effort requires a *shift from consumption* to *investment activity.* This necessitates a prior increase in agricultural productivity, accompanied by measures that will transfer the food surplus from the peasant cultivator to workers on capital projects. This is an exceedingly difficult task to carry out.

4. In addition to shifting resources from agriculture to capital building tasks, a nucleus of *industrial equipment* must be brought in. This can be done by *international trade,* by *foreign investment,* or by *foreign aid.*

Imperialism

5. The channel of international trade is a difficult one for many backward nations, as a consequence of *imperialism.* Many underdeveloped nations have *"lopsided"* economies that sell one raw commodity in markets where demand is typically inelastic. Foreign investment has not produced much capital for the backward nations, partly because of their own suspicions of Western nations, partly because the West has not reinvested its earnings there. *Foreign aid* thus becomes a small but crucial avenue for the transfer of funds and skills. It should be noted that skill is often essential to acquire before funds can be absorbed.

Foreign aid

Rate of investment

6. Development hinges on three economic variables: the *rate of investment,* the *capital-output ratio* (the size of additional output yielded by net investment) and the *rate of population growth.* Given a 10 percent net investment rate and a one-third capital output ratio it should be possible to begin growth even against a 3 percent population increase.

7. The problem is that the economic effort is not detachable from the whole array of *social and political problems.* To mount a development program requires that many traditional institutions and ways be discarded for new and untried ones. This process of change occurred over several centuries in the West, but the exigencies of the population crisis make it necessary to compress it within a few generations today.

Marginal capital-output ratio

8. Constraints imposed by resource limitations impose ceilings on the material attainments open to the underdeveloped nations. At least in the long run, they will be forced to develop resource allocation patterns very different from ours. *Planned economies* are not a matter of choice, but necessity, for their futures.

Ecological constraints

9. The result is that the modernization of the backward areas is very likely to require *authoritarian measures,* both political and economic. The strains of maintaining a successful development program, no less than the initial problems of mounting one, are apt to lead to "strong-man" government and collectivist economic measures. In this light *we can see communism as a technique for attempting to bring about the deep-seated changes required for rapid modernization.*

Collectivism

Modernization

Q U E S T I O N S

1. In what ways do you think underdeveloped countries are different from the American Colonies in the mid-1600s? Think of literacy, attitudes toward work and thrift, and other such factors. What about the relationship to more advanced nations in each case?

2. Why do you think it is so difficult to change social attitudes at the lowest levels of society? At the upper levels? Are there different reasons for social inertia at different stations in society?

3. Does the United States have a population problem? Will population growth here affect economic or social aspects of life more? Do you think we should adopt an American population control policy? What sort of policy?

4. Many economists have suggested that all advanced nations should give about 1 percent of their GNP for foreign aid. In the U.S., that would mean a foreign aid appropriation of about $10 billion. Actually we appropriate about $2 billion. Do you think it would be practicable to suggest a 1 percent levy? How would the country feel about such a program?

5. What are the main variables in determining whether or not growth will be self-sustaining? If net investment were 8 percent of GNP and the capital output ratio were $\frac{1}{4}$, could a nation grow if its rate of population increase were $2\frac{1}{4}$ percent? What changes could initiate growth?

6. What do you think is the likelihood of the appearance of strong-arm governments and collectivist economies in the underdeveloped world? For the appearance of effective democratic governments? For capitalist economies? Socialist ones? Is it possible to make predictions or judgments in these matters that do not accord with your personal preferences?

7. If you had to plan the 50-year development of a nation like India, and if you knew that it would be essential to economize on the production and consumption of minerals, how would you suggest that patterns of consumption be changed to effect major resource savings? To what extent would such changes impose further changes in the pattern of social life?

With this somber look at the underdeveloped areas we bring to a conclusion our overview of general economic history. Throughout the pages behind us we followed a majestic theme of economic development in the West; and now in the twentieth century, this same long process is stirring in the East and South. Thus, from our vantage point, we can see the beginning of worldwide economic development as a genuine watershed in human history. An active and dynamic form of economic life, until recently the distinctive characteristic of the industrial West, is about to be generalized over the face of the globe. The process of diffusion will take generations, but it marks a profound, irreversible, and truly historic alteration in the economic condition of man.

Yet, if the process of economic growth is henceforth to be carried out on a global scale, it is also clear that there will be significant change in the auspices under which this process is likely to unfold. As we have seen, it is command rather than the market system which is in the ascendant as the driving force in the underdeveloped regions. And when we combine the geographic extent of these regions with those in which communism has become firmly entrenched, it seems that command now bids fair to become *the* dominant means of organizing economic activity on this planet, as tradition was not very long ago.

But again there is a difference. During the centuries in which tradition held sway over most of the world, the economies run by the market system were the locus of progress and motion. Today and in the future, one cannot with assurance say the same. For a pre-eminent motive of the rising economies of command is to *displace* the market societies as the source of the world's economic vitality.

Does this mean that economic history now writes finis to the market system? Does it mean that the market, as a means of solving the economic problem, is about to be relegated to the museum of economic antiquities, or at best limited to the confines of North America and Western Europe? The question brings to a focus our continuing concern with the market system through history. Let us attempt in these last pages to give an appraisal of its prospects.

Stages of Economic Development

We might well begin such an appraisal by taking a last survey of the array of economic systems which marks our times. It is, at first glance, an extraordinary assortment: we find, in these mid-years of the twentieth century, a spectrum of economic organization that represents virtually every stage in economic history from the earliest and most primitive. But at second look, a significant pattern can be seen within this seemingly disordered assemblage. The few remaining wholly traditional economies, such as those of the Near East or tribal Africa, have not yet begun to move into the mainstream of economic development. A much larger group of underdeveloped nations, in which institutions of economic command are now rising amid a still traditional environment, have just commenced their development efforts and are now coping with the initial problems preparatory to eventual all-out industrialization. Going yet further along we find the economies of iron command, such as China and to a much lesser extent Russia; here we find national communities that are (or recently were) wrestling with the gigantic task of rapid massive modernization. Finally, we pass to the market economies of the West, to encounter societies with their developmental days behind them, now concerned with the operation of high-consumption economic systems.*

The categorization suggests a very important general conclusion. *The economic structures of nations today bear an integral relation with their stage of economic development.* Acts of foreign intervention aside, the choice of command or market systems is not just the outcome of political considerations, or ideologies and preferences. It is also, and perhaps primarily, the result of functional requirements which are very different at different levels of economic achievement.

* A map on pp. 232-33 is keyed to these economic differences. Needless to say, the map gives no more than a subjective interpretation of the extent of Tradition, Command, and Market in the various countries of the world.

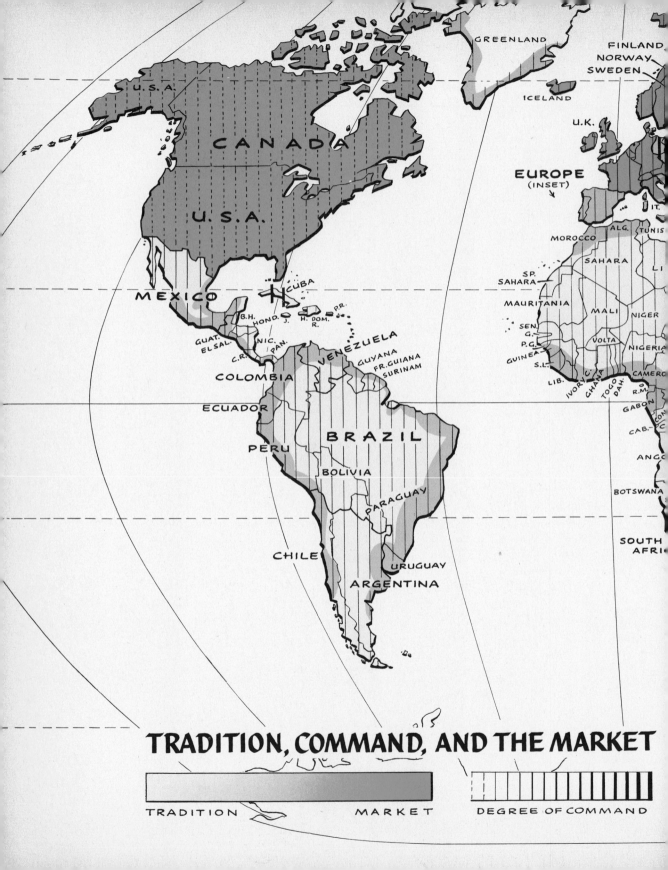

TRADITION, COMMAND, AND THE MARKET

TRADITION   MARKET   DEGREE OF COMMAND

GREENLAND

FINLAND
NORWAY
SWEDEN

ICELAND

U.S.A.

CANADA

U.S.A.

U.K.

EUROPE
(INSET)

MOROCCO

ALG.   TUNIS

IT.

SP.
SAHARA

SAHARA

LI

MEXICO

CUBA

MAURITANIA

MALI

NIGER

B.H.

HOND.

J.

P.R.

SEN.

G.

P.G.

GUINEA

S.L.

VOLTA

NIGERIA

GUAT.
ELSAL.

NIC.

H. DOM.
R.

PAN.

C.R.

VENEZUELA

GUYANA

FR. GUIANA

SURINAM

LIB.

IVORY C.

GHANA

TOGO

DAH.

R.M.

CAMERO

COLOMBIA

GABON

ECUADOR

BRAZIL

CAB.

ANG

PERU

BOLIVIA

BOTSWANA

PARAGUAY

SOUTH
AFRI

CHILE

URUGUAY

ARGENTINA

We have already noted this connection in our discussion of the under-developed areas. Now, however, we can place what we have learned into a wider frame of reference. For if we compare the trend of events in the underdeveloped economies with the "equivalent" stage of development in Western history, we see a significant point of resemblance between the two. The emergence of command in the development-minded countries today has a parallel in the mercantile era, when the Western nation also received a powerful impetus toward industrialization under the organizing influence of the "industry-minded" governments of that period.

Thereafter, to be sure, the resemblance ceases. In the West, following the first push of mercantilism, it was the market mechanism that provided the main directive force for growth; in the underdeveloped lands, as we have seen, this influence is likely to be preempted to a much larger extent by political and economic command.

Three main reasons lie behind this divergence of paths. *First, the underdeveloped areas today start from a lower level of preparedness* than did the West in the seventeenth and eighteenth centuries. Not only have the actual institutions of the market not yet appeared in many backward lands, but the whole process of acculturation has failed to duplicate that of the West. In many ways—not all of them economic—the West was "ready" for economic development, as Chapter 4 sought to make clear. A similar readiness is not in evidence in the majority of the backward lands today, with the result that development, far from evincing itself as a spontaneous process, comes about as the result of enforced and imposed change.

Second, the *West was able to mount its development effort in leisurely tempo.* This is not to say that its rate of growth was slow or that strong pressures did not weigh upon many Western countries, arousing within them feelings of dissatisfaction with their progress. Yet the situation was unlike that of the backward areas today. Here immense pressures, both of population growth and of political impatience, create an overwhelming need and desire for speed. As a result, the process of growth is not allowed to mature quietly in the background of history, as it did for much of the West, but has been placed at the very center of political and social attention.

Finally, the underdeveloped countries, who suffer from so many handicaps in comparison with the developmental days of the West, enjoy one not inconsiderable advantage. Because they are in the rear guard rather than the vanguard of history, they know where they are going. *In a manner denied to the West, they can see ahead of them the goal they seek to reach.* They do not wish to reach this goal, however, by retreading the painful and laborious path marked out by the West. Rather, they intend to shortcut it, to move directly to their destination by utilizing the mechanisms of command to bring about the great alterations that must be made.

Can economic command significantly compress and accelerate the growth process? The remarkable performance of the Soviet Union suggests that it can. In 1920 Russia was but a minor figure in the economic councils of the world. Today it is second only—though still a far second—to the United States. If Soviet production continues to gain on American production at the rate of the last ten years, in little more than another generation its industrial output (although not its per capita output) will be larger than our own. Not less important, Chinese growth, until the great famine disaster of 1959–1960, was two or three times faster than India's; and despite political turmoil, China's economic advantage over India still seems substantial.[1]

It is no doubt wise not to exaggerate the advantages of a command system. If it holds the potential for an all-out attack on backwardness, it also contains the possibilities for substantial failure, as in the very badly planned Cuban economy.[2] The mere existence of a will to plan is no guarantee that the plans will be well drawn, or well carried out, or reasonably well obeyed. Nonetheless, these caveats must be set against the dismal record of economies that continue to wallow in the doldrums of tradition, or that undertake the arduous transition into modernity under the inadequate stimulus of halfhearted regimes and half-formed market systems. In this comparison of alternatives, the advantage seems strongly on the side of those backward societies that are capable of mustering a strong central economic authority.

Once the development process is well under way, however, the relative functional merits of the market and the command mechanisms begin to change. After planning has done its massive tasks—enforcing economic and social change, creating an industrial sector, rationalizing agriculture—another problem begins to assume ever more importance. This is the problem of efficiency, of dovetailing the innumerable productive efforts of society into a single coherent and smoothly functioning whole.

In the flush period of middevelopment, the market mechanism easily outperforms the command apparatus as a means of carrying out this complex coordinating task. Every profit-seeking entrepreneur, every industrial salesman, every cost-conscious purchasing agent becomes in effect part of a gigantic and continuously alert planning system within the market economy. Command systems do not easily duplicate their efforts. Bottlenecks, unusable output, shortages, waste, and a cumbersome hierarchy of bureaucratic forms and officials typically interfere with the maximum efficiency of the planned economy in midgrowth.

ECONOMIES IN MID-DEVELOPMENT

[1] See Alexander Eckstein, *Communist China's Economic Growth and Foreign Trade* (New York: McGraw-Hill, 1966), pp. 45f. For problems of interpreting Russian statistics, see Alec Nove, *Communist Economic Strategy* (Washington, D.C.: National Planning Association, 1959), pp. 38–42.

[2] For a remarkable account of Cuban problems with planning, see the speech by Fidel Castro in the *New York Review of Books,* September 24, 1970.

What we see here is not just a passing problem, easily ironed out. One of the critical lessons of the twentieth century is that the word *planning* is exceedingly easy to pronounce and exceedingly difficult to execute. When targets are still relatively simple, and the priorities of action beyond dispute—as in the case of a nation wrenching itself from the stagnation of an ineffective regime—planning can produce miracles. But when the economy reaches a certain degree of complexity, in which the coordination of ten activities gives way to the coordination of ten thousand, innumerable problems arise, *because planned economies enjoy no "natural" congruence between private action and public necessity.*

Here is where the market comes into its own. As we know from our study of microtheory, each firm must combine its factors of production with one eye on their relative costs and the other on their respective productivities, finally bringing about a mix in which each factor is used as effectively as possible, given its cost. Thus in seeking only to maximize their own profits, the units in a market system inadvertently tend also to maximize the efficiency of the system as a whole.

Even more remarkable, one operating rule alone suffices to bring about this extraordinary conjunction of private aims and public goals. *That single rule is to maximize profits.* By concentrating on that one criterion of success and not by trying to maximize output in physical terms or by trying to live by a complicated book of regulations, entrepreneurs in a competitive environment do in fact bring the system to a peak of operating efficiency. In other words, *profits are not only a source of privileged income, but also an enormously versatile and useful "success indicator" for a system that is trying to squeeze as much output as possible from its given inputs.*

Furthermore, the market mechanism solves the economic problem *with a minimum of social and political controls.* Impelled by the drives inherent in a market society, the individual marketer fulfills his public economic function without constant attention from the authorities. In contradistinction to his counterpart in a centralized command society, who is often prodded, cajoled, or even threatened to act in ways that do not appeal to his self-interest, the classical marketer obeys the peremptory demands of the market as a voluntary exercise of his own economic "freedom."

Thus it is not surprising that we find many of the motivating principles of the market being introduced into command societies. For as these societies settle into more or less established routines, they too can utilize the pressure of want and the pull of pecuniary desire to facilitate the fulfillment of their basic plans.

Economic freedom, as we know it in the West, is not yet a reality, or even an official objective, in any of these countries. The right to strike, for example, is not recognized, and nothing like the fluid consumer-responsive market system is allowed to exert its unimpeded influence on the general direction of economic development. But the introduction of more and more discretion at the factory level argues strongly that the principles of the market society are apt to find their place in planned societies at an appropriate stage of economic development.

Thus our survey of successive stages of development brings us to a consideration of Western economic society—that is, to the advanced economies which have progressed beyond the need for forced industrialization and now enter the stage of high consumption.

From our foregoing discussion, it is clear that the market mechanism finds its most natural application in this fortunate period of economic evolution. Insofar as the advanced Western societies have reached a stage in which the consumer is not only permitted but encouraged to impose his wants on the direction of economic activity, there is little doubt that the market mechanism fulfills the prevailing social purpose more effectively than any other.

Nonetheless, the market is not without its own grave problems, even in this regard. For one thing, *it is an inefficient instrument for provisioning societies*—even rich societies—*with those goods and services for which no "price tag" exists,* such as education or local government services or public health facilities.

A market society "buys" such public goods by allocating a certain amount of taxes for these purposes. Its citizens, however, tend to feel these taxes as an exaction in contrast with the items they voluntarily buy. Typically, therefore, a market society underallocates resources to education, city government, public health or recreation, since it has no means of "bidding" funds into these areas, in competition with the powerful means of bidding them into autos or clothes or personal insurance.

A second and perhaps even deeper-seated failing of the market system is its application of a strictly economic calculus to the satisfaction of human wants and needs. As we said before, the market is an assiduous servant of the wealthy, but an indifferent servant of the poor. Thus it presents us with the anomaly of a surplus of luxury housing existing side-by-side with a shortage of inexpensive housing, although the social need for the latter is incontestably greater than the former. Or it pours energy and resources into the multiplication of luxuries for which the wealthier classes offer a market, while allowing more basic needs of the poor to go unheeded and unmet.

Finally, these shortcomings are aggravated by *the inability of the market system to cope with certain social costs that the private sector thrusts on the public. Pollution, traffic congestion, and oil spills are familiar examples of such "externalities."* In one form or another, all indicate a central weakness of the market mechanism: *its inability to formulate effective stimuli or restraints other than those that arise from the marketplace itself.*

So long as the public need roughly coincides with the sum of the private interests to which the market automatically attends, this failing of the market system is a minor one. But in an advanced economic society, it tends to become ever more important. As primary wants become satisfied, the public aim turns toward stability and security, objectives not attainable without a degree of public control. As technological organization becomes more complex and massive, again a public need arises to contain the new agglomerations of economic power. So, too, as wealth increases, pressure for education, urban improvement, welfare and the like, comes to the fore, not only as an indication of the public conscience, but as a functioning requirement of a mature society. And finally, the public stimulus and management of continued growth take on increased political urgency as the ecological problems of industrial societies multiply.

We have already paid much attention to the rise of planning in the advanced market societies as a corrective force to deal with just such problems. Now we can go so far as to generalize the economic meaning of this trend. *Planning arises in the advanced market societies to offset their inherent goal-setting weaknesses, just as the market mechanism arises in advanced command societies to offset their inherent motivational weaknesses.* In other words, planning and market mechanisms, in those societies which have begun to enter the stage of high consumption, are not mutually incompatible. On the contrary, they powerfully supplement and support one another.

CONVERGENCE OF SYSTEMS

What seems to impend at the moment, then, is a *convergence of economic mechanisms* for the more advanced societies. In the planned economies the market is being introduced to facilitate the smoother achievement of established objectives, while in the market economies, a degree of planning is increasingly relied upon to give order, stability, and social direction to the outcome of private activity.

This does not imply that the two major systems today are about to become indistinguishable. The convergence of economic mechanisms may blur but not obliterate the basic distinctions between them. Nor does the convergence of mechanisms in itself portend profound changes in the larger social structures of socialism and capitalism. A gradual rapprochement of the economic mechanisms should not lead us to hasty conclusions about the rebirth of "capitalism" in the Soviet Union or the advent of "socialism" in the United States. This is a matter into which we will look more deeply in our last chapter.

COMMON PROBLEMS

There is another way in which the phenomenon of convergence reveals itself, in addition to that of a coming together of economic mechanisms. *It is the appearance of similar problems in advanced industrial societies.* When we examine capitalism and socialism, we will pay special attention to the problems that separate and distinguish these two kinds of societies. Here it is important to realize that they are also bound together by certain common difficulties.

What is the nature of these overarching problems? As we would expect, they stem from the very technical capability and social organization that bring similar economic mechanisms into being. Three problems in particular seem of major importance:

1. *The control over technology.*

One of the most important attributes of modern history is lodged in a striking difference between two kinds of knowledge: the knowledge we acquire in physics, chemistry, engineering, and other sciences, and that which we gain in the sphere of social or political or moral activity. The difference is that knowledge in some sciences is cumulative and builds on itself, whereas knowledge in the social sphere does not. The merest beginner in biology soon knows more than the greatest biologists of a century ago. By way of contrast, the veteran student (or practitioner) of government, of social relations, of moral philosophy is aware of his modest stature in comparison with the great social and moral philosophers of the past.

The result is that all modern societies tend to find that their technological capabilities are constantly increasing, while the social and political and moral institutions by which those capabilities are controlled cannot match the challenges with which they are faced. Television, for example, is an immense force for cultural homogenization; medical technology changes the composition of society by altering its age groups and life expectancy; rapid transportation vastly increases mobility and social horizons; and the obliterative power of nuclear arms casts a pervasive anxiety over all of life. All these technologically-rooted developments fundamentally alter the conditions and problems of life, but we do not know what social, political, and moral responses are appropriate to them. *As a result, all modern societies— socialistic and capitalistic—experience the feeling of being at the mercy of a technological and scientific impetus that shapes the lives of their citizens in ways that cannot be accurately foreseen nor adequately controlled.*

2. *The problem of participation.*

The second problem derives from the first. Because advanced societies are characterized by high levels of technology, they are necessarily marked by a high degree of organization. The technology of our era depends on the cooperation of vast masses of men, some at the levels of production, some at the levels of administration. The common undergirding of all advanced industrial or "postindustrial" societies lies not alone in their gigantic instrumentalities of production, but in their equally essential and vast instrumentalities of administration, whether these be called corporations, production ministries, or government agencies.

The problem is then how the citizen is to find a place for his individuality in the midst of so much organization; how he is to express his voice in the direction of affairs, when so much bureaucratic management is inescapable; how he is to "participate" in a world whose technological structure calls for ever more order and coordination. This is a matter which, like the sweeping imperative of technology, affects both capitalism and socialism. In both kinds of societies, individuals feel overwhelmed by the impersonality of the work process, impotent before the power of huge enterprises—above all, the state itself—and frustrated at an inability to participate in decisions that seem more and more beyond any possibility of personal influence.

No doubt much can be done to increase the feeling of individual participation in the making of the future, especially in those nations that still deny elementary political freedoms. *But there remains a recalcitrant problem of how the quest for increased individual decision making and participation can be reconciled with the organizational demands imposed by the technology on which all advanced societies depend.* This is a problem that is likely to trouble societies—capitalist or socialist—as long as technology itself rests on integrated processes of production and requires centralized organs of administration and control.

3. *The problem of work.*

Finally, we must raise a problem that has just begun to appear in the advanced countries of the West but that seems virtually certain soon to make its appearance in the advanced socialist nations as well. It is the problem of work, or rather the gradually diminishing need for work, and the rising question of what will take the place of work as the great object of human energy.

Work has always been considered the curse of man; and in most societies, where work is long and onerous, boring and monotonous, it fully deserves its bad reputation. Hence for most people, the vista of a society in which the need to work is progressively reduced—indeed, in which leisure rather than work is the central feature of every day—appears to be much more of a paradise than a problem.

For the great majority of humankind, who are born into societies from which there will be no escape from work for decades, that vista can remain an unquestioned dream. But for a growing number of advanced societies, socialist as well as capitalist, the dream has to be questioned more seriously. Under the combined influences of the labor-saving potential of automation, the braking force exerted by the environment, and perhaps a deep-rooted "antimaterialistic" change of life-style, the rich societies of the world may well be standing on the theshold of a substantial reduction in the number of work hours expected of an average citizen.

In the United States we are witnessing the beginning of a four-day week in certain industries. If the trend of the past century continues, a three-day week, possibly even a two-day week, will be the stint expected of our grandchildren. Will this explosive expansion of leisure come as a welcome release of creativity, or will it be only a stultifying bore? History gives us scant guidance, for if we look to the manner in which the leisured classes of the past have made use of their release from work, we find such extremes as the exquisite mandarin culture of China or the warlords of feudal Europe; the indolent nobility of Rome or the amateur scientists of the eighteenth-century British aristocracy.

All we can say is that leisure is a condition that can lead to destructive as well as constructive activities, and that its enlargement, on a hitherto unimagined scale, will present to all wealthy societies a mixed promise and problem of vast proportions. Along with the problem of controlling the onrush of technology or of securing democratic participation in a technocratic society, the challenge of coping with the vacuum left by the diminishing need to work bids fair to constitute another point of convergence between rich societies, socialist and capitalist.

CONVERGENCE AND HISTORY

In a larger sense, then, "convergence" brings us beyond economics to the common human adventure in which economic systems are only alternate routes conducting humanity toward much the same general direction and destination. Perhaps it is well that we end our survey of economic history with the recognition that the long trajectory of the market system does not bring us to a terminus of social history, but only to a state in which some kinds of problems—the pitifully simple problems of producing and distributing goods—begin to be solved, only to reveal vastly larger problems in the very technology and organization that prepared the means for solving them.

But those are problems for the future. Meanwhile it is the present that absorbs us, for it is in the present that we have our personal encounter with history. And so we cannot end our study of economics until we have considered a question that we posed many hundreds of pages back, but which has waited until now for a full scrutiny. This is the question of America Today, and of its prospects and problems. Many of these we have dealt with in the course of our text, but a central question remains. What of capitalism itself? To this last stage of our inquiry we are finally ready to turn.

Stages of development

1. The spectrum of economic systems in the world corresponds generally to their *stages of economic development.*

Mercantilism

2. The inception of growth seems to require a political stimulus. In the West, this was provided by *mercantilism,* after which the market took over the task of growth. The West was favored over the present underdeveloped areas by its ability to mount a *leisurely development,* and by its *vanguard position* vis-à-vis the rest of the world.

3. Today, *command economies* are attempting to push their societies off dead center and to initiate the process of growth. For these tasks, command seems a more appropriate system than the market.

Mid-development

4. *Economies in mid-development,* such as the Soviet Union, are characterized by mixtures of command and market systems. Command is best suited for massive economic and social reallocations, but not to the problems of running a smoothly integrated high-output economy. Bureaucratic inefficiency, and the absence of a congruence between private interest and public requirement, introduce many difficulties into the planning mechanism. Here the market begins to achieve a new relevance.

High consumption economies

5. *High consumption economies* are naturally suited to market guidance. However, these economies now suffer from the inability of the market to formulate public needs. *Thus, planning arises in market systems to offset their inherent goal-setting weaknesses, just as the market arises in command systems to offset their inherent motivational weaknesses.*

Market and goals

Convergence

6. Thus we see a *convergence of systems* in the more advanced nations. However, a convergence of economic systems does not mean that "capitalism" and "socialism" are becoming indistinguishable.

Cumulative vs. noncumulative

7. Convergence seems to mean, also, that all advanced industrial societies share certain overarching problems: (1) a noncumulative social or political or moral understanding trying to control the effects of a cumulative technology; (2) finding a place for the individual who wants to participate in a system that demands large-scale, coordinated processes of production and administration; and (3) coping with the promise or problems of an unprecedented rise in leisure. These problems manifest themselves differently in capitalism and socialism, but in neither does a solution seem to be in sight.

Participation

Leisure

QUESTIONS

1. How do you account for the simultaneous existence in the world of such radically different economic systems?

2. In what ways was the early growth experience of the West unlike the present growth prospects of the backward world? Do you think these differences will have a substantial effect on the choice of economic systems for the backward countries?

3. Discuss the difference in social goals and priorities between a nation that is just beginning its development and one in mid-development. Between one in mid-development and one at a stage of high mass consumption. What is the relevance of planning techniques for each of these stages of development? Would you expect the techniques of planning to be similar in all stages? What differences would you look for?

4. What is meant by the congruence of self-interest and public requirement in a market system? Is this what we mean by the "invisible hand"? How can this congruence be reconciled with the fact that the market has no means of establishing public priorities?

5. What are the advantages of the market system for economic freedom? Do you think the market system is also productive of political freedom? Draw a scatter diagram showing on one axis the degree of planning and on the other axis your estimate of relative political freedoms for the following nations: Sweden, England, U.S., France, South Africa. Is there much, if any, relationship between the two variables?

6. Do you think there can be a convergence of economic systems without a convergence of social and political systems?

7. What specific technological processes seem to defy social control? How about the effect of television? Urbanization? The arms race? Can you think of others?

8. Why do you think that knowledge accumulates more easily in science than it does in the areas of morality or politics or social activities?

9. Do you think that bureaucracy is an avoidable aspect of industrial society? If so, how? If not, what problems does it pose?

10. Do you think that the freedom to choose one's profession, to go to graduate school "to see how you like it," to become a hippie, etc., makes life easier or more difficult? Do you think your parents would agree?

We have reached the final stage in our inquiry; and now, as in our introductory pages, let me again speak in the first person, because what I have to say should not be given the authority that rightly or wrongly seems to adhere to statements made in the impersonal third person of textbook prose. What follows is no more than the fruit of personal reflection, offered not to settle matters, but only to make explicit my own convictions and to give student and instructor an opportunity to discuss the most important social issue with which economics is ultimately concerned. As the title of this chapter indicates, that ultimate problem is capitalism itself, and the extent to which it must be held responsible for the troubles of our country.

DEFINITIONS: WHAT IS CAPITALISM? SOCIALISM?

We had better begin with definitions. If we are now to ask whether America's troubles are due to capitalism, we should know what we mean by that crucial word.

It is surprisingly difficult to find a succinct definition of capitalism.[1] But I think that all shades of opinion, from right to left, would agree that its essential characteristics are these:

1. *The legal right to private ownership of the means of production.*

Under capitalism, the capital equipment of society is owned by a minority of individuals (capitalists) who have the right to use this property for private gain.

2. *The market determination of distribution.*

Capitalism relies primarily on the market system, not only to allocate its

---

[1] One of the few clear-cut definitions is in Max Weber's *General Economic History* (New York: The Free Press, 1950), Chapters 22 and 30. The Marxian definition is more diffuse, referring at different times to an *economic system,* to the *bourgeois society* built on that system, and occasionally to a *stage of Western civilization.* See George Lichtheim, *Marxism* (New York: Praeger, 1961), p. 164, note 4.

resources among various uses, but also to establish the levels of income (such as wages, rents, profits) of different social classes.

What is the corresponding definition of socialism? As we might expect, it is something of a mirror image of capitalism. "In its primary usage," writes Paul M. Sweezy, a leading Socialist theoretican, "the term 'socialism' means a social system which is differentiated from other social systems by the character of its property relations. ... Capitalism recognizes a relatively unrestricted right of private ownership in the means of production, while socialism denies this right and reserves such ownership to public bodies."[2]

Thus Sweezy, like most socialists, makes the crucial distinction between capitalism and socialism the question of *property ownership*—to which I think most socialists would also add that socialism, unlike capitalism, depends primarily on *planning*, rather than on the market, both for its overall allocation of resources and for its distribution of income.

IDEAL TYPES VS. REAL CASES

These definitions are what the sociologist Max Weber called "ideal types." They are meant to summarize and abstract out of the enormous variety of actual institutions and historical experiences those essential elements that make up a pure model of the institution or activity in which we are interested. We dealt with such an ideal type when we studied the operation of a "market" under pure competition, knowing full well that no market was in fact ever free of all imperfections. In the same fashion, the emphasis on public vs. private property, and on market vs. planned distribution serves to sharpen our conception of the "irreducible" elements of capitalism and socialism that are to be discovered behind their many variations in actual history.

But no sooner do we create these ideal types than we find ourselves in something of a quandary. For the question then arises as to what practical

[2] Paul M. Sweezy, *Socialism* (New York: McGraw-Hill, 1948), p. 3.

function these models of capitalism and socialism serve. For example, if one asks a dedicated humanitarian socialist if "socialism" is better than "capitalism," he will unhesitatingly tell you that it is, basing his reply on the superiority of public over private ownership and on the preference to be accorded to planning over the market. But the same humanitarian socialist recoils in horror at the repressiveness of Russia and looks with approval on the humaneness of (capitalist) Denmark. How does he reconcile this contradiction? By telling you that Russia is not "really" socialist, but only a grim travesty of socialism; and that Denmark is not "really" capitalist but a modified socialist version of capitalism. Yet, unquestionably, the Soviet Union has public ownership of property and a thorough-going system of planning, and Denmark has private ownership of property and a general market determination of incomes and outputs.

The point of this disconcerting confrontation is clear. It is that the elements that all agree are decisive in defining capitalism and socialism as "ideal types" do not tell us very much about the societies that display those characteristic elements. As a matter of fact, thinking about the differences among capitalist nations—compare Sweden and the Union of South Africa—or among socialist countries—contrast Russia and China—we begin to wonder if the words *capitalism* and *socialism* mean anything at all.

CAPITALISM
AND SOCIALISM
AS ECONOMIC
SYSTEMS

I think the answer is that the terms *do* mean something, although perhaps less than we often assume. As we shall see, there are crucial areas of life to which they add little if any understanding. But there are other areas where they add a good deal, and it is to these that we now direct our attention.

The first such area should be obvious. It is that of economics proper. *Capitalism and socialism as ideal types identify for us a series of economic problems that we find among all members of each type.*

What are these problems? For capitalism, the answer lies in a series of problems with which much of formal economics is concerned: disequilibrium, instability, misallocation of resources, and inequality of incomes. For these are results of the economic process in *every* society in which there is private ownership of property and a market determination of prices. Whether we look to Japan or Sweden, the Union of South Africa or the United States, we see similar tendencies toward too much or too little growth, inflation or unemployment, a struggle between the private and the public sector, and a highly uneven division of incomes between the property-owning and the working classes. These are problems as specific to capitalism as the problems of guild life were specific to feudalism.

Can we apply the same general finding to socialism? To a certain extent our comparison is muddied by the fact that so many socialist systems are still in (or only very recently out of) a period of forced economic growth. Hence we do not really have "mature" socialisms to compare with mature capitalisms.

Nonetheless, there seems to be a set of common economic problems that is built into socialism in much the same fashion as the problems that are intrinsically part of the capitalist mechanism. As we would expect, these are problems of public ownership and planning—in particular, the problem of controlling unwieldy state bureaucracies and avoiding inefficient production and distribution directives. Indeed, one of the most brilliant socialist economic theoreticians, the late Oskar Lange, wrote presciently in 1938: *"The real danger of socialism is that of the bureaucratization of economic life. . . ."*[3]

We shall return to a consideration of what these deep-rooted problems imply for capitalism and socialism.* But first let us ask if we find a parallel to the economic attributes of the two systems in their political characteristics. Some eminent political economists, Milton Friedman prominent among them, believe that we do. Friedman believes that the *existence of a market mechanism separate from the state provides the necessary basis for a free political life.* He does not insist that every capitalist society is therefore a free one—indeed, he specifically singles out Fascist Italy and Nazi Germany and Spain and Tsarist Russia as societies in which capitalist economic structures did *not* provide political freedom. But he is firm in his conviction that the existence of capitalism is a *necessary*, even if not a sufficient, condition for political freedom.

Friedman spells out his argument forcefully:

One feature of a free society is surely the freedom of individuals to advocate and propagandize openly for a radical change in the structure of society. . . . It is a mark of the political freedom of a capitalist society that men can openly advocate and work for socialism. . . . How could the freedom to advocate capitalism be preserved and protected in a socialist society?

In order for men to advocate anything, they must in the first place be able to earn a living. This already raises a problem in a socialist society, since all jobs are under the direct control of political authorities. It would take an act of self-denial whose difficulty is underlined by experience in the United States after World War II with the problem of "security" among Federal employees, for a socialist government to permit its employees to advocate policies directly contrary to official doctrine.

But let us suppose this act of self-denial to be achieved. For advocacy of capitalism to mean anything, the proponents must be able to finance their cause—to hold public meetings, publish pamphlets, buy radio time, issue newspapers and magazines and so on. How could they raise the funds?[4]

[3] Oskar Lange and Fred M. Taylor, *On the Economic Theory of Socialism* (New York: McGraw-Hill, 1956), p. 109.

* It is equally obvious that the phenomenon of convergence in the economic mechanisms of the two systems tends to bring the problems of one system into the other.

[4] *Capitalism and Freedom*, pp. 10, 16–18.

Does Friedman's logic establish a second fundamental dividing line between capitalism and socialism? It may. There *is* a certain refuge for the dissident individual in the free-for-all of the market that may be missing in socialism for the very reasons that Friedman suggests. Indeed, as M. A. Adelman has written, one main objection to socialist society is that it too much resembles the company town under capitalism, in which one employer has power over everyone within his jurisdiction.[5]

Yet I do not think that the issue has the clarity of the economic differences between capitalist and socialist societies. Certainly it weakens Friedman's position that among capitalist societies—that is, in the spectrum of systems relying on private property and the market system—*there seems to be no correlation whatsoever between the degree of political freedom and the use of "socialistic" limitations of property rights or the market mechanism.* Indeed, the most "socialistic" capitalisms, such as the Scandinavian bloc, England, or New Zealand, are probably the world's freest political societies.

Second, it should be pointed out that in the provision of a *guaranteed income* to all citizens, there is available a protection against the very kind of political vulnerability Friedman warns us about. As we have seen, the United States seems to be moving slowly toward such a system, and there is no reason why a socialist system could not adopt one very easily. A guaranteed income under socialism would free the dissident citizen from political pressure, just as private employment offers him this freedom under capitalism.

To be sure, such a system also requires that a socialist state value political liberty so highly that it would not cut off the income of an agitator for capitalism. Certainly no socialist state today displays any such easy tolerance—just as very few capitalist states allow complete liberty for agitators against capitalism. In all societies there is a natural "defensive" reaction against hostile ideas, and there is no reason to suppose that socialist authorities will be more tolerant of dissent than are capitalist ones. Indeed, in the present stage of historical development it is doubtful that socialist governments in general can be expected to be as politically tolerant as capitalist ones, partly because many socialist economies are in the throes of forced growth, and partly because most socialist governments feel insecure in a world in which capitalist power is still dominant.

Whether socialism will continue to be less politically free than the most liberal capitalisms is a question about which little can be said at present. As we have seen, it is possible to guard against the company-town aspect of socialism by means of a guaranteed income. But that is not to say that even a wealthy and self-assured socialist society will *wish* to put political liberty, with all its risks, high on its agenda. In the final analysis, I suspect that the

---

[5] Cited in *The Business Establishment,* ed. Earl Cheit (New York: Wiley, 1964), p. 217, note 17.

degree of political liberty will vary from nation to nation under socialism, as it does under capitalism; and that the *economic* framework will have very little to do with the quality of political life in either system.

This complex relationship between economic structures and political liberty brings us deeper into the question of how "capitalism" as an ideal type differs from "socialism." Specifically it leads to the question of whether we can discover a basis for *social* difference between the two systems— differences in values or life styles that might find their origins in the economic systems characteristic of each.

At first glimpse, there seems no relationship whatsoever between the two. Indeed, if we were to compare "socialist" Yugoslavia with "capitalist" Italy we would probably find many *more* similarities of social tone, cultural life, and general atmosphere, than if we compared "socialist" Yugoslavia with "socialist" China. And in the same way, "capitalist" West Germany probably more closely resembles "socialist" East Germany in general life style than it does "capitalist" Australia. *National* differences in culture and tradition seem so overwhelmingly important that any common social traits traceable to capitalism or socialism recede far into the background, if indeed they are discoverable at all.*

This emphasis on national differences is, I believe, of the greatest importance, and we will return to it in full measure when we inquire further into the problems of American capitalism. Yet at this stage of our inquiry, while we are still seeking to divide all capitalisms from all socialisms, perhaps one distinctive element should be noted. It is the presence within all socialist countries of an ideal not to be found in any capitalist country. This is the ideal of Socialist Man—of man transformed from the competitive, acquisitive being that he is (and that he is *encouraged* to be) under all property-dominated, market-oriented systems, into the cooperative human being who finds fulfillment in unselfishness and who presumably can develop only in the benign environment of a propertyless, nonmarket social system.

It need hardly be said that this ideal of Socialist Man remains an unrealized goal in any socialist society, and may perhaps even be an unrealizable goal, comparable to the ideal of a truly religious community vainly pursued by centuries of Christianity. Yet, however distant, however vulgar-

---

* Merely as one indication of this diversity, let us look into the much discussed matter of suicide rates. Does "welfare capitalism" bring a high suicide rate, as President Eisenhower once suggested? The evidence does not show it. Suicides per 100,000 population are higher (18.5 per 100,000) in Sweden than in the U.S. (10.4 per 100,000), but they are higher here than in Norway (7.9) or the Netherlands (6.6 per 100,000). Denmark, on the other hand, has an even higher rate—20.3 per 100,000—but it suffered from this rate *before* it became a welfare state. See Alan Gruchy, *Comparative Economic Systems* (Boston: Houghton, 1966), p. 436.

ized in practice, however abused as a mere slogan for social manipulation, the conception of Socialist Man provides a spiritual basis for an ideology that is powerfully persuasive. Capitalist nations may be efficient, humane, democratic, permissive, creative, but they do not have a "vision" built on the elements of property ownership and the market—a vision comparable to that which is founded on the ideal of common ownership and sharing.

This absence of a capitalist ideal may strike some as a fact little to be regretted, in view of the human suffering that so many official ideals have brought in the past. But if we suspend our judgments and merely ask whether there is an ultimate difference between the worlds of socialist and capitalist values and goals, I think the answer must be yes, that socialism has a sense of high human mission—perhaps even redemption—that capitalism, even at its best, cannot quite match.

PROBLEMS AND SOLUTIONS

Our discussion suggests that the ideal types of "capitalism" and "social-ism" *are* useful because they indicate different kinds of problems that the two systems tend to generate. But we have not yet inquired into an extreme-ly important question that our findings pose. Granted that capitalism and socialism have common problems, *does this mean that they all find similar solutions to these problems?*

To ask the question is to answer it. Obviously, different capitalisms respond to their economic and social and political problems in very different ways, as do different socialisms. Take capitalism as an example. Two well-known Marxist critics of capitalism have written that genuine planning or resolute action to provide housing would be impossible in America because "such planning and such action ... will never be undertaken by a govern-ment run by and for the rich, as every capitalist government is and must be."[6] They have obviously concentrated on the lack of an effective social sector in the U.S., and overlooked the planning and housing undertaken by Norway, Sweden, Denmark, New Zealand, Netherlands, and other govern-ments presumably run by and for the rich, since they are certainly countries in which private ownership of the means of production prevails.

In the same way, because all capitalist systems do suffer from macro-instabilities, it does not follow that all therefore suffer from the same degree of unemployment. As we have previously seen, during the 1960s when unemployment here and in Canada reached levels over 5 percent, in West Germany unemployment never rose over 1 percent of the labor force, and in New Zealand it was considerably less than that.

This same variety of responses can be found in socialist economies. Oskar Lange's diagnosis of bureaucracy has proved all too true within all socialisms, but some have responded with a reliance on market socialism

---

[6] Paul Sweezy and Paul Baran, *Monopoly Capital* (New York: *Monthly Review Press,* 1966), p. 300.

(Yugoslavia or pre-invasion Czechoslovakia); others, in efforts to solve the problem with better computer-planning (U.S.S.R.); and still others, with a search for "moral incentives" (Cuba or China).

American Capitalism in Crisis

All this has an obvious relevance to the central issue with which we began this chapter. For we can see now that whereas many of the problems that beset America undoubtedly have their roots in our capitalist institutions, the fact that we have coped with them so inadequately is not a matter that can be blamed on capitalism as such.

Take, for example, the question of social neglect that is so dismaying an aspect of American life. If we compare the United States with, say, Norway in terms of various indicators of social well-being, there is no doubt that we show up poorly. Infant mortality in the United States is a full 50 percent higher than it is in Norway. Norway spends a higher proportion of its GNP on education than we do, even though Norway has a much smaller per capita GNP. Norway has more hospital beds per thousand population than we do. It allocates a larger proportion of its GNP to social security expenditures than does the United States. Its cities are essentially free of all slums. Although Norwegian citizens have a much lower GNP than American citizens, "poverty" as a relative condition—or poverty as a human condition of neglect by society—has been virtually eliminated there.

If we are willing to grant on the basis of these and other indicators that Norway has a record of social welfare superior to that of the United States, we would expect large differences in the economic structures of the two countries; for instance, in their income distributions. Yet, as Table 14-1 shows, there are not!

What the table shows is that the pre-tax distribution of income—that is the relative shares of rich and poor as determined by the market mecha-

TABLE 14 • 1

PRE-TAX INCOME DISTRIBUTION: UNITED STATES AND NORWAY

PERCENT OF INCOME GOING TO PERCENTILE GROUPS				
	Lowest 20% of population	Second 20%	Third 20%	Fourth 20%	Top 20%
Norway (1950)	5.5	10.4	15.4	23.7	45.0
United States (1963)	5.1	12.1	17.6	23.6	41.6

Sources: Norway: Simon Kuznets, "Quantitative Aspects of the Economic Growth of Nations (VIII), Distribution of Income by Size," *Economic Development and Cultural Change* (January 1963). United States: U.S. Census Bureau, *Trends in the Income of Families and Persons in the U.S.: 1947 to 1964*, Technical Paper No. 17. Note that the years are not identical, but in view of the extreme slowness of movements in income distribution, this is not a serious consideration.

nism—is much the same in both nations. Indeed, in the United States the pre-tax share of the rich is *smaller* than it is in Norway, and the relative share of the second and third groups from the bottom (which includes the bulk of the working class) is *larger* than Norway.

But this surprising result would be totally altered if we now took into account the distribution of income *after* taxes and subsidies. In contrast to the generally nonprogressive structure of U.S. taxes, the Norwegian tax structure is one of the most progressive in the world and this progressive tax incidence is further emphasized by a system of subsidies to low income groups, which greatly lightens their net tax burden. The point, of course, is clear. It is that *the original capitalist dispositions of the marketplace do not leave an irretrievable mark on their societies, but can be radically modified by taxes and transfers.*[7]

CAPITALISM OR AMERICAN CAPITALISM

All this has a sobering, as well as an encouraging, implication. It is that much of what troubles America seems to be related to factors that, however much exacerbated by our economic system, cannot be uniquely attributed to capitalism as such. The low level of social services in America, the enormous role played by the military, the "rat-race" tempo of American life, the extent of our slums, the callous treatment of criminals, the obsession with "communism," and many other unlovely aspects of our social system are not predominant in many other capitalist systems.

The problem, in other words, resides more in those elements of our society that are *American* than in those that are capitalist. To put it differently, the significant question for us is to understand why capitalism here has not achieved the possibilities realized by capitalism elsewhere, rather than to compare the deficiencies of life in America with the presumed advantages that "socialism" might bring. For unless we understand and correct the failures of *American* capitalism, the likelihood is that a change of economic systems in this country would produce only an *American* socialism that would manifest many of the very failings of American capitalism.

Can we identify the elements in America that have brought about the failure of capitalism here to match the social achievements of similar systems abroad? Here we move from the reasonably firm grounds of empirical evidence to the quicksand regions of social conjecture. There are, perhaps, no "right" or "wrong" answers to this crucial question—only answers that are more or less useful in helping us think about an immensely complex and elusive problem. But with all the difficulties, let me try to suggest some possible explanations for the failures of our system.

[7] See Gruchy, *Comparative Economic Systems*, p. 338. See also his discussion of Swedish tax incidence, p. 402.

We might start by asking what is the most striking difference between the United States and the more socially responsive capitalisms we have referred to. One such difference that immediately suggests itself is sheer *size*. Is the greater social neglect of American capitalism simply the result of the scale of our continental country? Are we too big to create a genuine sense of community?

It is certainly plausible that a large country, with its variations in regions and interests, is less apt to feel a sense of shared responsibility than a small one. And yet at best, the explanation of size can be only a partial one. Canada, which is geographically larger than the United States, has a considerably more highly developed social welfare program and "point of view" than we do. Australia is another example of a large, regionally variegated nation with a high level of social services. Perhaps more to the point, our density of population (which is the way that "size" becomes translated into human experience) is 25 percent *greater* than Sweden and double that of New Zealand, so that our continental expanse does not physically separate man from man to a degree that might explain the lack of our "communal feelings."

A second hypothesis seems more convincing. It would explain the failures of American capitalism by the extreme diversity of our population— the many ethnic and cultural groups that have obstructed the formation of a socially-minded single community, comparable to the Danes or the Swedes.

Yet this hypothesis also loses much of its persuasiveness under scrutiny. Switzerland, for example, has three different language and nationality groups and yet maintains a very high level of communal concern. Canada, despite the political friction of its French- and English-speaking regions, has a well-developed social welfare system. Perhaps even more telling is a great deal of social neglect in certain areas of the United States where there *are* strong ethnic, regional, and racial bonds—the rich whites of Appalachia have paid little attention to the decline of their poor white kinsmen.

Yet, if our social heterogeneity does not provide a fully adequate reason for our inadequate social performance, it does point in one direction that sharply differentiates American capitalism from capitalism in other nations.* This is the fact that America is burdened with a *race problem* that is closely entwined with many areas of its laggard social performance.

There is no need at this point to rehearse the statistics of Negro poverty and neglect. Instead, it is necessary to link our deep-seated prejudice against the Negro with our national disregard of the (largely black) slums, our national neglect of the prisons (disproportionately filled with blacks), the

* With the exception of the Union of South Africa, which significantly also displays many of the same symptoms of social neglect that we do—and for the same reasons.

low level of welfare provision (roughly half of which goes to Negroes). To put it bluntly, one very likely reason for the continued failure of American society to clean up its ghettos, improve its prisons, and liberalize antipoverty programs is the unwillingness of many white Americans to allow their hard-earned dollars to be taxed and spent in ways that will tend to benefit black Americans more than white ones.

THE TRADITION OF DEMOCRATIC INDIVIDUALISM

The race issue, so central a part of our history, reaches deep into the core of American social neglect, but it does not account for every aspect of our problems. Racism does not explain our reluctance to deal generously with white poverty through higher Social Security levels, nor our militarism, nor our failure to cope effectively with the deterioration of the environment. To what special factors in American experience might we attribute these weaknesses of American capitalism?

The first answer I will suggest may be a surprising one. It is America's tradition of *democratic individualism*—a tradition born and nurtured on our frontiers, and perpetuated in the image of the town meeting as the ideal, democratic mode of government.

This is surely an odd suggestion, in that it is precisely this tradition that is one of the proudest claims of American society—indeed, the genuinely democratic quality of American life continues to impress visitors even from the most socially advanced European nations.

Yet, there is a price to be paid for this heritage. It is the lack of a tradition of strong central government and *noblesse oblige,* the duty of the benevolent ruler to provide for his less fortunate subjects. Both these traditions are woven into the cultural traditions of most European nations and have helped them create *welfare* capitalisms.

Alexis de Tocqueville, the great nineteenth-century French sociologist, wrote perceptively about the difference in traditions when he visited America in the 1830s:

Aristocracy [he wrote] links everybody, from peasant to king, in one long chain. Democracy breaks the chain and frees each link. As social equality spreads, there are more and more people who, though neither rich nor powerful enough to have much hold over others, have gained or kept enough wealth and enough understanding to look after their own needs. Such folk owe no man anything and hardly expect anything from anybody. They form the habit of thinking of themselves in isolation and imagining that their whole destiny is in their own hands. Thus, not only does democracy make men forget their ancestors, it also clouds their view of their descendants, and isolates them from their contemporaries. Each man is forever thrown back on himself alone, and there is a danger that he may be shut up in the solitude of his heart.[8]

---

[8] Alexis de Tocqueville, *Democracy in America* (New York: Harper, 1966), p. 478.

This is not to claim that European aristocracies were in fact more solicitous of their peoples in the nineteenth century than was democratic America. On the contrary, as the direction of immigration showed, quite the opposite was the case. Nonetheless, with eloquence and perception, Tocqueville points to a deep difference between democratically based and aristocratically based social systems. It is the presence, within the older governments of Europe, of a *legitimacy of authority* that, in the changed conditions of the twentieth century, made possible a much more vigorous and direct governmental attack on social problems than was possible in the American democratic-individualist environment.

But it is not only our tradition of small-scale local government that has handicapped us in dealing with large-scale, national problems. What Tocqueville alerts us to is an inhibition in the *feeling of social responsibility* of a democratic society, compared with one of more aristocratic lineage. This suggests that one of the reasons that Americans have not developed an effective attack on social problems is that there is no popular support for the idea that government should help the needy. The result has not only been an anaesthetizing of the American social conscience, but a paralysis of the mechanism by which that conscience might have been best expressed.*

To this possibly heretical suggestion, let me now add a second, which applies to America at the other end of the socio-political scale. It is that American capitalism, unlike its European counterparts, never developed much of a tradition of *democratic socialism as a reformist force.*

Many observers have commented on the failure of the socialist ideal to implant itself in America, a failure due in part to our economic success and in part to our political (if not economic) stress on equality, at least for whites. "On reefs of roast beef and apple pie," as the economic historian Werner Sombart put it, "socialistic utopias of every sort [were] sent to their doom."[9]

It has been customary for Americans to congratulate themselves on the absence of a native socialist movement, for socialism has certainly brought sharp conflicts and severe social tensions within many nations. Yet, it has also brought an impetus for social change and a widened agenda for

---

* Sociologist Seymour Martin Lipset gives a telling illustration of the difference in national attitude between our highly individualist tradition and that of a more aristocratic society. Both the United States and Canada have created national folk-heros connected with the frontier that was so important for both societies. How suggestive that America should have chosen the free-wheeling cowboy and that Canada should have picked the scarlet-clad Canadian mounted police, representative of central authority and law and order! See Lipset, *The First New Nation* (New York: Basic Books, 1963), p. 251.

[9] Quoted in Daniel Bell, *Marxian Socialism in the United States* (Princeton, N.J.: Princeton University Press, 1967), p. 4.

discussion that has been missing from America. In Sweden, Norway, Denmark, England, Netherlands, New Zealand—in short, virtually everywhere that capitalism has achieved a high level of social welfare—the driving force for change has been a democratic socialist party, pushing against the limits of conservative capitalism. In America, with the important exception of the early New Deal, no such "socialistic" enlargement of the conception of what a society might achieve has ever significantly enlarged the conception of what "capitalism" meant. Hence measures such as the nationalization of industry where that might be useful, or the massive redistribution of income—both measures used by a number of capitalist nations—are avoided in America because they smack of "socialism."*

THE PROBLEM OF MILITARY POWER

There remains, however, one vast problem to which neither of the preceding suggestions directly applies. It is the question of the relationship of capitalism to the rise of an aggressive American military state.

Is militarism itself a specifically capitalist phenomenon? The evidence of history would hardly indicate as much. There have been pacific capitalisms (Sweden, Switzerland) and aggressive ones (prewar Germany, postwar United States); and the actions of the Soviet Union in its invasion of Hungary and Czechoslovakia or its border clashes with China are enough to indicate that capitalism has no monopoly on international violence.

Yet there is no doubt that in recent years American capitalism has become a military state that feels itself impelled to police the world. Since World War II, the United States has intervened in Lebanon, the Dominican Republic, Cuba, South Vietnam, Cambodia, and Laos; has clandestinely overthrown at least one government (Guatemala), and probably another (Iran); has actively supported repressive right-wing regimes in Greece and Brazil; has entered into a worldwide system of secret military arrangements even extending to the support of the government of Ethiopia; and (as we mentioned in Chapter 1) has "shown the flag" on a total of 50 occasions.

Whence derives this military commitment? The answer is not easy to give. In part it lay in a genuine fear of postwar Soviet intentions, hardly reassured by Russia's general truculence, by its walling-off East Berlin, and by its anticapitalist rhetoric. Yet, compared with the reaction of many European nations, the American response to these threats was exaggerated—indeed, so exaggerated that it undoubtedly helped to provoke the very Soviet (and later Chinese) belligerency by which Americans could then justify their uncompromising stand.

---

* The political scientist Robert A. Dahl has written that Americans are "half colorblind" when they think about such problems as how to control giant corporations. "An important reason," he writes, "is that our history has left us without a socialist tradition. . . . The consequence, I think, is a serious limit to our capacity for clearheaded consideration of how economic enterprises should be governed. Because we have no socialist tradition, our debates about economic institutions nearly always leave some major alternatives—chiefly 'socialist' alternatives—unexplored." (*After the Revolution?* New Haven: Yale University Press, 1970, p. 119).

The sources of this American response are many: clergymen who equated the rise of communism with the anti-Christ and who stirred the fears of fundamentalist religious groups; labor unions whose anticommunist feelings reached such irrational levels that longshoremen refused to unload Polish merchandise at the very time that Poland was trying to break *away* from the Soviet bloc; veterans organizations to whom patriotism meant an uncritical support of American "might"; Congressmen who subscribed to the belief that America must defend "freedom" everywhere, except perhaps for selected members of their own constituencies; military leaders who gradually enlarged the conception of American "defense" to the ability to wage two major wars and one minor war *simultaneously*; industrial circles for whom the arms economy provided a seemingly inexhaustible source of revenue; high government officials who saw America as the world's bulwark against "international communism," even after international communism had dissolved into mutually hostile nation-states; intellectuals and professors who applied the cool logic of "maximizing" national security but never questioned the premises on which security might be based.

In this multiplicity of causes, each of which has played its part in the American anticommunist stance, the role of "capitalism" is both central and elusive. Certainly capitalism all over the world has felt itself menaced by the rise of powerful socialist governments in Russia and China and the prospect of revolutionary socialism in the underdeveloped areas, much as the Catholic Church once felt menaced by the rise of Protestantism; or the British aristocracy, by the rise of democracy in France. Yet, as we know, Catholicism made its peace with Protestantism—differently, to be sure, in different countries—and the aristocracies made their peace with democracy—also differently in different countries. That private property and the market mechanism can also make a peace with public property and planning seems equally evident—but that, too, will take place differently in different countries.

In many capitalist nations that process of peacemaking seems now fairly far advanced. Various capitalist nations have long carried on trade freely with Russia, have begun to invest in communist nations, have recognized and traded with China, and while maintaining a healthy skepticism toward the national policies of these nations, have felt no need to mount an anticommunist crusade against them. Now, after the disastrous Indo-Chinese War that has been the price America has paid for its blind anticommunism, we shall have to see if here, too, we cannot find a pragmatic mode of coexistence, and become once again a citizen, and not the policeman, of the world.

WHAT SHOULD BE DONE?

If our discussion points to any conclusion, it is that we must seek to change many aspects of American capitalism in the direction that capitalism in other nations has indicated. This does not mean, of course, that America could or should set out to "copy" the achievements of other lands. Institutions, like good wines, do not always travel easily. We shall have to find our own ways of coping with the problems of health and the cities and national planning and the arts and pollution and education—ways that may take inspiration from foreign accomplishments, but that must in the end reflect our own ways of doing things.

Yet it may help if we have at least a general idea of what such a major effort would look like. There is such a "preview" in the proposed budget of government expenditure for the year 1976, drawn up by the National Urban Coalition. Envisaging a new program of National Health insurance, public service employment, family assistance for the poor, aid to students from preschool to college, grants for improving police departments, taxes to curb pollution, plus a wide range of other social services, the Coalition looks ahead to a total federal government expenditure in 1976 of $354 billion,[10] compared with $206 billion today.

Is such an enormous increase in expenditure imaginable in a capitalist society? Comparisons are helpful here. In 1967 the United States used 18.8 percent of its GNP for nonwar public purposes. The proposals above would raise the nonwar proportion of GNP used by government to only 20 percent, assuming that GNP will grow very rapidly (about 5 percent per year) under the many-sided stimulus of this new program.

But if GNP grew at only 3 percent, the "burden" of the proposed nonwar expenditures on GNP would be only 26 percent of GNP (and the addition of the defense portion would raise it to only 30 percent). In Table 14-2, compare the portion of GNP used by other nations for nonwar purposes only.

TABLE 14•2

NONWAR USES OF GNP, SELECTED NATIONS (1967)

Canada	26.7%	Italy	27.6%
France	31.6	Sweden	36.8
West Germany	30.9	United Kingdom	27.0

Source: *Counterbudget*, p. 313.

The problem, then, is not one of economics, but of politics, of will. The program will require increased tax revenues, and the Coalition proposals call for graduated increases in taxes on incomes over about $10,200, plus the closing of many tax loopholes. Thus a family earning $11,000 a year would pay about $100 more in taxes; one earning $20,000 would pay roughly $1,000 more; one earning $35,000 might pay as much as $2,500 more.[11]

[10] *Counterbudget*, p. 300. (The 1976 figure includes $94 billion of purchases of goods and services, $50 billion of which are allocated for military expenditure, and $260 billion of transfers to individuals and states and localities.)

[11] *Ibid.*, p. 10.

Will those influential Americans who constitute the 40 percent of all families above the $10,000 line assent to such an increase in their taxes to bring about a new America? Only time and effort will tell. Many Americans, particularly those who find themselves in the influential upper echelons in the nation, are not deeply disturbed by the problems of the remaining 60 percent, much less those of peoples many thousand miles away. Yet, others—including sizeable numbers who are aware of their good fortune—feel the urgency of the problems and the inadequacy of the American response. Indeed, if we judge by the past, the leadership for the reform of America's backwardness will come from those very groups who will have to make some sacrifice of their private income to achieve a greater public good.

Textbooks are not proper places for expression of political sentiment. They are not improper places, however, in which to give vent to moral sentiments, provided these are properly identified. Hence let me end our long discussion of the origins and character and problems and promise of our society by saying that I believe that American capitalism stands at the threshold of a crucial decade. For almost a generation our society has been identified in the eyes of much of the world as a nation that is rich but indifferent; peace-loving in rhetoric but aggressive in behavior; boastful of its economic strength, blind to the misuse of that strength. Now the years are at hand in which that image—and the realities that are uncomfortably close to the image—can be changed. We will continue to be a rich nation; we must cease to be in so many ways a poor one. We will continue to be a powerful nation; we must learn the limits of our power. We will continue to be an economic colossus, but our economic system must now become the undergirding for a good society.

In view of our heritage, our traditions, our deeply-rooted failings, this will not be an easy transformation for America to make. It may even prove to be an impossible one, although I strongly believe that this is not the case. But in any event, the all-important thing is to make the effort. The challenge is to change America today into a different and much better America tomorrow. In my view, this will be the most searching test of its character that American society has ever faced.

THE MORAL
CHALLENGE

Index

INDEX

Business management, 110–12, 125–26,
  131–33, 201f.
Business responsibility, 130–36
Business schools, 168

CALVINISM, 61–63
Cannon, W., Rep., 167–68
Capital:
  defined, 92–94
  and development, 211, 216–18, 221–22
  emergence of, as a factor of production,
    66, 69–71
  formation, 147–50 (*see also* Investment)
  goods, 92
  output ratio, 222
  and productivity, 92–94, 221–22
  and saving, 94–95, 147–50
Capital formation and growth, 147–50,
  218–19, 221–22
Capitalism:
  American, 2–11, 172, 251
  defined, 244f.
  early, and social justice, 89–90
  early industrial, 78ff.
  European, 172f.
  evolution of, 155ff., 238–41
  and freedom, 247–49
  growth process in, 91–95
  guided, 151ff., 163, 238–41
  as ideal type, 245–46
  and life styles, 249
  and militarism, 256–57
  rise of, 73–74, 78ff.
  and socialism, 177f., 238–41, 244f.
  and unemployment, 250–51
Capital movements, international, 194ff.
Carlyle, Thomas, 84
Carnegie, Andrew, 110, 125

Cartels, 174–75, 175n.
Castro, Fidel, 235n.
Catholicism, 46–47, 61–62
"Center," (of market structure), 120–23, 127
Chandler, Alfred, 198n.
Cheit, Earl, 248n.
Child labor, 88, 90–91
China, 227–28, 230–35
Choice and economics, 17
Chrematistike, 39–40
Church and medieval economics, 46–48,
    60–61
Cicero, 37
Cities (*see also* Urbanization):
  in antiquity, 34–35
  in feudalism, 34–35, 56–57
  and monarchy, 59–60
Clayton Antitrust Act, 119
Clubok, Alfred B., 211n.
Coal and Steel Community, 179–80
Cochran, Thomas, 115, 116n., 117n., 174n.
Coeur, Jacques, 65, 65n.
Colbert, J. B., 74, 75
Collectivism, 224–27, 231–35
Collectivization, 184–85
Collegia, 35
Collusion, 128n.
Colt, Samuel, 198
Colton, David, 112
Combination Laws, 106
Command:
  and development, 224–27, 231–35
  as economic system, 21, 23–25, 96
  and efficiency, 236–37
  and growth, 95–97, 224–27, 231–35
Commercial revolution, 65–75, 81
Commodity stabilization, 219–20
Common Market, 179–81
Commoner, Barry, 8

Welfare state:
  in Europe, 179, 181–82, 258
  in U.S., 153–59, 258–59
Wilkins, Mira, 199n.
Wilkinson, John, 82–83
Wilson, Woodrow, 118
Wit, Daniel, 211n.
Work:
  and alienation, 103–4, 166–67, 240–41
  industrialism and, 103
  problem of, 240–41

Worker representation, 134–35, 191n.
World War II, 159–61
Wykes, Thomas, 59

XEROX, 132

YARMOLINSKY, ADAM, 6n., 7n.
Yugoslavia, 190–91, 249